Pantry Vinaigrette, 340

Buttery Parmesan
Garlic Bread, 339

EASY
WEEKNIGHT
DINNERS

READER'S DIGEST — RDA ENTHUSIAST BRANDS, LLC

P9-DHH-947

Favorite Skillet Lasagna, 31

Taste of Home   Reader's digest

A TASTE OF HOME/READER'S DIGEST BOOK

©2014 RDA Enthusiast Brands, LLC, 1610 N. 2nd St., Suite 102, Milwaukee WI 53212-3906. All rights reserved.
Taste of Home and Reader's Digest are registered trademarks of The Reader's Digest Association, Inc.

EDITORIAL

Editor-in-Chief: Catherine Cassidy
Creative Director: Howard Greenberg
Editorial Operations Director: Kerri Balliet

Managing Editor, Print & Digital Books: Mark Hagen
Associate Creative Director: Edwin Robles Jr.

Editor: Janet Briggs
Art Director: Maggie Conners
Layout Designer: Nancy Novak
Contributing Layout Designer: Siya Motamedi
Editorial Production Manager: Dena Ahlers
Copy Chief: Deb Warlaumont Mulvey
Copy Editor: Mary C. Hanson
Content Operations Manager: Colleen King
Content Operations Assistant: Shannon Stroud
Executive Assistant: Marie Brannon

Chief Food Editor: Karen Berner
Food Editors: James Schend; Peggy Woodward, RD
Associate Food Editor: Krista Lanphier
Recipe Editors: Mary King; Annie Rundle; Jenni Sharp, RD; Irene Yeh

Test Kitchen and Food Styling Manager: Sarah Thompson
Test Cooks: Nicholas Iverson (lead), Matthew Hass, Lauren Knoelke
Food Stylists: Kathryn Conrad (senior), Leah Rekau, Shannon Roum
Prep Cooks: Megumi Garcia, Melissa Hansen, Bethany Van Jacobson, Sara Wirtz

Photography Director: Stephanie Marchese
Photographers: Dan Roberts, Jim Wieland
Photographer/Set Stylist: Grace Natoli Sheldon
Set Stylists: Stacey Genaw, Melissa Haberman, Dee Dee Jacq
Creative Contributors: Mark Derse (photographer), Rachel Lewis (food stylist)

Editorial Business Manager: Kristy Martin
Billing Specialist: Mary Ann Koebernik

BUSINESS

Vice President, Chief Sales Officer: Mark S. Josephson
Vice President, Business Development & Marketing: Alain Begun
General Manager, Taste of Home Cooking Schools: Erin Puariea
Vice President, Digital Experience & E-Commerce: Jennifer Smith
Vice President, Direct to Consumer Marketing: Dave Fiegel

THE READER'S DIGEST ASSOCIATION, INC.

Chairman of the Board: Robert E. Guth
President and Chief Executive Officer: Bonnie Kintzer
Vice President, Chief Operating Officer, North America: Howard Halligan
President & Publisher, Books: Harold Clarke
Vice President, North American Operations: Philippe Cloutier
Vice President, Chief Marketing Officer: Leslie Doty
Vice President, North American Human Resources: Phyllis E. Gebhardt, SPHR
Vice President, Consumer Marketing Planning: Jim Woods

For other **Taste of Home books** and products, visit us at **tasteofhome.com.**

For more **Reader's Digest** products and information, visit **rd.com** (in the United States) or **rd.ca** (in Canada).

Library of Congress Number: 2014931434

Paperback
International Standard Book Number: 978-1-61765-280-6
1 3 5 7 9 10 8 6 4 2
Printed in U.S.A.

Hard Cover
International Standard Book Number: 978-1-61765-344-5
Component Number: 116000212H00
1 3 5 7 9 10 8 6 4 2
Printed in U.S.A.

Pictured on front cover: BBQ Yumburgers, page 12, Spicy Barbecued Chicken, page 167, Spinach Pizza, page 55, Chipotle-Black Bean Chili, page 236, Ravioli Skillet, page 93
Pictured on back cover: Easy Stuffed Shells, page 67, Balsamic-Glazed Beef Skewers, page 145, Shrimp Fried Rice, page 136, Shortcut Strawberry-Vanilla Dessert, page 331

Broccoli Chicken Casserole, 81

Smothered Burritos, 63

CONTENTS

CONTENTS

DINNER IN SHORT ORDER

Does the question "What's for dinner?" make your head spin? Do thoughts like *I'm way too busy to make dinner...I've got to drive the kids around*...run through your mind? Good news! You're holding the solution in your hands.

Taste of Home Easy Weeknight Dinners features **316** simple, family-pleasing dishes perfect for today's time-starved cook. This collection was created *by* busy home cooks *for* busy home cooks. It has **284 entrees**—over a year's worth of weeknight dinners!

Easy Weeknight Dinners recipes are so easy. They won't keep you in the kitchen for long. There are quick weeknight entrees, slow cooked meals and dishes suitable for a relaxed Sunday supper. The reasons they're so perfect for busy cooks are:

• Short ingredient lists that use everyday items.

• No-fuss preps that take 30 minutes or less.

• Clear, easy-to-follow directions.

• Simple cooking methods—skillet, oven, grill or slow cooker.

In addition, the collection has **a photo of every recipe** to allow you to quickly find a dish that appeals to your family. For quick reference, the beginning of each chapter has a **convenient recipe index**. The **Cook to Cook tip boxes** have comments from real home-cooks who have tried the recipe and changed it up a bit to suit their family's tastes. If you like to cook once and eat twice, look for the **freezer icon** **FREEZE IT**. These recipes give freezing and reheating directions. Turn to the **Jazz it Up** chapter for super-easy ideas to **add some interest to plain sides**.

And finally, the **dishes are just delicious**, and you can be assured they'll turn out perfectly time after time. The family-pleasing recipes in ***Taste of Home Easy Weeknight Dinners*** were sent in by family cooks and tested by the professionals in *Taste of Home* kitchens. When you serve your family one of these quick-to-fix dinners, you know you're giving them a wonderful meal...even when time is tight!

Chipotle-Black Bean Chili, 236

Savory Crescent Turkey Potpies, 209

Loaded Flank Steak, 148

1

30 MINUTES TO DINNER

Start here if you have only a half hour until dinnertime.

30 MINUTES TO DINNER INDEX

Cook to Cook

Look for
THESE boxes
for helpful tidbits!

BBQ MEAT LOAF MINIS

These are so simple—even kids can prepare meat loaf in muffin cups. But depending on their ages, you might want to do the actual baking. For extra spice, add 2 teaspoons chili powder and serve with mild or moderate salsa.

— LINDA CALL FALUN, KANSAS

START TO FINISH: 30 MIN.
MAKES: 6 SERVINGS

- 1 **package (6 ounces) stuffing mix**
- 1 **cup water**
- 2 **tablespoons hickory smoke-flavored barbecue sauce**
- 1 **pound ground beef**
- 1 **cup (4 ounces) shredded cheddar cheese**
  Additional hickory smoke-flavored barbecue sauce, optional

1. Preheat oven to 375°. In a large bowl, combine stuffing mix, water and 2 tablespoons barbecue sauce. Add the beef; mix lightly but thoroughly. Place ⅓ cup beef mixture into each of 12 ungreased muffin cups, pressing lightly.

2. Bake, uncovered, 18-22 minutes or until a thermometer reads 160°. Sprinkle tops with cheese; bake 2-4 minutes or until the cheese is melted. If desired, serve with additional barbecue sauce.

BASIL-BUTTER STEAKS WITH ROASTED POTATOES

A few items and 30 minutes are all you'll need for this incredibly satisfying meal. The two-ingredient basil butter gives these steaks a very special flavor.

—TASTE OF HOME TEST KITCHEN

START TO FINISH: 30 MIN.
MAKES: 4 SERVINGS

- 1 package (15 ounces) frozen Parmesan and roasted garlic red potato wedges
- 4 beef tenderloin steaks (1¼ inches thick and 6 ounces each)
- ½ teaspoon salt
- ½ teaspoon pepper
- 5 tablespoons butter, divided
- 2 cups grape tomatoes
- 1 tablespoon minced fresh basil

1. Preheat oven to 425°. Bake potato wedges according to time given on package directions.

2. Meanwhile, sprinkle steaks with salt and pepper. In a 10-in. cast-iron skillet, brown steaks in 2 tablespoons butter. Add the tomatoes to skillet. Bake, uncovered, 15-20 minutes or until meat reaches desired doneness (for medium-rare, a thermometer should read 145°; medium, 160°; well-done, 170°).

3. In a small bowl, combine basil and remaining butter. Spoon over steaks and serve with potatoes.

SOUTHWESTERN GOULASH

I had some extra cilantro in the fridge and didn't want to throw it away. Instead, I came up with a Southwest-inspired soup using ingredients I had on hand. The whole family liked it.

—VIKKI REBHOLZ WEST CHESTER, OH

START TO FINISH: 30 MIN.
MAKES: 6 SERVINGS

- 1 **cup uncooked elbow macaroni**
- 1 **pound lean ground beef (90% lean)**
- 1 **medium onion, chopped**
- 1 **can (28 ounces) diced tomatoes, undrained**
- ⅔ **cup frozen corn**
- 1 **can (8 ounces) tomato sauce**
- 1 **can (4 ounces) chopped green chilies**
- ½ **teaspoon ground cumin**
- ½ **teaspoon pepper**
- ¼ **teaspoon salt**
- ¼ **cup minced fresh cilantro**

1. Cook macaroni according to package directions. Meanwhile, in a Dutch oven over medium heat, cook beef and onion until meat is no longer pink; drain. Stir in the tomatoes, corn, tomato sauce, chilies, cumin, pepper and salt. Bring to a boil. Reduce heat; simmer, uncovered, 3-5 minutes to allow flavors to blend.
2. Drain macaroni; add to meat mixture. Stir in cilantro; heat through.

FREEZE OPTION *Freeze individual portions of cooled goulash in freezer containers. To use, partially thaw in refrigerator overnight. Heat through in a saucepan, stirring occasionally and adding a little water if necessary.*

NOTES

Cook to Cook

Loved it! I used ground sausage instead of beef. I also added red pepper flakes and black beans! Very good, easily adaptable to whatever you have in the house. **—KHAL8**

MEDITERRANEAN STEAK & EGG PITAS

Steak and eggs, a traditional standby, gets a Mediterranean makeover in this oh- so-easy entree. Hearty and fun, these pitas are loaded with taste!

—TASTE OF HOME TEST KITCHEN

START TO FINISH: 25 MIN.
MAKES: 4 SERVINGS

- 1   beef top sirloin steak (1 pound), cut into ½-inch cubes
- ½   teaspoon Greek seasoning
- ¼   teaspoon salt
- ¼   teaspoon pepper
- 2   teaspoons olive oil
- 4   eggs
- 4   whole pita breads, warmed
- 2   medium tomatoes, chopped
- 1   can (2¼ ounces) sliced ripe olives, drained
- ⅔   cup crumbled garlic and herb feta cheese

1. Sprinkle the beef with the Greek seasoning, salt and pepper. In a large skillet, saute beef in oil 4-6 minutes or until no longer pink. Remove from heat and keep warm.

2. In a large nonstick skillet coated with cooking spray, fry eggs as desired. Spoon steak over pita breads; top with tomatoes, olives, cheese and eggs.

ITALIAN BEEF AND SHELLS

Put together a hearty entree with this veggie-and-pasta combo. Wine lends an extra touch of flavor to the sauce and makes this main dish a winner.

—MIKE TCHOU PEPPER PIKE, OHIO

START TO FINISH: 30 MIN.
MAKES: 4 SERVINGS

- 1½ cups uncooked medium pasta shells
- 1 pound lean ground beef (90% lean)
- 1 small onion, chopped
- 1 garlic clove, minced
- 1 jar (23 ounces) marinara sauce
- 1 small yellow summer squash, quartered and sliced
- 1 small zucchini, quartered and sliced
- ¼ cup dry red wine or reduced-sodium beef broth
- ½ teaspoon salt
- ½ teaspoon Italian seasoning
- ½ teaspoon pepper

1. Cook pasta according to package directions.

2. Meanwhile, in a Dutch oven, cook the beef, onion and garlic over medium heat until meat is no longer pink; drain. Stir in the marinara sauce, squash, zucchini, wine and seasonings. Bring to a boil. Reduce the heat; simmer, uncovered, 10-15 minutes or until thickened.

3. Drain pasta; stir into beef mixture and heat through.

Cook to Cook

Very good and easy. I also added chopped carrots. —JILLANGLEMYER

30 MINUTES TO DINNER

FREEZE IT

BBQ YUMBURGERS

If you top these with extra barbecue sauce, you'll get onions and sauce both inside and out of these burgers.

—**DONNA HOYE** WHITMORE LAKE, MI

START TO FINISH: 30 MIN.
MAKES: 4 SERVINGS

- 1 **large onion, halved and sliced**
- 2 **teaspoons canola oil**
- 1 **pound lean ground beef (90% lean)**
- 2 **tablespoons finely chopped onion**
- 2 **tablespoons barbecue sauce**
- 2 **garlic cloves, minced**
- 1 **teaspoon onion powder**
- ½ **teaspoon salt**
- ¼ **teaspoon pepper**
- 4 **whole wheat hamburger buns, split**
  Optional toppings: tomato slices, lettuce leaves and additional barbecue sauce

1. In a skillet, cook and stir sliced onion in hot oil 4-6 minutes or until tender.
2. In a bowl, combine beef, chopped onion, barbecue sauce, garlic, onion powder, salt and pepper, mixing lightly but thoroughly. Shape into four ½-in.-thick patties.
3. Grill burgers, covered, over medium heat 4-6 minutes on each side or until a thermometer reads 160°. Serve on buns with cooked onions and, if desired, optional toppings.

FREEZE OPTION *Place patties on a plastic wrap-lined baking sheet; wrap and freeze until firm. Transfer patties to a large resealable plastic bag; return to freezer. To use, prepare sliced onions. Grill frozen patties as directed, increasing time as necessary for a thermometer to read 160°.*

BLUE CHEESE-TOPPED STEAKS

Tenderloin steaks are lightly crusted with blue cheese and bread crumbs in my recipe. These steaks are quick enough for a weeknight dinner and special enough for holiday dining.

—**TIFFANY VANCIL** SAN DIEGO, CA

START TO FINISH: 30 MIN.
MAKES: 4 SERVINGS

- 2 tablespoons crumbled blue cheese
- 4½ teaspoons dry bread crumbs
- 4½ teaspoons minced fresh parsley
- 4½ teaspoons minced chives
  Dash pepper
- 4 beef tenderloin steaks (4 ounces each)
- 1½ teaspoons butter
- 1 tablespoon all-purpose flour
- ½ cup reduced-sodium beef broth
- 1 tablespoon Madeira wine
- ⅛ teaspoon browning sauce, optional

1. Preheat oven to 350°. In a small bowl, combine the blue cheese, bread crumbs, parsley, chives and pepper. Press onto one side of each steak.

2. In a large nonstick skillet coated with cooking spray, cook steaks over medium-high heat for 2 minutes on each side. Transfer to a 15x10x1-in. baking pan coated with cooking spray.

3. Bake 6-8 minutes or until the steaks reach desired doneness (for medium-rare, a thermometer should read 145°; medium, 160°; well-done, 170°).

4. Meanwhile, in a small saucepan, melt butter. Whisk in the flour until smooth. Gradually whisk in broth and wine. Bring to a boil; cook and stir 2 minutes or until thickened. Stir in the browning sauce if desired. Serve with the steaks.

Cook to Cook

I made this for my husband's birthday dinner and it was perfect! Delicious, tender, great combination of flavors! I did not have any red wine so I used a good quality dark balsamic vinegar—and the gravy was amazing.
—**GEORGIAJAMMY**

BLACK BEAN TACO SALAD

Here's a delicious entree salad that will please even your pickiest eaters. It's mild, pleasant and fun.

—TASTE OF HOME TEST KITCHEN

START TO FINISH: 20 MIN.
MAKES: 4 SERVINGS

- 1 **pound ground beef**
- 4 **cups torn leaf lettuce**
- 1 **large tomato, chopped**
- 1 **cup canned black beans, rinsed and drained**
- ½ **cup Catalina salad dressing**
- 4 **cups nacho-flavored tortilla chips**

1. In a large skillet, cook beef over medium heat until no longer pink; drain. In a large bowl, combine the lettuce, tomato, beans and beef. Drizzle with dressing and toss to coat.
2. Arrange tortilla chips on a serving plate; top with beef mixture.

> **Cook to Cook**
>
> I enjoyed this recipe. The 2nd time I made it I used ground chicken instead of beef and liked it even more. **—LEE907**

NOTES

FREEZE IT

HEARTY PENNE BEEF

Turn to this dish when you are looking for a comforting meal! The best of everything is found here—it's tasty, easy and also a great way to sneak in some spinach for extra nutrition.

—TASTE OF HOME TEST KITCHEN

START TO FINISH: 30 MIN.
MAKES: 4 SERVINGS

- 1¾ cups uncooked penne pasta
- 1 pound ground beef
- 1 teaspoon minced garlic
- 1 can (15 ounces) tomato puree
- 1 can (14½ ounces) beef broth
- 1½ teaspoons Italian seasoning
- 1 teaspoon Worcestershire sauce
- ¼ teaspoon salt
- ¼ teaspoon pepper
- 2 cups chopped fresh spinach
- 2 cups (8 ounces) shredded part-skim mozzarella cheese

1. Cook pasta according to package directions. Meanwhile, in a Dutch oven, cook beef over medium heat until no longer pink. Add garlic; cook 1 minute longer. Drain. Stir in the tomato puree, broth, Italian seasoning, Worcestershire sauce, salt and pepper.
2. Bring to a boil. Reduce heat; simmer, uncovered, 10-15 minutes or until slightly thickened. Add spinach; cook 1-2 minutes or until the spinach is wilted.
3. Drain pasta; stir into beef mixture. Sprinkle with cheese; cover and cook 3-4 minutes or until cheese is melted.

FREEZE OPTION *Cool and transfer to freezer containers. Freeze up to 3 months. To use, thaw in refrigerator overnight. Place in a Dutch oven and heat through. Sprinkle with some additional cheese.*

STOVETOP HAMBURGER CASSEROLE

Serve this skillet and watch your family come running to the table. It's not only loaded with ground beef, pasta, veggies and cheddar cheese, but it also goes together in a jiffy.

—EDITH LANDINGER LONGVIEW, TX

START TO FINISH: 25 MIN.
MAKES: 6 SERVINGS

- 1 **package (7 ounces) small pasta shells**
- 1½ **pounds ground beef**
- 1 **large onion, chopped**
- 3 **medium carrots, chopped**
- 1 **celery rib, chopped**
- 3 **garlic cloves, minced**
- 3 **cups cubed cooked red potatoes**
- 1 **can (15¼ ounces) whole kernel corn, drained**
- 2 **cans (8 ounces each) tomato sauce**
- 1½ **teaspoons salt**
- ½ **teaspoon pepper**
- 1 **cup (4 ounces) shredded cheddar cheese**

1. Cook pasta according to package directions.

2. Meanwhile, in a large skillet, cook beef and onion over medium heat until the meat is no longer pink; drain. Add the carrots and celery; cook and stir for 5 minutes or until vegetables are crisp-tender. Add garlic; cook 1 minute.

3. Stir in the potatoes, corn, tomato sauce, salt and pepper; heat through.

4. Drain pasta and add to skillet; toss to coat. Sprinkle with cheese. Cover and cook until cheese is melted.

FREEZE IT

CHIMICHANGAS

My cousin is of Mexican heritage, and I've watched her make these crunchy and delicious wraps for years. The first time I made them for my own family, they became an instant favorite.

—**DEBI LANE** CHATTANOOGA, TN

START TO FINISH: 30 MIN.
MAKES: 6 SERVINGS

- 1 **pound ground beef**
- 1 **envelope taco seasoning**
- 1 **can (16 ounces) refried beans**
- 6 **flour tortillas (12 inches), warmed**
- 1 **cup (4 ounces) shredded Colby-Monterey Jack cheese**
- 4 **teaspoons canola oil Sour cream and salsa**

1. In a large skillet, cook beef over medium heat until no longer pink; drain. Stir in taco seasoning. In a small saucepan, cook refried beans over medium-low heat 2-3 minutes or until heated through.

2. Spoon about ⅓ cup of beans off-center on each tortilla; top with ¼ cup beef mixture. Sprinkle with cheese. Fold sides and ends of tortilla over filling and roll up.

3. In a large skillet over medium-high heat, brown burritos in oil on all sides. Serve with sour cream and salsa.

FREEZE OPTION *Individually wrap cooled chimichangas in paper towels and foil; freeze in a resealable plastic freezer bag. To use, remove foil; place paper towel-wrapped burrito on a microwave-safe plate. Microwave on high 3-4 minutes or until heated through, turning once. Let stand 20 seconds.*

Cook to Cook

My husband and I love these! They're very easy to make, and you can substitute different kinds of meat for the ground beef. We often make them with shredded or ground chicken, and they're wonderful. These also freeze well, too. I always have to keep my eye on the freezer to make sure I get the leftovers before my husband eats them all!
—**CAREE929**

NOTES

30 MINUTES TO DINNER

FREEZE IT

ITALIAN-STYLE SALISBURY STEAKS

This is my husband's favorite meal. He loves it! If you like, top each serving with mozzarella or Parmesan cheese.

—HEATHER NALLEY EASLEY, SC

START TO FINISH: 25 MIN.
MAKES: 4 SERVINGS

- 1 egg, beaten
- 1 teaspoon Worcestershire sauce
- ½ cup seasoned bread crumbs
- ½ teaspoon garlic powder
- ½ teaspoon pepper
- 1 pound ground beef
- 1 tablespoon canola oil
- 1 can (14½ ounces) diced tomatoes with basil, oregano and garlic, undrained
- 1 can (8 ounces) Italian tomato sauce

1. In a large bowl, combine the first five ingredients. Crumble beef over mixture and mix well. Shape into four oval patties. In a large skillet, brown patties in oil on both sides. Drain.

2. In a small bowl, combine diced tomatoes and tomato sauce. Pour over patties. Bring to a boil. Reduce heat; cover and simmer 10-15 minutes or until meat is no longer pink.

FREEZE OPTION *Freeze individual cooled steaks with some tomato mixture in resealable freezer bags. To use, partially thaw in the refrigerator overnight. Microwave, covered, on high in a microwave-safe dish until heated through, gently stirring and adding a little water if necessary.*

SLOPPY JOES

Everybody in the family will be delighted with the zesty flavor of this yummy sandwich. Try it spooned over warmed corn bread if you don't have buns.

—**KAREN ANDERSON** CUYAHOGA FALLS, OH

START TO FINISH: 30 MIN.
MAKES: 6 SERVINGS

- 1½ **pounds ground beef**
- 1 **can (10 ounces) diced tomatoes and green chilies, undrained**
- 1 **can (6 ounces) tomato paste**
- ¼ **cup ketchup**
- 2 **tablespoons brown sugar**
- 1 **tablespoon spicy brown mustard**
- ¼ **teaspoon salt**
- 6 **sandwich buns, split**

In a large skillet, cook beef over medium heat until no longer pink; drain. Stir in the tomatoes, tomato paste, ketchup, brown sugar, mustard and salt. Bring to a boil. Reduce heat; simmer, uncovered, 5 minutes. Serve on buns.

FREEZE OPTION *Freeze cooled meat mixture in freezer containers. To use, partially thaw in the refrigerator overnight. Heat through in a saucepan, stirring occasionally and adding a little water if necessary. Serve on buns.*

Cook to Cook

My family LOVES this. All I add is a slice of cheese for my picky 5- and 8-year-old boys, and they eat it up! We have this a minimum of twice a month...sometimes more if we're pressed for time. We usually use beef but occasionally make it with ground turkey instead. —**BIRDY3**

FAMILY-FAVORITE CHEESEBURGER PASTA

I created this recipe to satisfy a cheeseburger craving. What a delicious, healthy classic!

—**RAQUEL HAGGARD** EDMOND, OK

START TO FINISH: 30 MIN.
MAKES: 4 SERVINGS

- 1½ cups uncooked whole wheat penne pasta
- ¾ pound lean ground beef (90% lean)
- 2 tablespoons finely chopped onion
- 1 can (14½ ounces) no-salt-added diced tomatoes
- 2 tablespoons dill pickle relish
- 2 tablespoons prepared mustard
- 2 tablespoons ketchup
- 1 teaspoon steak seasoning
- ¼ teaspoon seasoned salt
- ¾ cup shredded reduced-fat cheddar cheese
  Chopped green onions, optional

1. Cook pasta according to package directions.
2. Meanwhile, in a large skillet, cook beef and onion over medium heat until meat is no longer pink; drain. Drain pasta; add to meat mixture.
3. Stir in the tomatoes, relish, mustard, ketchup, steak seasoning and seasoned salt. Bring to a boil. Reduce heat; simmer, uncovered, 5 minutes.
4. Sprinkle with cheese. Remove from heat; cover and let stand until the cheese is melted. Garnish with green onions if desired.

TORTELLINI AND HAM

A couple of convenience items form the basis for this no-fuss meal. It's sure to become a staple when you need a great last-minute weeknight supper.

—TASTE OF HOME TEST KITCHEN

START TO FINISH: 25 MIN.
MAKES: 4 SERVINGS

- 1 **package (19 ounces) frozen cheese tortellini**
- 1 **cup frozen pepper strips, thawed**
- 3 **tablespoons butter**
- 1¼ **cups cubed fully cooked ham**
- 1 **teaspoon minced garlic**
- 1½ **teaspoons cornstarch**
- ½ **cup chicken broth**
- 1 **teaspoon dried basil**
- ½ **teaspoon dried parsley flakes**
- ¼ **teaspoon pepper**
- 4 **tablespoons grated Parmesan cheese, divided**

1. Cook tortellini according to package directions.

2. Meanwhile, in a large skillet, saute pepper strips in butter until crisp-tender. Add ham and garlic; saute 1 minute longer.

3. Combine the cornstarch, broth, basil, parsley and pepper; stir into pepper mixture. Bring to a boil; cook and stir 2 minutes or until thickened.

4. Add 2 tablespoons cheese. Drain tortellini; toss with ham mixture. Sprinkle with remaining cheese.

Cook to Cook

This was really good! I hate to revamp a recipe and rate it, but I stayed really close to this. I ran out of Parmesan and parsley. I omitted the parsley and basil and added one teaspoon of Italian seasoning. I used fresh Romano cheese in place of Parmesan. The flavor was amazing and lighter without a traditional cream sauce :). **—BOOSBUG**

NOTES

_____
_____
_____
_____
_____
_____
_____

30 MINUTES TO DINNER

SMOKED KIELBASA WITH RICE

With a little bit of zip and just the right amount of smokiness, this sausage-and-rice medley is an easy way to please the household. You can also omit the rice and serve the sausage pieces with toothpicks as an appetizer.

—NICOLE JACKSON EL PASO, TX

START TO FINISH: 25 MIN.
MAKES: 6 SERVINGS

- 2 pounds smoked kielbasa or Polish sausage, halved lengthwise and cut into ¼-inch slices
- ¼ cup finely chopped onion
- 3 bacon strips, finely chopped
- ¾ cup honey barbecue sauce
- ¼ cup packed brown sugar
- 1 tablespoon prepared horseradish
- 2 teaspoons water
- 2 teaspoons minced garlic
- ½ teaspoon crushed red pepper flakes
  Hot cooked rice

In a Dutch oven, saute the kielbasa, onion and bacon until onion is tender; drain. Add the barbecue sauce, brown sugar, horseradish, water, garlic and pepper flakes. Bring to a boil; cook and stir 2-3 minutes or until sauce is thickened. Serve with rice.

FREEZE OPTION *Place cooled individual portions in freezer containers without rice. Freeze up to 3 months. To use, thaw in the refrigerator overnight. Place in a saucepan; heat through, gently stirring and adding a water if necessary. Serve with rice.*

KIELBASA BOW TIE SKILLET

Dinner in one pan is my type of meal! It freezes and reheats beautifully, too, so you'll want to fix extras for a fast entree later. My daughters are picky eaters, but this reminds them of macaroni and cheese. I toss in some of their favorite veggies, and they devour it!

—LORI DANIELS BEVERLY, WV

START TO FINISH: 25 MIN.
MAKES: 4 SERVINGS

- 8 ounces uncooked bow tie pasta
- 1 pound smoked kielbasa or smoked Polish sausage, cut into ¼-inch slices
- 1 jar (4½ ounces) sliced mushrooms, drained
- 2 tablespoons butter
- 2 teaspoons minced garlic
- 1 tablespoon cornstarch
- 1½ cups milk
- 1½ cups fresh or frozen snow peas
- 1 cup (4 ounces) shredded cheddar cheese

1. Cook pasta according to package directions.
2. Meanwhile, in a large skillet, saute sausage and mushrooms in butter. Add garlic; cook 1 minute longer.
3. Combine cornstarch and milk until smooth; gradually add to the skillet. Bring to a boil; cook and stir 2 minutes or until thickened. Drain pasta; add to sausage mixture. Stir in the peas and cheese; cook until cheese is melted.

FREEZE OPTION *Cool pasta; transfer to freezer containers. Freeze for up to 3 months. To use, thaw in refrigerator overnight. Place in a Dutch oven; heat through. Sprinkle with additional cheese.*

Cook to Cook

All I can say is that this is FABULOUS! I wouldn't change a thing besides adding 8 ounces of fresh mushrooms instead of the 4.5-ounce jar of mushrooms and another ¼ cup of shredded cheddar cheese! This is a GREAT RECIPE and a QUICK ONE! —EQUESTSARAH81

30 MINUTES TO DINNER

Cook to Cook

My husband—who typically doesn't like this type of "helper-like" dinner—went back for seconds. I made it with ground turkey, and yes, I did add a little more taco seasoning to the mix. I added the sauce and seasonings to the meat in the pan after browning the meat. It was super fast and yummy! I'm adding it to my "make-again-dinner" list.
—LISA HANSON

FREEZE IT

TACO MAC

Pork sausage, taco seasoning and taco sauce add plenty of zip to easy macaroni and cheese. This zesty dish is just as yummy the next day.
—JOLYNN FRIBLEY NOKOMIS, IL

START TO FINISH: 30 MIN.
MAKES: 6 SERVINGS

- 1 **package (24 ounces) shells and cheese dinner mix**
- ½ **pound bulk pork sausage, cooked and drained**
- ⅓ **cup taco sauce**
- 1 **tablespoon taco seasoning**
- 4 **cups shredded lettuce**
- 2 **medium tomatoes, chopped**
- 1 **cup (4 ounces) shredded cheddar cheese, optional**

Prepare the shells and cheese mix according to the package directions. Stir in the sausage, taco sauce and seasoning; cook until heated through. Garnish with lettuce, tomatoes and cheddar cheese if desired.

FREEZE OPTION *Freeze individual portions of the cooled pasta mixture in freezer containers up to 3 months. To use, partially thaw in refrigerator overnight. Heat mixture through in a saucepan, stirring occasionally and adding a little milk if necessary. Garnish as directed.*

NOTE *This recipe was tested with Kraft Velveeta Family-Size Shells & Cheese.*

_____

_____

_____

_____

_____

_____

DOWN-HOME PORK CHOPS

A zippy sauce made of brown sugar, crushed red pepper flakes and soy sauce adds personality to this otherwise straightforward main dish.

—DENISE HRUZ GERMANTOWN, WI

START TO FINISH: 25 MIN.
MAKES: 4 SERVINGS

- 4 **boneless pork loin chops (4 ounces each)**
- 1 **tablespoon canola oil**
- 1 **garlic clove, minced**
- ½ **cup beef broth**
- 2 **tablespoons brown sugar**
- 1 **tablespoon soy sauce**
- ¼ **teaspoon crushed red pepper flakes**
- 2 **teaspoons cornstarch**
- 2 **tablespoons cold water**

1. In a large skillet over medium-high heat, brown pork chops on both sides in oil; remove and set aside. Add the garlic to pan; saute 1 minute. Stir in broth, brown sugar, soy sauce and pepper flakes.

2. Return chops to pan; cover and simmer 8-10 minutes or until meat reaches desired doneness (for medium-rare, a thermometer should read 145°; medium, 160°). Let stand 5 minutes before serving

3. Mix cornstarch and water until smooth; stir into the broth mixture. Bring to a boil; cook and stir 1 minute or until thickened. Serve with chops.

SAUSAGE POTATO SUPPER

One Saturday night a few years ago, I came up with this meal idea on the spur of the moment. It was dinnertime, I had to use what I had on hand—and this turned out to be a real winner.

—NANCY RUSSELL ENGLEWOOD, CO

START TO FINISH: 25 MIN.
MAKES: 2 SERVINGS

- 2 **small red potatoes, cubed**
- 1 **small zucchini, cut into ¼-inch slices**
- ¼ **to ½ teaspoon garlic salt**
- 1 **tablespoon butter**
- ½ **pound smoked sausage, cut into ½-inch slices**
- 4 **tablespoons grated Parmesan cheese, divided**
- ⅛ **to ¼ teaspoon pepper**

1. Place potatoes in a small saucepan and cover with water. Bring to a boil. Reduce heat; cover and cook 15-20 minutes or until tender.
2. Meanwhile, sprinkle zucchini with garlic salt. In a small skillet, stir-fry zucchini in butter until crisp-tender. Add sausage; cook until browned.
3. Drain potatoes; add to skillet. Sprinkle with 2 tablespoons Parmesan cheese and pepper; heat through. Sprinkle with remaining cheese.

APPLE-CHERRY PORK CHOPS

You'll never want pork chops any other way once you try this recipe! I season the juicy chops with a fragrant herb rub and serve them with a scrumptious apple-and-cherry sauce.

—DORIS HEATH FRANKLIN, NC

START TO FINISH: 30 MIN.
MAKES: 2 SERVINGS

- 2 **boneless pork loin chops** (½ inch thick and 5 ounces each)
- ¼ **teaspoon dried thyme**
- ⅛ **teaspoon salt**
- 1 **tablespoon olive oil**
- ⅔ **cup apple juice**
- 1 **small red apple, sliced**
- 2 **tablespoons dried cherries or cranberries**
- 2 **tablespoons chopped onion**
- 1 **teaspoon cornstarch**
- 1 **tablespoon cold water**

1. Sprinkle pork chops with thyme and salt. In a large skillet, cook pork in oil 3-4 minutes on each side or until the meat reaches desired doneness (for medium-rare, a thermometer should read 145°; medium, 160°). Remove and let meat stand 5 minutes.

2. Meanwhile, in the same skillet, combine the apple juice, apple, cherries and onion. Bring to a boil. Combine cornstarch and water until smooth; stir into skillet. Cook and stir 1-2 minutes or until thickened. Spoon over pork chops.

Cook to Cook

Very quick and tasty! Served it with brown ready-to-serve rice and fresh steamed broccoli. Thyme is my favorite spice on pork! **—DAISYSHAE99**

NOTES

30 MINUTES TO DINNER

MEDITERRANEAN PORK AND ORZO

All of the food groups are represented in this fresh and fabulous meal. It's one that my family requests time and again.

—MARY RELYEA CANASTOTA, NY

START TO FINISH: 30 MIN.
MAKES: 6 SERVINGS

- 2 **pork tenderloins (¾ pound each)**
- 1 **teaspoon coarsely ground pepper**
- 2 **tablespoons olive oil**
- 3 **quarts water**
- 1¼ **cups uncooked orzo pasta**
- ¼ **teaspoon salt**
- 1 **package (6 ounces) fresh baby spinach**
- 1 **cup grape tomatoes, halved**
- ¾ **cup crumbled feta cheese**

1. Rub pork with pepper; cut pork into 1-in. cubes. In a large nonstick skillet, heat oil over medium heat. Add pork; cook and stir 8-10 minutes or until no longer pink.

2. Meanwhile, in a Dutch oven, bring water to a boil. Stir in orzo and salt; cook, uncovered, 8 minutes. Stir in spinach; cook 45-60 seconds longer or until orzo is tender and spinach is wilted. Drain.

3. Add tomatoes to pork; heat through. Stir in orzo mixture and cheese.

NOTES

BLT WITH PEPPERED BALSAMIC MAYO

Here's my twist on a classic. Creamy avocado, balsamic mayo and crisp salad greens make this version legendary in my book. For a lighter take, use turkey bacon.

—**AMI BOYER** SAN FRANCISCO, CA

START TO FINISH: 25 MIN.
MAKES: 4 SERVINGS

- 8 **bacon strips, halved**
- ½ **cup mayonnaise**
- 1 **tablespoon balsamic vinegar**
- ½ **teaspoon pepper**
- ⅛ **teaspoon salt**
- 8 **slices bread, toasted**
- 2 **cups spring mix salad greens**
- 8 **cherry tomatoes, sliced**
- 1 **medium ripe avocado, peeled and sliced**

1. In a large skillet, cook bacon over medium heat until crisp. Remove to paper towels to drain.

2. In a small bowl, mix mayonnaise, vinegar, pepper and salt. Spread half of the mixture over four toast slices. Layer with the bacon, salad greens, tomatoes and avocado. Spread the remaining mayonnaise over remaining toast; place over top.

Cook to Cook

Loved this recipe! It was the first one that really caught my eye when I was looking through my *Taste of Home* magazine. The peppered balsamic mayo is sooo good, and I'm already thinking of other ways to use it....It made a nice complement to a regular BLT, along with the avocados, which added a real creaminess. A great light summer meal along with a bowl of gazpacho!

—VALANDDANSMITH

MINI HAM 'N' CHEESE PIZZAS

With ham, cheese and creamy Alfredo sauce, these little pizzas are sure to please. Best of all, they're kid-friendly.

—TASTE OF HOME TEST KITCHEN

START TO FINISH: 20 MIN.
MAKES: 4 SERVINGS

- ¼ cup refrigerated Alfredo sauce
- 4 pita breads (6 inches)
- 1 cup (4 ounces) shredded Swiss cheese
- 1¾ cups cubed fully cooked ham
- ½ cup shredded part-skim mozzarella cheese
- 1 tablespoon minced chives

1. Preheat oven to 350°. Spread Alfredo sauce over pita breads. Top with Swiss cheese, ham, mozzarella cheese and chives.

2. Place on an ungreased baking sheet. Bake 10-15 minutes or until the cheese is melted.

Cook to Cook

I added Canadian back bacon and pineapple to this, and it was delicious. Fast and easy to make. Will make this more often. **—GALHALL**

FAVORITE SKILLET LASAGNA

Whole wheat noodles and zucchini pump up nutrition in this delicious, family-friendly dinner. Topped with dollops of ricotta cheese, it has an extra touch of decadence. No one will believe this one's lighter.

—**LORIE MINER** KAMAS, UT

START TO FINISH: 30 MIN.
MAKES: 5 SERVINGS

- ½ **pound Italian turkey sausage links, casings removed**
- 1 **small onion, chopped**
- 1 **jar (14 ounces) spaghetti sauce**
- 2 **cups uncooked whole wheat egg noodles**
- 1 **cup water**
- ½ **cup chopped zucchini**
- ½ **cup fat-free ricotta cheese**
- 2 **tablespoons grated Parmesan cheese**
- 1 **tablespoon minced fresh parsley or 1 teaspoon dried parsley flakes**
- ½ **cup shredded part-skim mozzarella cheese**

1. In a large nonstick skillet, cook sausage and onion over medium heat until no longer pink; drain. Stir in the spaghetti sauce, egg noodles, water and zucchini. Bring to a boil. Reduce heat; cover and simmer 8-10 minutes or until noodles are tender, stirring occasionally.

2. Combine ricotta, Parmesan cheese and parsley. Drop by tablespoonfuls over pasta mixture. Sprinkle with mozzarella cheese; cover and cook 3-5 minutes or until cheese is melted.

CURRY CHICKEN

This is a big hit at our house. My young son and daughter just gobble it up. Your family will appreciate its irresistible blend of curry and sweet coconut milk.

—TRACY SIMIELE CHARDON, OH

START TO FINISH: 30 MIN.
MAKES: 4 SERVINGS

- 1½ **cups uncooked instant rice**
- 1 **pound boneless skinless chicken breasts, cut into 1-inch pieces**
- 2 **teaspoons curry powder**
- ¾ **teaspoon salt**
- ¼ **teaspoon pepper**
- ½ **cup chopped onion**
- 1 **tablespoon canola oil**
- 1 **can (13.66 ounces) coconut milk**
- 2 **tablespoons tomato paste**
- 3 **cups fresh baby spinach**
- 1 **cup chopped tomato**

1. Cook rice according to package directions.
2. Meanwhile, sprinkle the chicken with curry, salt and pepper. In a large skillet, saute chicken and onion in oil until chicken is no longer pink.
3. Stir in coconut milk and tomato paste. Bring to a boil. Reduce heat; simmer, uncovered, 5 minutes or until thickened. Add spinach and tomato; cook 2-3 minutes or until spinach is wilted. Serve with rice.

NOTES

CHICKEN AND BOWS

I first made this recipe when I was a professional nanny. It comes together in a snap and is ideal for dinner when the kids are hungry and you're strapped for time.

—**DANETTE FORBES** OVERLAND PARK, KS

START TO FINISH: 25 MIN.
MAKES: 12 SERVINGS

- 1 **package (16 ounces) bow tie pasta**
- 2 **pounds boneless skinless chicken breasts, cut into strips**
- 1 **cup chopped sweet red pepper**
- ¼ **cup butter, cubed**
- 2 **cans (10¾ ounces each) condensed cream of chicken soup, undiluted**
- 2 **cups frozen peas**
- 1½ **cups 2% milk**
- 1 **teaspoon garlic powder**
- ¼ to ½ **teaspoon salt**
- ¼ **teaspoon pepper**
- ⅔ **cup grated Parmesan cheese**

1. Cook pasta according to package directions.
2. Meanwhile, in a Dutch oven, cook chicken and red pepper in butter over medium heat 5-6 minutes or until chicken is no longer pink.
3. Stir in the soup, peas, milk, garlic powder, salt and pepper. Bring to a boil. Reduce heat; simmer, uncovered, 1-2 minutes or until heated through. Stir in cheese. Drain pasta; add to chicken mixture and toss to coat.

FREEZE OPTION *Transfer individual portions of cooled mixture to freezer containers. Freeze up to 3 months. To use, thaw in refrigerator overnight. Transfer to an ungreased shallow microwave-safe dish. Cover and microwave on high until heated through, stirring occasionally.*

Cook to Cook

My children just LOVED this recipe! I sauteed a clove of garlic in the butter for 30 seconds before adding the red pepper and chicken. I also added ½ cup onion in with the pepper and chicken. I seasoned the chicken with seasoning salt and omitted the salt in the recipe. Also omitted the garlic powder since I used fresh garlic. Even omitted the Parmesan cheese. It was still delicious!
—**MOMMYAUSTIN**

FAST & FABULOUS THAI CHICKEN SALAD

This healthful recipe looks time-consuming, but it's as simple as can be. Aside from mixing, the only prep work is chopping a red pepper.

—ELINOR IVES FISKDALE, MA

START TO FINISH: 20 MIN.
MAKES: 6 SERVINGS

- 1 **package (14 ounces) coleslaw mix**
- ⅓ **cup sesame ginger salad dressing**
- 2 **cups cubed cooked chicken**
- ½ **cup Thai peanut sauce**
- 1 **medium sweet red pepper, julienned**
- ½ **cup chow mein noodles**
- 2 **green onions, chopped**

In a large bowl, combine coleslaw mix and salad dressing. Transfer to a serving platter. Combine chicken and peanut sauce; place over coleslaw mixture. Top with red pepper, noodles and onions.

Cook to Cook

Excellent! Topped it with some peanuts, and it was a hit. **—5173NANCY**

TURKEY DIVAN

It looks and tastes decadent, but at just 291 calories per serving, this classic entree isn't much of a splurge. Pair it with a side salad and slice of whole grain bread for a complete meal.

—TASTE OF HOME TEST KITCHEN

START TO FINISH: 30 MIN.
MAKES: 8 SERVINGS

- 1½ cups water
- 16 fresh asparagus spears, trimmed
- 2 egg whites
- 1 egg
- 2 tablespoons fat-free milk
- 1¼ cups seasoned bread crumbs
- 1 package (17.6 ounces) turkey breast cutlets
- ¼ cup butter
- 8 slices deli ham
- 8 slices reduced-fat Swiss cheese

1. In a large skillet, bring water to a boil. Add asparagus; cover and boil 3 minutes. Drain and pat dry.

2. In a shallow bowl, beat the egg whites, egg and milk. Place bread crumbs in another shallow bowl. Dip turkey in egg mixture, then coat with crumbs.

3. In a large skillet, cook turkey in butter in batches 2-3 minutes on each side or until no longer pink. Layer each cutlet with a ham slice, two asparagus spears and cheese. Cover and cook 1 minute or until cheese is melted.

30 MINUTES TO DINNER

Cook to Cook

I love this recipe and make it quite often. I typically double the recipe and make a few modifications. I use Jennie-O Italian Seasoned Ground Turkey and add yellow squash and zucchini for some more veggies. It is super healthy and very tasty. —STRWBRRYSHRTCAKE97

PASTA FAGIOLI SOUP

My husband enjoys my version of this dish so much, he doesn't order it at restaurants anymore. With fresh spinach, pasta and seasoned sausage, this fast-to-fix soup eats like a meal.

—**BRENDA THOMAS** SPRINGFIELD, MO

START TO FINISH: 30 MIN.
MAKES: 5 SERVINGS

- ½ **pound Italian turkey sausage links, casings removed, crumbled**
- 1 **small onion, chopped**
- 1½ **teaspoons canola oil**
- 1 **garlic clove, minced**
- 2 **cups water**
- 1 **can (15½ ounces) great northern beans, rinsed and drained**
- 1 **can (14½ ounces) diced tomatoes, undrained**
- 1 **can (14½ ounces) reduced-sodium chicken broth**
- ¾ **cup uncooked elbow macaroni**
- ¼ **teaspoon pepper**
- 1 **cup fresh spinach leaves, cut into strips**
- 5 **teaspoons shredded Parmesan cheese**

1. In a large saucepan, cook sausage over medium heat until no longer pink; drain and set aside. In the same pan, saute onion in oil until tender. Add garlic; saute 1 minute longer.

2. Add the water, beans, tomatoes, broth, macaroni and pepper; bring to a boil. Cook, uncovered, 8-10 minutes or until macaroni is tender.

3. Reduce heat to low; stir in sausage and spinach. Cook 2-3 minutes or until spinach is wilted. Garnish with cheese.

CHICKEN PROVOLONE

Chicken Provolone, though one of my simplest dishes, is also one of my husband's favorites. It's effortless but looks fancy. I like to serve it on a dark plate with a garnish of fresh parsley or basil.

—DAWN E. BRYANT THEDFORD, NE

START TO FINISH: 25 MIN.
MAKES: 4 SERVINGS

- 4 **boneless skinless chicken breast halves (4 ounces each)**
- ¼ **teaspoon pepper**
  Butter-flavored cooking spray
- 8 **fresh basil leaves**
- 4 **thin slices prosciutto or deli ham**
- 4 **slices provolone cheese**

1. Sprinkle chicken with pepper. In a large nonstick skillet coated with butter-flavored cooking spray, cook chicken over medium heat 4-5 minutes on each side or until a thermometer reads 165°.

2. Transfer to an ungreased baking sheet; top with the basil, prosciutto and cheese. Broil 6-8 in. from heat 1-2 minutes or until cheese is melted.

30 MINUTES TO DINNER

BALSAMIC CHICKEN FETTUCCINE

Skip the marinara and serve noodles an elegant new way! Not only is this balsamic-infused entree a meal in itself, it makes a different twist on an Italian classic.

—TASTE OF HOME TEST KITCHEN

START TO FINISH: 25 MIN.
MAKES: 5 SERVINGS

- 8 ounces uncooked fettuccine
- 1½ pounds boneless skinless chicken breasts, cut into strips
- 2 tablespoons plus ½ cup balsamic vinaigrette, divided
- ½ pound sliced fresh mushrooms
- 1 medium red onion, chopped
- 2 cans (14½ ounces each) diced tomatoes, undrained
- 2 cups frozen broccoli florets
- ½ teaspoon Italian seasoning

1. Cook fettuccine according to package directions.

2. Meanwhile, in a large skillet, saute the chicken in 1 tablespoon vinaigrette until no longer pink. Remove and keep warm.

3. In same skillet, saute mushrooms and onion in 1 tablespoon vinaigrette until tender. Add the tomatoes, broccoli, Italian seasoning and remaining vinaigrette; cook 5-6 minutes longer or until heated through.

4. Drain fettuccine. Add fettuccine and chicken to skillet and toss to coat.

HEARTY TURKEY & RICE

We love this tasty dinner. It's takes just minutes to make and is the perfect meal when you're running late. You'll love the easy cleanup, too!

—JOAN HALLFORD

NORTH RICHLAND HILLS, TX

START TO FINISH: 25 MIN.
MAKES: 4 SERVINGS

- 1½ **cups instant brown rice**
- 1 **pound extra-lean ground turkey**
- 1 **medium onion, chopped**
- 1½ **cups salsa**
- 1 **can (8 ounces) no-salt-added tomato sauce**
- 1 **teaspoon reduced-sodium chicken bouillon granules**
- ¼ **teaspoon salt**
- ¼ **cup shredded reduced-fat cheddar cheese**
- ¼ **cup reduced-fat sour cream**
  Chopped tomatoes, baked tortilla chips and sliced ripe olives, optional

1. Cook rice according to package directions.

2. Meanwhile, in a large nonstick skillet coated with cooking spray, cook turkey and onion over medium heat until meat is no longer pink. Add the salsa, tomato sauce, bouillon and salt; heat through.

3. Serve with rice; top with cheese and sour cream. Garnish with tomatoes, chips and olives if desired.

FREEZE OPTION *Transfer individual portions of cooled meat mixture to freezer containers. To use, partially thaw in the refrigerator overnight. Heat through in a saucepan, stirring occasionally and adding a little water if necessary. Serve with rice.*

Cook to Cook

I really enjoyed this recipe. Made plenty for leftovers the next day. I'm thinking of adding black beans to the next go round! **—ALMORMON**

SPEEDY CHICKEN MARSALA

I've ordered Marsala so often in restaurants that I decided to create a version I could make in a flash at home.

—TRISHA KRUSE EAGLE, ID

START TO FINISH: 30 MIN.
MAKES: 4 SERVINGS

- 8 **ounces uncooked whole wheat or multigrain angel hair pasta**
- 4 **boneless skinless chicken breast halves (5 ounces each)**
- ¼ **cup all-purpose flour**
- 1 **teaspoon lemon-pepper seasoning**
- ½ **teaspoon salt**
- 2 **tablespoons olive oil, divided**
- 4 **cups sliced fresh mushrooms**
- 1 **garlic clove, minced**
- 1 **cup dry Marsala wine**

1. Cook pasta according to package directions.
2. Meanwhile, pound chicken with a meat mallet to ¼-in. thickness. In a large resealable plastic bag, mix the flour, lemon-pepper and salt. Add chicken, one piece at a time; close bag and shake to coat.
3. In a large skillet, heat 1 tablespoon oil over medium heat. Add chicken; cook 4-5 minutes on each side or until no longer pink. Remove from pan.
4. In the same skillet, heat remaining oil over medium-high heat. Add the mushrooms; cook and stir until tender. Add garlic; cook 1 minute longer. Add wine; bring to a boil. Cook 5-6 minutes or until liquid is reduced by half, stirring to loosen browned bits from pan. Return chicken to pan, turning to coat with sauce; heat through.
5. Drain pasta; serve with chicken mixture.

Cook to Cook

This was really delicious and quick to do. I had the store flatten the chicken breasts for me, and the rest was easy. I made 2 times the sauce to put over sweet potatoes. **—SMASUE**

WALDORF TURKEY SALAD

Crisp apples, celery and walnuts teamed with lean poultry turn any meal into a picnic. The combination of tastes and textures makes this salad a cool classic.

—MITZI SENTIFF ANNAPOLIS, MD

START TO FINISH: 25 MIN.
MAKES: 4 SERVINGS

- 1 cup (8 ounces) plain yogurt
- 2 tablespoons honey
- ⅛ to ¼ teaspoon ground ginger
- ¼ teaspoon salt
- 2 cups cubed cooked turkey breast
- 1 cup cubed apple
- 1 cup seedless red grapes, halved
- ½ cup thinly sliced celery
- ½ cup raisins
- 4 lettuce leaves
- 2 tablespoons chopped walnuts

1. In a small bowl, whisk the yogurt, honey, ginger and salt. In a large bowl, combine the turkey, apple, grapes, celery and raisins; add yogurt mixture and toss to coat.
2. Serve on lettuce; sprinkle with walnuts.

BEST CHICKEN 'N' BISCUITS

Quick and comforting, this delicious dish is filled with chunky chicken, colorful veggies and spoonfuls of creamy flavor. It's sure to warm your family to their toes!

—JUDITH WHITFORD EAST AURORA, NY

START TO FINISH: 30 MIN.
MAKES: 6 SERVINGS

- 6 **individually frozen biscuits**
- 1 **can (49½ ounces) chicken broth, divided**
- 1½ **pounds boneless skinless chicken breasts, cubed**
- 5 **medium carrots, coarsely chopped**
- 2 **celery ribs, chopped**
- ½ **cup chopped onion**
- ½ **cup frozen corn**
- 3 **teaspoons dried basil**
- ¼ **teaspoon pepper**
- 1 **cup all-purpose flour**
- ¾ **teaspoon browning sauce, optional**

1. Bake biscuits according to package directions.
2. Meanwhile, in a Dutch oven, mix 4 cups broth, chicken, carrots, celery, onion, corn, basil and pepper. Bring to a boil. Reduce heat; cover and simmer 7-10 minutes or until the vegetables are tender.
3. In a small bowl, combine flour and remaining broth until smooth. Stir into chicken mixture. Bring to a boil; cook and stir 2 minutes or until thickened. Stir in browning sauce if desired. Split biscuits; top with chicken mixture.

Cook to Cook

I had never made chicken and biscuits before, and this was a fantastic recipe! I added some fresh herbs (thyme, parsley, basil) but that was the only thing I changed! It was the perfect meal for a rainy day. Will make again!
—AWESOME_ASHLEY41

AUTUMN TURKEY TENDERLOINS

This out-of-the-ordinary meal is perfect for cool nights with family, friends or company. With cinnamon and brown sugar, it's slightly sweet, and the walnuts add a wonderful toasty, nutty crunch.

—**BRENDA LION** WARREN, PA

START TO FINISH: 30 MIN.
MAKES: 5 SERVINGS

- 1¼ **pounds turkey breast tenderloins**
- 1 **tablespoon butter**
- 1 **cup unsweetened apple juice**
- 1 **medium apple, sliced**
- 1 **tablespoon brown sugar**
- 2 **teaspoons chicken bouillon granules**
- ¼ **teaspoon ground cinnamon**
- ¼ **teaspoon ground nutmeg**
- 1 **tablespoon cornstarch**
- 2 **tablespoons cold water**
- ½ **cup chopped walnuts, toasted**

1. In a large skillet, brown turkey in butter. Add the apple juice, apple, brown sugar, bouillon, cinnamon and nutmeg. Bring to a boil. Reduce heat; cover and simmer 10-12 minutes or until a thermometer reads 165°.

2. Using a slotted spoon, remove turkey and apple slices to a serving platter; keep warm.

3. Combine cornstarch and water until smooth; stir into pan juices. Bring to a boil; cook and stir 2 minutes or until thickened. Spoon over turkey and apple. Sprinkle with walnuts.

NOTES

PEPPERONI PENNE CARBONARA

Sun-dried tomatoes and turkey pepperoni lend fantastic flavor to this creamy, hearty pasta dish. It's a great change of pace from everyday spaghetti.

—TASTE OF HOME TEST KITCHEN

START TO FINISH: 30 MIN.
MAKES: 6 SERVINGS

- 3 **cups uncooked penne pasta**
- 2 **cups chopped sun-dried tomatoes (not packed in oil)**
- 3 **cups boiling water**
- ¼ **cup butter**
- ½ **teaspoon minced garlic**
- 1 **cup chopped turkey pepperoni**
- 1 **cup shredded Parmesan cheese**
- 1 **cup heavy whipping cream**
- 3 **tablespoons minced fresh basil**
- ½ **teaspoon salt**
- ¼ **teaspoon pepper**

1. Cook pasta according to package directions.
2. Meanwhile, soak tomatoes in boiling water 10 minutes; drain well.
3. In a large skillet, saute tomatoes in butter 3 minutes. Add garlic; cook 1 minute longer.
4. Stir in pepperoni, cheese, cream, basil, salt and pepper. Cook over low heat until heated through. Drain pasta; toss with sauce.

Cook to Cook

Delicious! I added bacon, just because bacon is wonderous!
—WILLIAMSEGRAVES

SALSA VERDE CHICKEN CASSEROLE

Here's a rich and tasty rendition of all my favorite Tex-Mex dishes rolled into one delectable casserole. Best of all, it's ready in no time!

—**JANET MCCORMICK** PROCTORVILLE, OH

START TO FINISH: 30 MIN.
MAKES: 6 SERVINGS

- 2 **cups shredded rotisserie chicken**
- 1 **cup (8 ounces) sour cream**
- 1½ **cups salsa verde, divided**
- 8 **corn tortillas (6 inches)**
- 2 **cups chopped tomatoes**
- ¼ **cup minced fresh cilantro**
- 2 **cups (8 ounces) shredded Monterey Jack cheese**
  Optional toppings: avocado slices, thinly sliced green onions or fresh cilantro leaves

1. Preheat oven to 400°. In a small bowl, combine the chicken, sour cream and ¾ cup salsa. Spread ¼ cup salsa on the bottom of a greased 8-in.-square baking dish.

2. Layer with half of the tortillas and chicken mixture; sprinkle with the tomatoes, minced cilantro and half of the cheese. Repeat layers with the remaining tortillas, chicken mixture and cheese.

3. Bake, uncovered, 20-25 minutes or until bubbly. Serve with remaining salsa and, if desired, optional toppings.

30 MINUTES
TO DINNER

SHRIMP & TOMATO LINGUINE TOSS

Looking for lighter fare for supper? Pair this fast and flavorful pasta toss with salad and breadsticks for a stress-free meal.

—LOUISE GILBERT QUESNEL, BC

START TO FINISH: 15 MIN.
MAKES: 3 SERVINGS

- **6 ounces uncooked linguine**
- **⅓ pound uncooked medium shrimp, peeled and deveined**
- **3 garlic cloves, minced**
- **1 tablespoon olive oil**
- **1 can (14½ ounces) fire-roasted diced tomatoes, undrained**
- **2 teaspoons minced fresh basil or ½ teaspoon dried basil**
- **Dash pepper**
- **½ cup crumbled feta cheese**
- **Additional minced fresh basil, optional**

1. Cook linguine according to package directions.

2. Meanwhile, in a large skillet, cook shrimp and garlic in oil over medium heat until shrimp turn pink. Add the tomatoes, basil and pepper. Bring to a boil; cook and stir 1-2 minutes or until heated through.

3. Drain linguine; toss with tomato mixture. Sprinkle with the feta and additional basil if desired.

SOUTHWESTERN SCALLOPS

My saucy sea scallops are popular at dinner parties, and they're in my collection of easy weekday meals. The seasoning gives the sweet shellfish a pleasant kick.

—**MAGGIE FONTENOT** THE WOODLANDS, TX

START TO FINISH: 20 MIN.
MAKES: 4 SERVINGS

- 2 **teaspoons chili powder**
- ½ **teaspoon ground cumin**
- ¼ **teaspoon salt**
- ⅛ **teaspoon pepper**
- 1 **pound sea scallops (about 12)**
- 2 **tablespoons butter, divided**
- ½ **cup white wine or chicken broth**

1. In a small bowl, combine the chili powder, cumin, salt and pepper. Pat scallops dry with paper towels. Rub seasoning mixture over scallops.

2. In a large heavy skillet over medium heat, melt 1 tablespoon butter. Cook scallops 2 minutes on each side or until opaque and golden brown. Remove from skillet; keep warm.

3. Add wine to skillet, stirring to loosen any browned bits from pan. Bring to a boil; cook until liquid is reduced by half. Stir in remaining butter until melted. Serve with the scallops.

Cook to Cook

This was fantastic! I served it with rice pilaf, tossed green salad and a bottle of wine. We drained the scallops and reserved the liquid. When we added the wine to the skillet, we added the liquid, too. We'll definitely make this again!
—**WI BUG**

TILAPIA FLORENTINE

Get a little more heart-healthy fish into your weekly diet with this quick and easy entree. Topped with fresh spinach and a splash of lime, it's sure to become a go-to recipe!

—MELANIE BACHMAN ULYSSES, PA

START TO FINISH: 30 MIN.
MAKES: 4 SERVINGS

- 1 package (6 ounces) fresh baby spinach
- 6 teaspoons canola oil, divided
- 4 tilapia fillets (4 ounces each)
- 2 tablespoons lime juice
- 2 teaspoons garlic-herb seasoning blend
- 1 egg, lightly beaten
- ½ cup part-skim ricotta cheese
- ¼ cup grated Parmesan cheese

1. Preheat oven to 375°. In a large nonstick skillet, cook spinach in 4 teaspoons oil until wilted; drain.
2. Meanwhile, place tilapia in a greased 13x9-in. baking dish. Drizzle with lime juice and remaining oil. Sprinkle with seasoning blend.
3. In a small bowl, mix egg, ricotta cheese and spinach; spoon over fillets. Sprinkle with Parmesan cheese.
4. Bake 15-20 minutes or until fish flakes easily with a fork.

NOTES

_____
_____
_____
_____
_____
_____

SPLIT-SECOND SHRIMP

The microwave cooks my shrimp scampi in short order and it also keeps the kitchen cool in summer. The buttery garlic flavor makes this entree super for dinner—or even as a special-occasion appetizer.

—JALAYNE LUCKETT MARION, IL

START TO FINISH: 10 MIN.
MAKES: 6 SERVINGS

- 2 **tablespoons butter**
- 1½ **teaspoons minced garlic**
- ⅛ to ¼ **teaspoon cayenne pepper**
- 2 **tablespoons white wine or chicken broth**
- 5 **teaspoons lemon juice**
- 1 **tablespoon minced fresh parsley**
- ½ **teaspoon salt**
- 1 **pound uncooked large shrimp, peeled and deveined**

1. In a 9-in. microwave-safe pie plate, combine butter, garlic and cayenne. Cover and microwave on high 1 minute or until butter is melted. Stir in wine, lemon juice, parsley and salt. Add shrimp; toss to coat.

2. Cover and microwave on high for 2½ to 3½ minutes or until shrimp turn pink. Stir before serving.

NOTE *This recipe was tested in a 1,100-watt microwave.*

Cook to Cook

I love this recipe! So simple, with tasty results. I like to serve it atop angel hair pasta along with a green salad.
—LORI KOSTECKI

30 MINUTES TO DINNER

49

DIJON-CRUSTED FISH

Dijon, Parmesan and a hint of horseradish give this toasty fish lots of flavor. The prep is so simple, it just takes about 5 minutes to get four servings ready for the oven.

—**SCOTT SCHMIDTKE** CHICAGO, IL

START TO FINISH: 25 MIN.
MAKES: 4 SERVINGS

- 3 tablespoons reduced-fat mayonnaise
- 2 tablespoons grated Parmesan cheese, divided
- 1 tablespoon lemon juice
- 2 teaspoons Dijon mustard
- 1 teaspoon horseradish
- 4 tilapia fillets (5 ounces each)
- ¼ cup dry bread crumbs
- 2 teaspoons butter, melted

1. Preheat oven to 425°. In a small bowl, mix mayonnaise, 1 tablespoon cheese, lemon juice, mustard and horseradish. Place fillets on a baking sheet coated with cooking spray. Spread mayonnaise mixture evenly over fillets.

2. In a small bowl, combine the bread crumbs, butter and remaining cheese; sprinkle over fillets.

3. Bake 13-18 minutes or until the fish flakes easily with a fork.

Cook to Cook

My family loved this. Since I didn't have any Dijon mustard, I used yellow mustard with seasoning and it still turned out great. We all thought that the Dijon would make it even better.
—**MODOGEIST**

SOUTHWEST FISH TACOS

These fish tacos are an adaptation of a dish I was served in Bermuda. There is almost no prep work, which makes them an ideal recipe when time is tight .

—JENNIFER REID FARMINGTON, ME

START TO FINISH: 20 MIN.
MAKES: 4 SERVINGS

- 1½ **pounds sole fillets, cut into 1-inch strips**
- 1 **tablespoon taco seasoning**
- ¼ **cup butter, cubed**
- 1 **package (10 ounces) angel hair coleslaw mix**
- ½ **cup minced fresh cilantro**
- ½ **cup reduced-fat mayonnaise**
- 1 **tablespoon lime juice**
- 1 **teaspoon sugar**
- ¼ **teaspoon salt**
- ¼ **teaspoon pepper**
- 8 **taco shells, warmed**
- 8 **lime wedges**

1. Sprinkle fish with taco seasoning. In a large skillet over medium heat, cook fish in butter 3-4 minutes on each side or until fish flakes easily with a fork.
2. Meanwhile, in a small bowl, mix coleslaw, cilantro, mayonnaise, lime juice, sugar, salt and pepper.
3. Place fish in taco shells. Top with coleslaw mixture; serve with lime wedges.

30 MINUTES TO DINNER

SESAME NOODLES WITH SHRIMP & SNAP PEAS

Stir-fries and busy nights are a meal match made in heaven. For a boost of vibrant color and freshness, I sometimes stir in chopped cilantro just before serving it.

—**NEDRA SCHELL** FORT WORTH, TX

START TO FINISH: 25 MIN.
MAKES: 4 SERVINGS

- 8 **ounces uncooked whole wheat linguine**
- 1 **tablespoon canola oil**
- 1 **pound uncooked medium shrimp,** peeled and deveined
- 2 **cups fresh sugar snap peas,** trimmed
- ⅛ **teaspoon salt**
- ⅛ **teaspoon crushed red pepper flakes**
- ¾ **cup reduced-fat Asian toasted sesame salad dressing**

1. Cook linguine according to package directions for al dente.

2. Meanwhile, in a large skillet, heat oil over medium-high heat. Add shrimp, peas, salt and pepper flakes; stir-fry 2-3 minutes or until shrimp turn pink and peas are crisp-tender.

3. Drain linguine, reserving ¼ cup pasta water. Add pasta, pasta water and salad dressing to shrimp mixture; toss

Cook to Cook

A great, quick meal! I used regular pasta and added some onion and red bell pepper to the stir-fry and it was delicious! —**CAST_IRON_KING**

NOTES

_____

_____

_____

_____

_____

BROCCOLI CHEESE TORTELLINI

When we lived in Seattle, my favorite restaurant served a wonderful dish I ordered every time I ate there. When we moved away, I came up with this to satisfy my craving.

—DARLENE BRENDEN SALEM, OR

START TO FINISH: 25 MIN.
MAKES: 6 SERVINGS

- 2 **cups heavy whipping cream**
- 1 **cup fresh broccoli florets**
- 2 **packages (9 ounces each) refrigerated cheese tortellini**
- 2½ **cups shredded Parmesan cheese, divided**
- ¼ **teaspoon coarsely ground pepper**
- 2 **teaspoons minced fresh parsley**

1. In a large saucepan, cook cream and broccoli, uncovered, over medium-low heat 5-6 minutes or until broccoli is crisp-tender.
2. Meanwhile, cook the tortellini according to package directions.
3. Stir 2 cups cheese and pepper into broccoli mixture. Bring to a boil. Reduce heat; simmer, uncovered, 8-10 minutes or until mixture is thickened, stirring occasionally.
4. Drain tortellini; add to sauce and toss to coat. Sprinkle with parsley and remaining cheese.

PASTA CARBONARA

My hungry clan can't get enough of this creamy, cheesy recipe. Serve it with a side salad and your favorite rolls to round out the meal.

—**CINDI BAUER** MARSHFIELD, WI

START TO FINISH: 30 MIN.
MAKES: 4 SERVINGS

- 2½ cups uncooked mostaccioli
- 8 bacon strips, diced
- 1 jar (4½ ounces) whole mushrooms, drained
- ¾ cup half-and-half cream
- ⅓ cup butter, cubed
- 1 teaspoon dried parsley flakes
- 1 teaspoon minced garlic
- 6 to 8 drops hot pepper sauce
- ½ teaspoon salt, optional
- ⅓ cup grated Parmesan cheese
- ¼ cup sliced green onions

1. Cook mostaccioli according to package directions.
2. Meanwhile, in a large skillet, cook bacon over medium heat until crisp. Using a slotted spoon, remove to paper towels to drain. Brown mushrooms in drippings; remove to paper towels. Drain drippings from pan.
3. Add the cream, butter, parsley, garlic, pepper sauce and, if desired, salt to skillet; cook and stir over medium heat until butter is melted.
4. Drain mostaccioli; add to cream mixture. Stir in bacon, mushrooms and cheese; heat through. Remove from the heat. Sprinkle with green onions.

Cook to Cook

I am SO impressed with this recipe. I made it in a flash, and it was gone even faster. Restaurant quality flavor and texture. My changes were just slight, because I had the stuff lying around, but I used fresh crimini mushrooms instead of canned and added some fresh chopped spinach. It was AMAZING. This one slid into the "favorites" folder within an hour. Thanks to the originator for making my day! —**10SCHICK**

SPINACH PIZZA

Looking for a meatless dinner? Here's a vegetarian pizza that is so easy to prepare. What a delicious way to make a veggie—filled meal!

—DAWN BARTHOLOMEW RALEIGH, NC

START TO FINISH: 25 MIN.
MAKES: 4-6 SERVINGS

- 1 **package (6½ ounces) pizza crust mix**
- ½ **cup Alfredo sauce**
- 2 **medium tomatoes**
- 4 **cups chopped fresh spinach**
- 2 **cups (8 ounces) shredded Italian cheese blend**

1. Preheat oven to 450°. Prepare pizza dough according to package directions. With floured hands, press dough onto a greased 12-in. pizza pan.

2. Spread Alfredo sauce over dough to within 1 in. of edges. Thinly slice or chop tomatoes; top pizza with spinach, tomatoes and cheese.

3. Bake 10-15 minutes or until cheese is melted and crust is golden brown.

ROASTED PEPPER TORTELLINI

Convenient refrigerated pasta can turn any time at all into pasta time.

—TASTE OF HOME TEST KITCHEN

START TO FINISH: 25 MIN.
MAKES: 6 SERVINGS

- 1 **package refrigerated cheese tortellini**
- 1 **pound bulk Italian sausage**
- ½ **cup chopped onion**
- 2 **jars roasted sweet red peppers, drained**
- 1 **can pizza sauce**
  Shredded part-skim mozzarella cheese

1. Cook tortellini according to package directions.

2. Meanwhile, cook sausage and onion in a large skillet over medium heat until meat is no longer pink; drain.

3. Process peppers in a food processor until smooth. Add the peppers, pizza sauce and drained tortellini to skillet; heat through. Sprinkle with the mozzarella cheese.

NOTES

5 SIMPLE INGREDIENTS

Take a look at what five readily available ingredients can make!

5 SIMPLE INGREDIENTS INDEX

Cook to Cook

Look for
THESE boxes
for helpful tidbits!

TORTILLA BEEF BAKE

My family loves Mexican food, so I devised this simple satisfying casserole that gets its spark from salsa. We like it so much that there are rarely any leftovers.

— KIM OSBURN LIGONIER, IN

PREP: 10 MIN. **BAKE:** 30 MIN.
MAKES: 6 SERVINGS

- 1½ **pounds ground beef**
- 1 **can (10¾ ounces) condensed cream of chicken soup, undiluted**
- 2½ **cups crushed tortilla chips, divided**
- 1 **jar (16 ounces) salsa**
- 1½ **cups (6 ounces) shredded cheddar cheese**

1. Preheat oven to 350°. In a large skillet, cook beef over medium heat until no longer pink; drain. Stir in soup.
2. Sprinkle 1½ cups tortilla chips in a greased shallow 2½-qt. baking dish. Top with the beef mixture, salsa and cheese.
3. Bake, uncovered, 25-30 minutes or until bubbly. Sprinkle with remaining chips. Bake 3 minutes longer or until chips are lightly toasted.

BALSAMIC-SEASONED STEAK

A tasty marinade makes this sirloin so delicious! You'll love its simple preparation and scrumptious Swiss-cheese topping.

—TASTE OF HOME TEST KITCHEN

START TO FINISH: 25 MIN.
MAKES: 4 SERVINGS

- 2 **tablespoons balsamic vinegar**
- 2 **teaspoons steak sauce**
- 1 **beef top sirloin steak (1 pound)**
- ¼ **teaspoon coarsely ground pepper**
- 2 **ounces reduced-fat Swiss cheese, cut into thin strips**

1. In a small bowl, combine vinegar and steak sauce; set aside. Rub steak with pepper. Place on a broiler pan. Broil 4 in. from heat for 7 minutes.

2. Turn; spoon half of the steak sauce mixture over steak. Broil 5-7 minutes longer or until the meat reaches desired doneness (for medium-rare, a thermometer should read 145°; medium, 160°; well-done, 170°).

3. Remove steak to a cutting board; cut across the grain into ¼-in. slices. Place on a foil-lined baking sheet; drizzle with juices from cutting board and remaining steak sauce mixture. Top with cheese.

4. Broil 1 minute or until the cheese is melted.

NOTES

_____
_____
_____
_____
_____
_____

CREAMY BEEF & POTATOES

One of my husband's favorite childhood memories was eating his Grandma Barney's Tater Tot Casserole. We've found that the dish is just as comforting when made with O'Brien potatoes.

— HEATHER MATTHEWS KELLER, TX

START TO FINISH: 20 MIN.
MAKES: 4 SERVINGS

- 4 **cups frozen O'Brien potatoes**
- 1 **tablespoon water**
- 1 **pound ground beef**
- ½ **teaspoon salt**
- ¼ **teaspoon pepper**
- 2 **cans (10¾ ounces each) condensed cream of mushroom soup, undiluted**
- ⅔ **cup 2% milk**
- 2 **cups (8 ounces) shredded Colby-Monterey Jack cheese**

1. Place potatoes and water in a microwave-safe bowl. Microwave, covered, on high 8-10 minutes or until tender, stirring twice.

2. Meanwhile, in a Dutch oven, cook beef over medium heat 6-8 minutes or until no longer pink, breaking into crumbles; drain. Stir in salt and pepper.

3. In a small bowl, whisk soup and milk until blended; add to beef. Stir in potatoes. Sprinkle with cheese. Reduce heat to low; cook, covered, until cheese is melted.

NOTE *This recipe was tested in a 1,100-watt microwave.*

Cook to Cook

Pretty good and super-quick and easy. I will probably add more veggies like corn or peas next time, but definitely not bad for something to make in a pinch when you really don't feel like cooking.
—SCHAPDEL

5 SIMPLE INGREDIENTS

MARMALADE-GLAZED STEAKS

Marmalade and mustard? They may sound like strange bedfellows, but this tasty main course proves they're a match made in mouthwatering heaven.

—**MIKE TCHOU** PEPPER PIKE, OH

START TO FINISH: 20 MIN.
MAKES: 4 SERVINGS

- ½ cup orange marmalade
- 2 tablespoons spicy brown mustard
- 2 tablespoons cold butter
- 1 beef top sirloin steak (1¼ pounds), cut into four steaks
- 2 green onions, chopped

1. In a small saucepan, heat marmalade and mustard over low heat. Whisk in butter until melted. Set aside ¼ cup glaze for serving.

2. Broil steaks 4 in. from heat 5-7 minutes on each side or until meat reaches desired doneness (for medium-rare, a thermometer should read 145°; medium, 160°; well-done, 170°), basting occasionally with remaining glaze.

3. Spoon reserved glaze over steaks; sprinkle with onions.

SMOTHERED BURRITOS

This recipe is quick and easy and will satisfy even the pickiest of eaters! Salsa verde is spicy. You can reduce the amount of salsa verde to make a milder version.

—KIM KENYON GREENWOOD, MO

START TO FINISH: 25 MIN.
MAKES: 4 SERVINGS

- 1 **can (10 ounces) green enchilada sauce**
- ¾ **cup salsa verde**
- 1 **pound ground beef**
- 4 **flour tortillas (10 inches), warmed**
- 1½ **cups (6 ounces) shredded cheddar cheese**

1. Preheat oven to 375°. Combine enchilada sauce and salsa verde in a small bowl. In a large skillet, cook beef over medium heat until no longer pink; drain. Stir in ½ cup sauce mixture.

2. Spoon ⅔ cup beef mixture off center on each tortilla; sprinkle each with 3 tablespoons cheese. Fold sides and ends over filling and roll up.

3. Transfer to a greased 11x7-in. baking dish. Pour remaining sauce mixture over burritos; sprinkle with remaining cheese. Bake, uncovered, 10-15 minutes or until cheese is melted.

Cook to Cook

I have tried many, many different burrito recipes—only to be disappointed. This one is a keeper for me. It is delicious and so, so simple! I wasn't sure about the salsa verde, so I substituted regular salsa in this recipe. It turned out great! **—RRVAUGHAN**

5 SIMPLE INGREDIENTS

BACON CHEESEBURGER PASTA

I try to make foods that are not only kid-friendly but also easy to reheat, since my husband works long hours and often eats later than our children. If you like, use reduced-fat cheese and ground turkey for a lighter version.

—MELISSA STEVENS ELK RIVER, MN

START TO FINISH: 30 MIN.
MAKES: 4 SERVINGS

- 8 **ounces uncooked penne pasta**
- 1 **pound ground beef**
- 6 **bacon strips, diced**
- 1 **can (10¾ ounces) condensed tomato soup, undiluted**
- ½ **cup water**
- 1 **cup (4 ounces) shredded cheddar cheese**
  Barbecue sauce and prepared mustard, optional

1. Cook pasta according to package directions.

2. Meanwhile, in a large skillet, cook beef over medium heat until no longer pink; drain and set aside.

3. In same skillet, cook bacon until crisp; remove with a slotted spoon to paper towels to drain. Discard drippings. Drain pasta; add to skillet. Stir in the soup, water, beef and bacon; heat through.

4. Remove from heat and sprinkle with cheese. Cover and let stand 2-3 minutes or until the cheese is melted. If desired, serve with barbecue sauce and mustard.

CAESAR STRIP STEAKS

I season New York strip steaks with a Caesar dressing mixture, then grill them for a tasty entree that's ready in minutes. As a side dish, I serve baked potatoes topped with chunky salsa and sour cream.

—MELISSA MORTON PHILADELPHIA, PA

START TO FINISH: 20 MIN.
MAKES: 4 SERVINGS

- 4 **tablespoons creamy Caesar salad dressing, divided**
- 2 **teaspoons garlic powder**
- 1 **teaspoon salt**
- 1 **teaspoon coarsely ground pepper**
- 2 **boneless beef top loin steaks (12 ounces each)**

1. In a small bowl, mix 2 tablespoons salad dressing, garlic powder, salt and pepper. Spoon over both sides of the steaks.

2. Grill, covered, over medium heat or broil 4 in. from heat 7-9 minutes on each side or until meat reaches desired doneness (for medium-rare, a thermometer should read 145°; medium, 160°; well-done, 170°), basting occasionally with remaining salad dressing. Cut steaks in half to serve.

NOTE *Top loin steak may be labeled as strip steak, KS City steak, NY strip steak, ambassador steak or boneless club steak in your region.*

Cook to Cook

Who would put Caesar dressing on a NYS (New York strip) steak? This was very good. I definitely will make it again!
—MSHELL5701

NOTES

5 SIMPLE INGREDIENTS

EASY & ELEGANT TENDERLOIN ROAST

I love the simplicity of these ingredients—olive oil, garlic, salt and pepper—and how they make such a scrumptious roast. Once it's in the oven, you'll have time to attend to other matters. Serve it with pearl onions.
—MARY KANDELL HURON, OH

PREP: 10 MIN. • **BAKE:** 50 MIN. + STANDING
MAKES: 12 SERVINGS

- 1 **beef tenderloin roast (5 pounds)**
- 2 **tablespoons olive oil**
- 4 **garlic cloves, minced**
- 2 **teaspoons sea salt**
- 1½ **teaspoons coarsely ground pepper**

1. Preheat oven to 425°. Place roast on a rack in a shallow roasting pan. In a small bowl, mix the oil, garlic, salt and pepper; rub over roast.

2. Roast 50-70 minutes or until meat reaches desired doneness (for medium-rare, a thermometer should read 145°; medium, 160°; well-done, 170°). Remove from the oven; tent with foil. Let stand 15 minutes before slicing.

Cook to Cook

I made this for our family Christmas dinner and could not be happier with it! The simple garlic rub was perfect. Served it with horseradish cream and sauteed mushrooms. To make the rub, I put the whole garlic cloves with the rest of the rub ingredients in a food processor. —MARTINNA

EASY STUFFED SHELLS

One day when we had unexpected guests, I just put this recipe together on the spot. It was an immediate hit and is now a family favorite. Let your kids can help by placing the meatballs in the shells.
—**DOLORES BETCHNER** CUDAHY, WI

PREP: 20 MIN. • **BAKE:** 40 MIN.
MAKES: 12 SERVINGS

- 1 package (12 ounces) jumbo pasta shells
- 1 jar (26 ounces) spaghetti sauce
- 36 frozen fully cooked Italian meatballs (½ ounce each), thawed
- 2 cups (8 ounces) shredded part-skim mozzarella cheese

1. Preheat oven to 350°. Cook pasta according to package directions; drain and rinse in cold water.

2. Place ½ cup sauce in a greased 13x9-in. baking dish. Place a meatball in each shell; transfer to prepared dish. Top with remaining sauce and sprinkle with cheese.

3. Cover and bake for 35 minutes. Uncover; bake 5-10 minutes longer or until bubbly and cheese is melted.

BEEFY FRENCH ONION POTPIE

My husband loves French Onion Soup, and I thought it could make a tasty base for a hearty, beef potpie. And was I right!

—SARA HUTCHENS DU QUOIN, IL

START TO FINISH: 30 MIN.
MAKES: 4 SERVINGS

- 1 **pound ground beef**
- 1 **small onion, chopped**
- 1 **can (10½ ounces) condensed French onion soup**
- 1½ **cups (6 ounces) shredded part-skim mozzarella cheese**
- 1 **tube (12 ounces) refrigerated buttermilk biscuits**

1. Preheat oven to 350°. In a large skillet, cook beef and onion over medium heat 6-8 minutes or until meat is no longer pink, breaking beef into crumbles; drain. Stir in soup; bring to a boil.

2. Transfer to an ungreased 9-in. deep-dish pie plate; sprinkle with cheese. Bake 5 minutes or until cheese is melted. Top with biscuits. Bake 15-20 minutes longer or until biscuits are golden brown.

Cook to Cook

Made this last night for a neighbor who stopped over at the last minute. I added a little garlic powder and a couple of splashes of Worchestershire sauce to the recipe, plus some chopped chives on top of the biscuits. It was liked by all. Quick, easy and delicious! **—KUIPO**

BREADED PORK CHOPS

A new zippy version of an old standby, this pork chop recipe is guaranteed to bring your family to the dinner table.

—**ANN INGALLS** GLADSTONE, MO

START TO FINISH: 30 MIN.
MAKES: 6 SERVINGS

- 1 **cup seasoned bread crumbs**
- 2 **tablespoons grated Parmesan cheese**
- ⅓ **cup prepared ranch salad dressing**
- 6 **bone-in pork loin chops (½ inch thick and 8 ounces each)**

1. Preheat oven to 375°. In a shallow bowl, combine bread crumbs and cheese. Place dressing in another shallow dish. Dip pork chops in dressing, then roll in crumb mixture.

2. Place in an ungreased 13x9-in. baking pan. Bake, uncovered, for 25 minutes or until meat reaches desired doneness (for medium-rare, a thermometer should read 145°; medium, 160°). Let stand 5 minutes before serving

NOTES

5 SIMPLE INGREDIENTS

69

SAVORY PORK ROAST

I enjoy this herbed roast so much that I make it as often as I can. It's wonderful for company, particularly when served with sweet potatoes and corn muffins.
—EDIE DESPAIN LOGAN, UT

PREP: 5 MIN. • **BAKE:** 80 MIN. + STANDING
MAKES: 12 SERVINGS

- 1 garlic clove, minced
- 2 teaspoons dried marjoram
- 1 teaspoon salt
- 1 teaspoon rubbed sage
- 1 boneless whole pork loin roast (4 pounds)

1. Preheat oven to 350°. Combine the seasonings; rub over roast. Place on a rack in a shallow roasting pan.
2. Bake, uncovered, 80 minutes or until meat reaches desired doneness (for medium-rare, a thermometer should read 145°; medium, 160°). Tent with foil; let stand 10-15 minutes before slicing.

SAUSAGE MANICOTTI

Manicotti has never been easier to make. This recipe comes together in a snap, but tastes like it took hours.

—CAROLYN HENDERSON MAPLE PLAIN, MN

PREP: 15 MIN. • **BAKE:** 65 MIN.
MAKES: 7 SERVINGS

- 1 **pound bulk pork sausage**
- 2 **cups (16 ounces) 4% cottage cheese**
- 1 **package (8 ounces) manicotti shells**
- 1 **jar (24 ounces) marinara sauce**
- 1 **cup (4 ounces) shredded part-skim mozzarella cheese**

1. Preheat oven to 350°. In a large bowl, combine sausage and cottage cheese. Stuff into manicotti shells. Place in a greased 13x9-in. baking dish. Top with marinara sauce.
2. Cover and bake 55-60 minutes or until a meat thermometer inserted into the center of a shell reads 160°.
3. Uncover; sprinkle with mozzarella cheese. Bake 8-10 minutes or until cheese is melted. Let stand 5 minutes before serving.

FREEZE OPTION *Transfer individual portions of cooled manicotti to freezer containers. To use, partially thaw in refrigerator overnight. Transfer to a microwave-safe dish and microwave on high, stirring occasionally and adding a little spaghetti sauce if necessary.*

Cook to Cook

This is by far the easiest, quickest and most tasty manicotti that I have ever made....and I have been cooking for my husband for 43 years! All I can say about this recipe is, it's a real keeper.
—KIRCHNER

NOTES

5 SIMPLE INGREDIENTS

FREEZE IT

RIGATONI & SAUSAGE

To serve a dozen people without much extra effort, simply double the recipe and prepare two of these hearty pasta casseroles at once.

—ELAINE NEUKIRCH GENOA, IL

PREP: 20 MIN. • **BAKE:** 15 MIN.
MAKES: 6 SERVINGS

- 3¾ cups uncooked rigatoni
- 5 Italian sausage links (4 ounces each), sliced
- 1 jar (24 ounces) spaghetti sauce
- ¼ cup dry red wine
- 2 cups (8 ounces) shredded Italian cheese blend

1. Preheat oven to 350°. Cook rigatoni according to package directions.
2. Meanwhile, in a Dutch oven, cook sausage over medium heat until no longer pink; drain. Add spaghetti sauce and wine.
3. Drain rigatoni; add to sausage mixture and toss to coat.
4. Transfer to a greased 13x9-in. baking dish; sprinkle with cheese. Bake, uncovered, 15-20 minutes or until cheese is melted.

FREEZE OPTION *Transfer individual portion of cooled pasta mixture to freezer containers. To use, partially thaw in refrigerator overnight. Heat through in a saucepan, stirring occasionally and adding a little spaghetti sauce if necessary.*

SPINACH RAVIOLI BAKE

This entree is unbelievably simple to prepare and tastes delicious. The fact that you use frozen ravioli—straight from the bag without boiling or thawing—saves so much time.

—SUSAN KEHL PEMBROKE PINES, FL

PREP: 5 MIN. • **BAKE:** 40 MIN.
MAKES: 6 SERVINGS

- 2 **cups spaghetti sauce**
- 1 **package (25 ounces) frozen sausage ravioli or ravioli of your choice**
- 2 **cups (8 ounces) shredded part-skim mozzarella cheese**
- 1 **package (10 ounces) frozen chopped spinach, thawed and squeezed dry**
- ¼ **cup grated Parmesan cheese**

1. Preheat oven to 350°. Place 1 cup spaghetti sauce in a greased shallow 2-qt. baking dish. Top with half of the ravioli, mozzarella cheese, spinach and Parmesan cheese. Repeat layers.
2. Bake, uncovered, 40-45 minutes or until heated through and cheese is melted.

Cook to Cook

This is great! I did increase the sauce by about a cup. I used shredded Parmesan instead of grated, but just because I had it on hand, and an Italian blend cheese instead of mozzarella, which I think added more flavor than mozzarella would. I baked 20 minutes covered and uncovered for the last 20-25 minutes, this helped to retain moisture. Awesome dish that my picky husband devoured!
—TSTREICH

5 SIMPLE INGREDIENTS

ONION-DIJON PORK CHOPS

Coated in a flavorful sauce, these chops are cooked to tender perfection. Serve with rice and carrots for a full meal.

—TASTE OF HOME TEST KITCHEN

START TO FINISH: 25 MIN.
MAKES: 4 SERVINGS

- 4 **boneless pork loin chops (5 ounces each)**
- ¼ **teaspoon salt**
- ¼ **teaspoon pepper**
- ¾ **cup thinly sliced red onion**
- ¼ **cup water**
- ¼ **cup cider vinegar**
- 3 **tablespoons brown sugar**
- 2 **tablespoons honey Dijon mustard**

1. Sprinkle pork chops with salt and pepper. In a large nonstick skillet coated with cooking spray, cook pork over medium heat 4-6 minutes on each side or until lightly browned. Remove and keep warm.

2. Add the remaining ingredients to the skillet, stirring to loosen browned bits from pan. Bring to a boil; cook and stir 2 minutes or until thickened.

3. Return chops to the pan. Reduce heat; cover and simmer 3-4 minutes or until meat reaches desired doneness (for medium-rare, a thermometer should read 145°; medium, 160°). Let stand 5 minutes before serving.

Cook to Cook

I replace the red onion with a sweet yellow onion. Sometimes I make this with chicken instead of pork, but it's delicious both ways. My family loved the recipe, too. I've made it quite a few times and it is always well-received.
—LMW238

CORN DOG TWISTS

Kids will have as much fun making this cute twist on hot dogs and buns as they will have eating them! Set out bowls of relish, mustard and ketchup for easy dipping.

—**MELISSA TATUM** GREENSBORO, NC

START TO FINISH: 25 MIN.
MAKES: 8 SERVINGS

- 1 **tube (11½ ounces) refrigerated corn bread twists**
- 8 **hot dogs**
- 1 **tablespoon butter, melted**
- 1 **tablespoon grated Parmesan cheese**

1. Preheat oven to 375°. Separate corn bread twists; wrap one strip around each hot dog. Brush strips with butter; sprinkle with cheese. Place on a lightly greased baking sheet.
2. Bake 11-13 minutes or until golden brown.

NOTES

5 SIMPLE INGREDIENTS

BARBECUE JACK CHICKEN

Pepper jack cheese from the deli and bottled barbecue sauce are all you need to dress up these grilled chicken breasts.

—TASTE OF HOME TEST KITCHEN

START TO FINISH: 25 MIN.
MAKES: 4 SERVINGS

- 4 **boneless skinless chicken breast halves (6 ounces each)**
- 4 **slices pepper jack cheese**
- 1 **cup barbecue sauce**

1. Carefully cut a pocket in each chicken breast half. Place a slice of cheese in each pocket. Secure with wooden toothpicks.

2. Grill chicken, covered, over medium heat or broil 4 in. from the heat 6-8 minutes on each side or until a thermometer reads 165º, basting frequently with barbecue sauce. Discard toothpicks before serving.

Cook to Cook

Very easy and a simple recipe to make on the fly. I switched the cheese to shredded Monterey Jack with jalapeno pepper; it gave the chicken some pop. Broiling this recipe worked out better then expected. —COUNTRYCOOKER75

CURRIED COCONUT CHICKEN

Looking for a new way to fix chicken breasts? This no-fuss recipe is a nice change of pace. It's sweet, savory and a little exotic. Serve it over rice or couscous.

—BECKY WALCH MANTECA, CA

PREP: 10 MIN. • **BAKE:** 30 MIN.
MAKES: 4 SERVINGS

- 3 **tablespoons butter, melted**
- 1 **cup flaked coconut**
- 2 **teaspoons curry powder**
- 4 **boneless skinless chicken breast halves (6 ounces each)**
- ¼ **teaspoon salt**
- 1 **cup apricot preserves, warmed**

1. Preheat oven to 350°. Place butter in a shallow bowl. In another shallow bowl, combine the coconut and curry powder. Dip chicken in butter, then coat with coconut mixture.

2. Place in a greased 13x9-in. baking dish; sprinkle with the salt. Bake, uncovered, 30-35 minutes or until a thermometer reads 165°. Serve with preserves.

5 SIMPLE
INGREDIENTS

CHICKEN IN PUFF PASTRY

You'll never believe a dish this scrumptious, comforting and impressive-looking could be made with just five ingredients! It offers such an easy way to entertain friends.

—GINA HOBBS TIFTON, GA

PREP: 15 MIN. • **BAKE:** 20 MIN.
MAKES: 4 SERVINGS

- 4 **chicken tenderloins**
- ⅛ **teaspoon salt**
- ⅛ **teaspoon pepper**
- 1 **sheet frozen puff pastry, thawed**
- ½ **cup spreadable spinach and artichoke cream cheese**
- 4 **slices Muenster cheese, halved**
- 1 **egg**
- 1 **tablespoon water**

1. Preheat oven to 400°. Sprinkle chicken with salt and pepper; set aside. On a lightly floured surface, roll puff pastry into a 14-in. square. Cut into four squares.
2. Spoon 2 tablespoons cream cheese onto the center of each square; top with Muenster cheese and chicken.
3. Whisk egg and water; lightly brush over edges. Bring opposite corners of pastry over each bundle; pinch seams to seal. Place seam side down on a greased baking sheet; brush with remaining egg mixture.
4. Bake 18-22 minutes or until golden brown.

NOTES

APRICOT-ALMOND CHICKEN BREASTS

This chicken dish is so delicious, even my picky eaters clamor for it! It takes only minutes to prepare, so on busy weeknights I can put a healthy supper on the table.

—**TRISHA KRUSE** EAGLE, ID

PREP: 10 MIN. • **BAKE:** 30 MIN.
MAKES: 4 SERVINGS

- 4 **boneless skinless chicken breast halves (6 ounces each)**
- ½ **teaspoon salt**
- ¼ **teaspoon pepper**
- ¾ **cup apricot preserves**
- ¼ **cup reduced-sodium chicken broth**
- 1 **tablespoon honey mustard**
- ¼ **cup sliced almonds**

1. Preheat oven to 350°. Sprinkle chicken with salt and pepper. Place in a 13x9-in. baking dish coated with cooking spray. Bake, uncovered, 15 minutes.

2. In a small bowl, mix the preserves, broth and mustard. Pour over chicken; sprinkle with almonds. Bake 15-20 minutes longer or until the chicken juices run clear.

Cook to Cook

Peach preserves can be substituted for apricot preserves, and the recipe is equally delicious. Also, toasting the almonds in the oven before using gives them more flavor. I have used this recipe over and over and have received numerous requests for it. Absolutely delicious!
—**CATERING**

LEMON BASIL CHICKEN

Here's a recipe for tender, fragrant chicken that will make Sunday dinner—or any time, special. Fresh basil makes all the difference.

—MARIE MARSHALL CHURCH POINT, LA

PREP: 15 MIN.
BAKE: 1¼ HOURS + STANDING
MAKES: 6 SERVINGS

- 1 **medium lemon**
- 2 **garlic cloves, peeled, divided**
- ¼ **cup minced fresh basil, divided**
- 1 **broiler/fryer chicken (3 to 4 pounds)**
- 2 **tablespoons butter, melted**
- ½ **teaspoon salt**
- ¼ **teaspoon pepper**

1. Preheat oven to 375°. Finely grate enough peel from lemon to measure 2 teaspoons. Cut the lemon in half; squeeze juice from one half. Set aside. Slice one garlic clove; place sliced garlic, 2 tablespoons basil and the remaining lemon half in chicken cavity.
2. Place on a rack in a shallow roasting pan; rub with reserved lemon juice. Mince remaining garlic; combine with butter and reserved lemon peel. Rub mixture over chicken. Sprinkle with salt, pepper and remaining basil.
3. Bake, uncovered, 1¼ to 1½ hours or until a thermometer inserted in thickest part of a thigh reads 170-175°. Tent with foil; let stand 15 minutes before carving.

Cook to Cook

When I made this recipe the first time, my family loved it. Turns out just like the picture. Now when my husband makes it, he cooks two. Love the flavor and taste. YUM. —PAT VELLINO

BROCCOLI CHICKEN CASSEROLE

All ages really seem to go for this comforting, scrumptious meal in one. It takes just a handful of ingredients and minutes to put together. I've found that adding dried cranberries to the stuffing mix also adds flavor and color!

—JENNIFER SCHLACHTER BIG ROCK, IL

PREP: 15 MIN. • **BAKE:** 30 MIN.
MAKES: 6 SERVINGS

- 1½ **cups water**
- 1 **package (6 ounces) chicken stuffing mix**
- 2 **cups cubed cooked chicken**
- 1 **cup frozen broccoli florets, thawed**
- 1 **can (10¾ ounces) condensed broccoli cheese soup, undiluted**
- 1 **cup (4 ounces) shredded cheddar cheese**

1. Preheat oven to 350°. In a small saucepan, bring water to a boil. Stir in stuffing mix. Remove from heat; cover and let stand 5 minutes.

2. Meanwhile, layer chicken and broccoli in a greased 11x7-in. baking dish. Top with soup. Fluff stuffing with a fork; spoon over soup. Sprinkle with the cheese.

3. Bake, uncovered, 30-35 minutes or until heated through.

FREEZE OPTION *Transfer individual portions of cooled casserole to freezer containers. To use, partially thaw in refrigerator overnight. Transfer to a microwave-safe dish and microwave, covered, on high until a thermometer inserted in center reads 165°, stirring occasionally and adding a little broth if necessary.*

5 SIMPLE INGREDIENTS

CHIP-CRUSTED CHICKEN

Dijon-mayo and barbecue potato chips might sound strange together, but the flavors combine beautifully in this entree. And the chicken is so tender!

—**MIKE TCHOU** PEPPER PIKE, OH

START TO FINISH: 30 MIN.
MAKES: 6 SERVINGS

⅔ **cup Dijon-mayonnaise blend**

6 **cups barbecue potato chips, finely crushed**

6 **boneless skinless chicken breast halves (5 ounces each)**

1. Preheat oven to 375°. Place the mayonnaise blend and potato chips in separate shallow bowls. Dip chicken in mayonnaise blend, then coat with the chips.

2. Place chicken on an ungreased baking sheet. Bake 20-25 minutes or until a thermometer reads 165°.

Cook to Cook

When cooking this recipe, place the chicken on a cooling rack over a baking sheet. This allows the chicken to crisp up.
—**ONEINA1000**

CHICKEN FETTUCCINE ALFREDO WITH VEGGIES

I especially like to use frozen California-blend veggies when making this dish. If you prefer, you can substitute fresh garden vegetables, but it will add a little time. Simply start them in boiling water before adding the pasta. Then add the pasta to the boiling water 3 minutes before the veggies are done. This makes an easy, colorful and delicious entree!

—**TALENA KEELER** SILOAM SPRINGS, AR

START TO FINISH: 15 MIN.
MAKES: 4 SERVINGS

- 1 **package (9 ounces) refrigerated fettuccine**
- 3 **cups frozen mixed vegetables**
- 1 **package (9 ounces) ready-to-serve roasted chicken breast strips**
- 1½ **cups Alfredo sauce**
- ½ **cup shredded Parmesan cheese**

1. Fill a Dutch oven two-thirds full with water; bring to a boil. Add fettuccine and vegetables; return to a boil. Cook on high 2-3 minutes or until tender; drain.

2. Stir in chicken and Alfredo sauce; heat through. Sprinkle with cheese.

5 SIMPLE INGREDIENTS

PARMESAN CHICKEN NUGGETS

My 3-year-old is going through a stage where he'll eat only chicken nuggets and French fries. I like to make these golden nuggets for him so I know what he's eating. They're so good, and we like them, too!

—**AMANDA LIVESAY** MOBILE, AL

START TO FINISH: 30 MIN.
MAKES: 8 SERVINGS

- ¼ cup butter, melted
- 1 cup panko (Japanese) bread crumbs
- ½ cup grated Parmesan cheese
- ½ teaspoon kosher salt
- 1½ pounds boneless skinless chicken breasts, cut into 1-inch cubes
  Marinara sauce, optional

1. Preheat oven to 375°. Place butter in a shallow bowl. Combine the bread crumbs, cheese and salt in another shallow bowl. Dip chicken in butter, then roll in crumbs.

2. Place chicken in a single layer on two 15x10x1-in. baking pans. Bake 15-18 minutes until no longer pink, turning once. Serve with marinara sauce if desired.

EASY BREEZY TURKEY LOAF

If you think you can't make meat loaf like Mom does, try this super-easy recipe. Your favorite store-bought spaghetti sauce flavors the moist loaf, and the ground turkey saves on calories.

—**JO ANN SHAPPARD** VINCENNES, IN

PREP: 10 MIN. • **BAKE:** 65 MINUTES
MAKES: 6 SERVINGS

- 1 **cup seasoned bread crumbs**
- 1 **cup garden-style spaghetti sauce, divided**
- 1 **medium onion, chopped**
- 1 **egg**
- 1 **teaspoon salt**
- 1 **teaspoon pepper**
- 1½ **pounds ground turkey**

1. Preheat oven to 350°. In a large bowl, mix bread crumbs, ½ cup spaghetti sauce, onion, egg, salt and pepper. Crumble turkey over mixture and mix well. Pat into an ungreased 9x5-in. loaf pan.

2. Bake, uncovered, 1 hour. Spread remaining spaghetti sauce over loaf. Bake 5-10 minutes longer or until a thermometer reads 165° and the juices run clear.

FREEZE OPTION *Securely wrap individual portions of cooled meat loaf in plastic wrap and foil. To use, partially thaw in refrigerator overnight. Unwrap meat loaf; reheat on a greased shallow baking pan in a preheated 350° oven until heated through and a thermometer inserted in center reads 165°.*

Cook to Cook

I used Ragu Parmesean and Romano sauce plus added chopped green pepper, and it was delicious! Super easy and doesn't even taste like turkey! Yummo! —STRNBEL08

5 SIMPLE INGREDIENTS

BROWN SUGAR-GLAZED SALMON

I pop protein-packed salmon fillets in the oven before whipping up a sweet basting sauce. Made in moments, this tangy entree is perfect for busy families and weekend guests alike.

—**DEBRA MARTIN** BELLEVILLE, MI

START TO FINISH: 25 MIN.
MAKES: 4 SERVINGS

- 1 **salmon fillet (1 pound)**
- ¼ **teaspoon salt**
- ¼ **teaspoon pepper**
- 3 **tablespoons brown sugar**
- 1 **tablespoon reduced-sodium soy sauce**
- 4 **teaspoons Dijon mustard**
- 1 **teaspoon rice vinegar**

1. Preheat oven to 425°. Cut salmon widthwise into four pieces. Place in a foil-lined 15x10x1-in. baking pan; sprinkle with salt and pepper. Bake, uncovered, 10 minutes.
2. Meanwhile, in a small saucepan, combine the brown sugar, soy sauce, mustard and vinegar. Bring to a boil. Brush evenly over salmon. Broil 6 in. from heat 1-2 minutes or until fish flakes easily with a fork.

RED PEPPER & PARMESAN TILAPIA

My husband and I are always looking for light fish recipes because of their health benefits. This one's a hit with him, and we've tried it at dinner parties, too!

—MICHELLE MARTIN DURHAM, NC

START TO FINISH: 20 MIN.
MAKES: 4 SERVINGS

- ¼ **cup egg substitute**
- ½ **cup grated Parmesan cheese**
- 1 **teaspoon Italian seasoning**
- ½ **to 1 teaspoon crushed red pepper flakes**
- ½ **teaspoon pepper**
- 4 **tilapia fillets (6 ounces each)**

1. Preheat oven to 425°. Place egg substitute in a shallow bowl. In another shallow bowl, mix cheese, Italian seasoning, pepper flakes and pepper. Dip fillets in egg substitute, then cheese mixture.

2. Place in a 15x10x1-in. baking pan coated with cooking spray. Bake 10-15 minutes or until the fish flakes easily with a fork.

Cook to Cook

Very tasty! I didn't have the egg substitute so used real egg instead, and it came out fine. Definitely a keeper in my recipe box. **—BRENDA526**

NOTES

5 SIMPLE INGREDIENTS

SIMPLE SHRIMP SCAMPI

Your guests will be impressed with my no-fuss scampi. You'll hear raves after they take the first bite!

—LISA BOEHM DEEPWATER, MO

START TO FINISH: 10 MIN.
MAKES: 6 SERVINGS

- ¾ **cup butter, cubed**
- 2 **pounds uncooked medium shrimp, peeled and deveined**
- 5 **teaspoons lemon-pepper seasoning**
- 2 **teaspoons garlic powder**
  Lemon wedges, optional

In a large skillet over medium heat, melt butter. Add the shrimp, lemon-pepper and garlic powder; cook 5-8 minutes or until shrimp turn pink. Serve with lemon wedges if desired.

Cook to Cook

This was great! I made it as written alongside some whole wheat linguine, mixed the pasta in with the shrimp once it was cooked (letting the butter sauce coat the pasta), emptied into a bowl and topped with fresh parsley. It was a hit! Thanks so much for sharing!
—CKELLEY116

NOTES

SKILLET MAC & CHEESE

This is so simple, it seems almost too easy! But you'll love it and fix it often.

—ANN BOWERS ROCKPORT, TX

START TO FINISH: 25 MIN.
MAKES: 4 SERVINGS

- 2 **cups uncooked elbow macaroni**
- 2 **tablespoons butter**
- 2 **tablespoons all-purpose flour**
- 1½ **cups half-and-half cream**
- ¾ **pound process cheese (Velveeta), cubed**

1. Cook macaroni according to the package directions.

2. Meanwhile, in a large nonstick skillet, melt butter over medium heat. Stir in flour until smooth. Gradually add cream; bring to a boil. Cook and stir 2 minutes or until thickened. Reduce heat. Add the cheese, stirring until melted.

3. Drain macaroni; add to cheese mixture. Cook and stir 3-4 minutes or until heated through.

5 SIMPLE INGREDIENTS

SPAGHETTI WITH BACON

As children, my sisters and brothers and I always requested this satisfying dish for our birthday dinners. The recipe was passed down from my grandmother, who prepared it when my mother was a child nearly 90 years ago. I've continued the tasty tradition with my own children.

—**RUTH KEOGH** NORTH ST. PAUL, MN

PREP: 15 MIN. • **BAKE:** 45 MIN.
MAKES: 4-6 SERVINGS

- ½ pound bacon, diced
- 1 medium onion, diced
- 1 can (14½ ounces) diced tomatoes, undrained
- 1 can (8 ounces) tomato sauce
- 8 ounces spaghetti, cooked and drained

1. Preheat oven to 350°. In a skillet, brown bacon and onion until bacon is crisp; drain. Add tomatoes and tomato sauce; bring to a boil.
2. Place cooked spaghetti in a 2-qt. baking dish. Pour sauce over, cover and bake 45 minutes.

Cook to Cook

My whole family adores this simple baked spaghetti dish. Over the years I have added garlic powder, oregano and a pinch each of allspice and cayenne to the sauce to brighten the flavor. Sometimes I sprinkle the top with grated Parmesan cheese and/or Italian-seasoned bread crumbs. But no matter how I make it, the pan is always emptied—pronto!
—**FRIEDAG**

SKILLET SENSATIONS

Saute, brown or stir-fry these quick-cooking entrees.

SKILLET SENSATIONS INDEX

Cook to Cook

Look for
THESE boxes
for helpful tidbits!

RAVIOLI SKILLET

Dress up store-bought ravioli to make it really special—prosciutto and mozzarella help to do the trick.

— TASTE OF HOME TEST KITCHEN

START TO FINISH: 30 MIN.
MAKES: 4 SERVINGS

- 1 **pound ground beef**
- ¾ **cup chopped green pepper**
- 1 **ounce prosciutto or deli ham, chopped**
- 3 **cups spaghetti sauce**
- ¾ **cup water**
- 1 **package (25 ounces) frozen cheese ravioli**
- 1 **cup (4 ounces) shredded part-skim mozzarella cheese**

1. In a large skillet, cook the beef, green pepper and prosciutto over medium heat until beef is no longer pink; drain.

2. Stir in spaghetti sauce and water; bring to a boil. Add ravioli. Reduce heat; cover and simmer 7-9 minutes or until ravioli is tender, stirring once. Sprinkle with the cheese. Simmer, uncovered, 1-2 minutes longer or until cheese is melted.

HARVEST STIR-FRY

I work full time outside the home, so I'm always trying fast-to-fix dishes. Here is a colorful skillet supper that appeals to young and old alike.

—KAY TOON WORTHINGTON, IN

START TO FINISH: 25 MIN.
MAKES: 8-10 SERVINGS

- 1 **pound ground beef**
- 1 **medium onion, chopped**
- 6 **small yellow summer squash, chopped**
- 6 **medium tomatoes, quartered**
- 1 **to 1½ cups whole kernel corn**
- 1 **tablespoon minced fresh oregano or 1 teaspoon dried oregano**
- 1 **teaspoon salt**
- ½ **teaspoon coarsely ground pepper**

1. In a large skillet, cook beef and onion over medium heat until meat is no longer pink; drain.

2. Add the squash, tomatoes, corn, oregano, salt and pepper. Cook and stir 5-10 minutes or until the vegetables are tender.

SWEET-AND-SOUR BEEF

This stir-fry recipe is a family favorite. I've used a variety of meats and apples and sometimes replace the green onion with yellow onion. It always tastes great!

—BRITTANY MCCLOUD KENYON, MN

START TO FINISH: 30 MIN.
MAKES: 6 SERVINGS

- 1 **tablespoon cornstarch**
- 2 **tablespoons cold water**
- 1 **pound beef top sirloin steak, cut into ½-inch cubes**
- 1 **teaspoon salt**
- ½ **teaspoon pepper**
- 3 **teaspoons canola oil, divided**
- 1 **large green pepper, cut into ½-inch pieces**
- 1 **large sweet red pepper, cut into ½-inch pieces**
- 2 **medium tart apples, chopped**
- ½ **cup plus 2 tablespoons thinly sliced green onions, divided**
- ⅔ **cup packed brown sugar**
- ½ **cup cider vinegar**
  Hot cooked rice, optional

1. In a small bowl, mix cornstarch and water until smooth. Sprinkle beef with salt and pepper. In a large nonstick skillet or wok coated with cooking spray, heat 2 teaspoons oil over medium-high heat. Add beef; stir-fry 2-3 minutes or until no longer pink. Remove from pan.

2. In same skillet, stir-fry peppers and apples in remaining oil 2 minutes. Stir in ½ cup green onions; stir-fry 1-3 minutes longer or until peppers are crisp-tender. Remove from pan.

3. Add brown sugar and vinegar to skillet; bring to a boil, stirring to dissolve sugar. Stir cornstarch mixture and add to pan. Return to a boil; cook and stir 1-2 minutes or until thickened.

4. Return beef and pepper mixture to pan; heat through. If desired, serve with rice. Sprinkle with the remaining green onion.

Cook to Cook

I have made this recipe with steak, with chicken, with shrimp and with a combination of shrimp and chicken all came out tasting delicious. This one is a staple at my house!**—LIZ-Z**

ASPARAGUS BEEF LO MEIN

Here is a stir-fry that is big on flavor but relatively low in cost. It's served over ramen noodles, which is a nice change from rice. To simplify preparation, I use store-bought garlic-infused olive oil instead of minced garlic and olive oil.

—DOTTIE WANAT MODESTO, CA

START TO FINISH: 20 MIN.
MAKES: 4 SERVINGS

- 1 **beef top sirloin steak (1 pound), thinly sliced**
- 2 **tablespoons olive oil**
- 1 **pound fresh asparagus, trimmed and cut into 2½-inch pieces**
- ¼ **teaspoon minced garlic**
- 2¼ **cups water, divided**
- 2 **packages (3 ounces each) beef ramen noodles**
- ⅔ **cup hoisin sauce**

1. In a large skillet or wok, stir-fry beef in oil 5 minutes or until meat is no longer pink. Add the asparagus and garlic; stir-fry 2 minutes or until asparagus is crisp-tender.

2. In a small bowl, combine ¼ cup water and ½ teaspoon seasoning from 1 ramen noodle seasoning packet; stir until dissolved. Add hoisin sauce; stir into the beef mixture. Bring to a boil; cook and stir 2 minutes or until thickened. (Discard remaining seasoning from opened packet.)

3. In a large saucepan, bring remaining water to a boil; add ramen noodles and contents of remaining seasoning packet. Cook 3 minutes. Remove from heat; cover and let stand until noodles are tender. Serve with beef mixture.

NOTES

_____

_____

_____

_____

_____

_____

PIEROGI BEEF SKILLET

From-scratch pierogies are a real treat. But who has the time to make them? This meal-in-one recipe combines frozen pierogies with mixed veggies and quick-cooking ground beef.

—TASTE OF HOME TEST KITCHEN

START TO FINISH: 30 MIN.
MAKES: 4 SERVINGS

- 1 **pound ground beef**
- ½ **cup chopped onion**
- ¼ **cup all-purpose flour**
- 1 **can (14½ ounces) beef broth**
- 1 **package (16 ounces) frozen cheese and potato pierogies, thawed**
- 2 **cups frozen mixed vegetables, thawed and drained**
- ½ **teaspoon salt**
- ½ **teaspoon pepper**
- ½ **teaspoon Italian seasoning**
- ½ **cup shredded cheddar cheese**

1. In a large skillet, cook beef and onion over medium heat until meat is no longer pink; drain, reserving 3 tablespoons drippings.

2. Sprinkle flour over beef and drippings; stir until blended. Gradually add beef broth. Bring to a boil; cook and stir 2 minutes or until thickened.

3. Stir in the pierogies, vegetables and seasonings. Cook, uncovered, for 4-5 minutes or until heated through. Sprinkle with cheese.

Cook to Cook

This was a very simple and easy meal to make on a working day. My husband and son loved it. I used leftover corn and lima beans for the vegetables because that's what my guys like.
—JANET BURKHART

RAMEN-VEGETABLE BEEF SKILLET

This combination of ingredients is unique and tasty. Using ramen noodles makes it easy on the grocery budget.

—MARLENE MCALLISTER PORTLAND, MI

START TO FINISH: 30 MIN.
MAKES: 4 SERVINGS

- 1 **pound ground beef**
- 1½ **cups sliced fresh carrots**
- ¾ **cup sliced onion**
- 1 **cup water**
- 1 **cup shredded cabbage**
- 1 **cup sliced fresh mushrooms**
- 1 **cup chopped green pepper**
- 3 **tablespoons soy sauce**
- 1 **package (3 ounces) beef ramen noodles**

1. In a large skillet, cook beef, carrots and onion over medium heat until meat is no longer pink and carrots are crisp-tender; drain.

2. Add water, cabbage, mushrooms, green pepper, soy sauce and contents of seasoning packet from the noodles. Break noodles into small pieces; add to pan. Cover and cook 10 minutes or until liquid is absorbed and noodles are tender.

GINGERED PEPPER STEAK

When my mother-in-law shared this recipe, she said it cooks up in no time—and she was right! The wonderfully tender steak seems like a special treat.

—SUSAN ADAIR SOMERSET, KY

START TO FINISH: 15 MIN.
MAKES: 4 SERVINGS

- 2 **teaspoons sugar**
- 2 **teaspoons cornstarch**
- ¼ **teaspoon ground ginger**
- ¼ **cup reduced-sodium soy sauce**
- 1 **tablespoon white wine vinegar**
- 1 **pound beef flank steak, thinly sliced**
- 2 **medium green peppers, julienned**
- 1 **teaspoon canola oil**
  Hot cooked rice, optional

1. In a large bowl, combine the sugar, cornstarch, ginger, soy sauce and vinegar until smooth. Add beef and toss to coat; set aside.

2. In a large skillet or wok, stir-fry green peppers in oil until crisp-tender, about 3 minutes. Remove with a slotted spoon and keep warm. Add beef with marinade to pan; stir-fry 3 minutes or until meat reaches desired doneness. Return peppers to pan; heat through. Serve over rice if desired.

Cook to Cook

Very good recipe—I'll definitely make it many times. The sauce is so good it could be used with chicken and any stir-fry vegetables you like—or even with rice noodles. **—MAHARAJIE**

FREEZE IT

HEARTY SALISBURY STEAKS

I pair these steaks with mashed potatoes and vegetables. With its down-home taste, this meal always disappears fast!

—DOROTHY BAYES SARDIS, OH

START TO FINISH: 30 MIN.
MAKES: 5 SERVINGS

- **1 medium onion, finely chopped**
- **½ cup crushed saltines (about 15 crackers)**
- **¼ cup egg substitute**
- **½ teaspoon pepper**
- **1 pound lean ground beef (90% lean)**
- **1 tablespoon canola oil**
- **2 cups water**
- **1 envelope reduced-sodium onion soup mix**
- **2 tablespoons all-purpose flour**

1. In a large bowl, combine onion, saltines, egg substitute and pepper. Add beef; mix lightly but thoroughly. Shape into five patties.

2. In a large skillet, heat oil over medium heat. Add patties; cook 3-4 minutes on each side or until lightly browned. Remove patties and keep warm; discard drippings.

3. Combine water, soup mix and flour; stir into skillet. Bring to a boil. Return patties to skillet. Reduce heat; simmer, covered, 5-7 minutes or until meat is no longer pink.

FREEZE OPTION *Freeze individual cooled steaks with some gravy in resealable freezer bags. To use, partially thaw in refrigerator overnight. Microwave, covered, on high in a microwave-safe dish until heated through, gently stirring and adding a little water if necessary.*

Cook to Cook

This was very good! I did change things a little bit—I didn't have onion soup mix on hand so I substituted with 4 tsp. beef bouillon granules, 8 tsp. dry onion flakes, 1 tsp. onion powder and ¼ tsp. pepper. I also added fresh mushrooms, as well as some Worcestershire sauce. Would make again! **—SOXFAN28**

NOTES

PIZZA JOES

If you're tired of the same old, boring sloppy joes, try this tasty twist. These messy, kid-friendly sandwiches have a definite pizza flavor that families will love, but be sure to serve them with a fork!

—**CONNIE PETTIT** LOGAN, OH

START TO FINISH: 30 MIN.
MAKES: 6 SERVINGS

- 1 **pound lean ground beef (90% lean)**
- 1 **medium onion, chopped**
- ¼ **cup chopped green pepper**
- 1 **jar (14 ounces) pizza sauce**
- 3 **ounces sliced turkey pepperoni (about 50 slices), chopped**
- ½ **teaspoon dried basil**
- ¼ **teaspoon dried oregano**
- 6 **hamburger buns, split**
- 6 **tablespoons shredded part-skim mozzarella cheese**

1. In a large nonstick skillet, cook the beef, onion and pepper over medium heat until meat is no longer pink. Drain if necessary. Stir in the pizza sauce, pepperoni, basil and oregano. Bring to a boil. Reduce heat; cover and simmer 10 minutes.

2. Spoon ⅔ cup beef mixture onto each bun; sprinkle with cheese. Place on a baking sheet. Broil 3-4 in. from heat 1 minute or until cheese is melted. Replace tops.

FREEZE OPTION *Freeze cooled meat mixture in freezer containers. To use, partially thaw in the refrigerator overnight. Heat through in a saucepan, stirring occasionally and adding a little water if necessary. Serve on buns.*

SKILLET SENSATIONS

TOASTED REUBENS

When New Yorkers taste my Reuben, they say it's like those served by delis in "The Big Apple." For a little less kick, omit the horseradish from the mayonnaise mixture.
—**PATRICIA KILE** ELIZABETHTOWN, PA

START TO FINISH: 20 MIN.
MAKES: 4 SERVINGS

- 8 **slices rye bread**
- 4 **teaspoons prepared mustard**
- 4 **slices Swiss cheese**
- 1 **pound thinly sliced deli corned beef**
- 1 **can (8 ounces) sauerkraut, rinsed and well drained**
- ½ **cup mayonnaise**
- 3 **tablespoons ketchup**
- 2 **tablespoons sweet pickle relish**
- 1 **tablespoon prepared horseradish**
- 2 **tablespoons butter**

1. Spread mustard over four slices of bread. Layer with cheese, corned beef and sauerkraut. In a small bowl, mix mayonnaise, ketchup, relish and horseradish; spread over remaining bread. Place over sauerkraut. Spread outsides of sandwiches with butter.

2. In a large skillet, toast sandwiches over medium heat 3-4 minutes on each side or until golden brown and cheese is melted.

Cook to Cook

Instead of sauerkraut, I used jarred sweet and sour red cabbage. —**LISALEI**

SKILLET BEEF AND POTATOES

Using unpeeled potato slices, which are precooked in the microwave, speeds up the cooking time for this meal. Fresh rosemary adds a nice savory accent.

—**TASTE OF HOME TEST KITCHEN**

START TO FINISH: 25 MIN.
MAKES: 4 SERVINGS

- 3 medium potatoes, halved and cut into ¼-inch slices
- ⅓ cup water
- ½ teaspoon salt
- 1 pound beef top sirloin steak, cut into thin strips
- 2 teaspoons garlic pepper blend
- ½ cup chopped onion
- 3 tablespoons olive oil, divided
- 1½ teaspoons minced fresh rosemary

1. Place potatoes, water and salt in a microwave-safe dish. Cover and microwave on high 6-10 minutes or until potatoes are tender; drain.

2. Season beef with pepper blend. In a large skillet, stir-fry beef and onion in 2 tablespoons of oil 5 minutes or until beef is no longer pink.

3. Meanwhile, in another skillet, stir-fry potatoes in the remaining oil 5 minutes or until browned. Stir in beef mixture. Sprinkle with rosemary.

NOTE *This recipe was tested in a 1,100-watt microwave.*

CRUMB-COATED CUBED STEAKS

I always buy steaks like this that are already cubed and tenderized at the meat counter. Fresh tomato slices, mashed potatoes and black-eyed peas complete the menu.

—**AGNES WARD** STRATFORD, ON

START TO FINISH: 30 MIN.
MAKES: 4 SERVINGS

- **1 egg**
- **½ cup milk**
- **23 saltines, crushed**
- **⅔ cup all-purpose flour**
- **¾ teaspoon salt**
- **¼ teaspoon baking powder**
- **¼ teaspoon cayenne pepper**
- **¼ teaspoon pepper**
- **4 beef cubed steaks (4 ounces each)**
- **3 tablespoons canola oil**

GRAVY
- **2 tablespoons all-purpose flour**
- **1⅓ cups milk**
- **¼ teaspoon salt**
- **¼ teaspoon pepper**

1. In a shallow bowl, whisk egg and milk. In another shallow bowl, combine the cracker crumbs, flour, salt, baking powder, cayenne and pepper. Dip steaks in egg mixture, then in crumb mixture.

2. In a large skillet, cook steaks in oil over medium heat 3-4 minutes on each side or until no longer pink. Remove and keep warm.

3. Add flour to the skillet, stirring to blend and loosen browned bits from pan. Gradually add milk. Bring to a boil; cook and stir 2 minutes or until thickened. Season with salt and pepper. Serve with steaks.

Cook to Cook

These were very good! We call them "chicken fried steaks" where I come from (Alabama). I had to use Ritz crackers because I didn't have saltines. Also, I will double the gravy next time so there will be a little to go with our mashed potatoes. Yum! I felt like I was back down South for a little while!
—**VALANDDANSMITH**

OPEN-FACED TEXAS BURGERS

Served on Texas toast, this open-faced burger will be the talk of the table tonight!
—**WILLIE DEWAARD** CORALVILLE, IA

START TO FINISH: 30 MIN.
MAKES: 2 SERVINGS

- 2 **tablespoons chopped onion**
- 1 **small garlic clove, minced**
- ⅛ **teaspoon dried thyme**
- ⅔ **cup shredded Colby-Monterey Jack cheese, divided**
- ⅔ **pound ground beef**
- 2 **slices frozen garlic Texas toast**
- ½ **cup tomato sauce**
- 1½ **teaspoons packed brown sugar**
- ½ **teaspoon Worcestershire sauce**
- ½ **teaspoon A.1. steak sauce**

1. In a large bowl, combine the onion, garlic, thyme and ½ cup cheese. Crumble beef over mixture and mix well. Shape into two oval patties.

2. In a large skillet, cook burgers over medium heat 5-6 minutes on each side or until meat is no longer pink.

3. Meanwhile, prepare Texas toast according to package directions.

4. Drain burgers; set aside and keep warm. Add the tomato sauce, brown sugar, Worcestershire sauce and steak sauce to skillet. Bring to a boil; cook and stir 1-2 minutes or until slightly thickened. Return burgers to skillet; turn to coat. Sprinkle with remaining cheese. Serve burgers on toast.

BACON CHEESEBURGER RICE

My husband and I thought the original skillet dish lacked pizzazz, so we created this tastier version. I've had teenage nieces and nephews request the recipe after their first bite.

—JOYCE WHIPPS WEST DES MOINES, IA

START TO FINISH: 30 MIN.
MAKES: 4 SERVINGS

- 1 pound ground beef
- 1¾ cups water
- ⅔ cup barbecue sauce
- 1 tablespoon prepared mustard
- 2 teaspoons dried minced onion
- ½ teaspoon pepper
- 2 cups uncooked instant rice
- 1 cup (4 ounces) shredded cheddar cheese
- ⅓ cup chopped dill pickles
- 5 bacon strips, cooked and crumbled

1. In a large skillet over medium heat, cook beef until no longer pink; drain. Add the water, barbecue sauce, mustard, onion and pepper.

2. Bring to a boil; stir in the rice. Sprinkle with cheese. Reduce heat; cover and simmer 5 minutes. Sprinkle with pickles and bacon.

Cook to Cook

Made this last night and then served the leftovers over shredded lettuce and tomato slices. Delish! I used ground turkey and instant brown rice for a healthy swap and will definitely make it again! **—HAZEL202**

HARVEST HAM STEAK

Sauteed onions top this smoky ham steak simmered with apple juice and topped with apple butter. If you have some on hand, use homemade apple butter for a personalized touch.

—TASTE OF HOME TEST KITCHEN

START TO FINISH: 20 MIN.
MAKES: 4 SERVINGS

- 1 **medium onion, halved and thinly sliced**
- ¼ **teaspoon pepper**
- 2 **tablespoons butter**
- 1 **boneless fully cooked ham steak (1 pound)**
- 1 **teaspoon cornstarch**
- ½ **cup unsweetened apple juice**
- ½ **cup apple butter**

1. In a large skillet, saute onion and pepper in butter until crisp-tender. Remove from pan and set aside. Cut ham steak into four pieces. In the same skillet, brown ham on both sides.

2. Meanwhile, in a small bowl, combine cornstarch and apple juice until smooth; pour over ham. Bring to a boil; cook and stir 1-2 minutes or until slightly thickened. Reduce heat; spread apple butter over ham. Top with onion. Cover and simmer 5-7 minutes or until heated through.

NOTE *This recipe was tested with commercially prepared apple butter.*

NOTES

ALMOND PORK CHOPS WITH HONEY MUSTARD

I love how crunchy almonds and sweet mustard sauce jazz up this tender pork dish. Usually, I double the recipe. One chop per person is never enough for my family.

—LILY JULOW LAWRENCEVILLE, GA

START TO FINISH: 25 MIN.
MAKES: 4 SERVINGS

- ½ cup smoked almonds
- ½ cup dry bread crumbs
- 2 eggs
- ⅓ cup all-purpose flour
- ¼ teaspoon salt
- ⅛ teaspoon pepper
- 4 boneless pork loin chops (1 inch thick and 6 ounces each)
- 2 tablespoons olive oil
- 2 tablespoons butter
- ½ cup reduced-fat mayonnaise
- ¼ cup honey
- 2 tablespoons Dijon mustard

1. In a food processor, process the almonds until finely chopped. Transfer to a shallow bowl; add bread crumbs. In another bowl, beat the eggs. In a large resealable plastic bag, combine flour, salt and pepper. Add pork chops, one at a time, and shake to coat. Dip in eggs, then coat with almond mixture.

2. In a large skillet over medium heat, cook chops in oil and butter 5 minutes on each side or until meat reaches desired doneness (for medium-rare, a thermometer should read 145°; medium, 160°). Let stand 5 minutes before serving

3. Meanwhile, in a small bowl, mix the mayonnaise, honey and mustard. Serve with pork chops.

Cook to Cook

Oh my, try this new favorite! I never really liked pork chops until now. The sauce is absolutely amazing, too, and I plan to use it for other dishes as well. I am sending this recipe to all my friends and family! **—KIPANY**

SAUSAGE 'N' SAUERKRAUT

Three young children involved in different activities keep me running year-round. I created this tasty, quick-and-easy dish so I can throw it together in no time on those extra-busy nights.

—**MARY LYON** SPOTSYLVANIA, VA

START TO FINISH: 30 MIN.
MAKES: 4 SERVINGS

- 4 **medium potatoes, peeled and cubed**
- 2 **tablespoons canola oil**
- 1 **small onion, halved and sliced**
- 1 **pound smoked sausage, cut into ¼-inch pieces**
- 1 **package (16 ounces) sauerkraut, rinsed and well drained**
- ¼ **teaspoon pepper**
- ⅛ **teaspoon salt**

In a large skillet, saute potatoes in oil 5-6 minutes or until lightly browned. Stir in onion; saute 3-4 minutes or until tender. Add sausage, sauerkraut, pepper and salt. Cook, uncovered, over medium heat 4-5 minutes or until heated through, stirring occasionally.

NOTES

PORK CHOPS IN HONEY-MUSTARD SAUCE

Pork chops are a great economical cut and cook up quickly, making them ideal for weeknight meals. But turning out tender chops can be tricky. Browning them first, then finishing them in this tangy, slightly sweet sauce results in perfectly cooked and delectable chops every time.

—SUSAN BENTLEY BURLINGTON, NJ

START TO FINISH: 30 MIN.
MAKES: 4 SERVINGS

- ¾ teaspoon garlic powder, divided
- ½ teaspoon salt
- ¼ teaspoon pepper
- 4 boneless pork loin chops (6 ounces each)
- 1 tablespoon olive oil
- ½ cup white wine or chicken broth
- ¼ cup chicken broth
- 2 tablespoons Dijon mustard
- 1 tablespoon honey
- ½ cup heavy whipping cream

1. Combine ½ teaspoon garlic powder, salt and pepper; sprinkle over pork chops. In a large skillet, brown pork chops in oil. Remove and keep warm.

2. Remove skillet from heat and add wine, stirring to loosen browned bits from pan. Bring to a boil; cook until liquid is reduced by half. Reduce heat to medium. Whisk in broth, mustard, honey and remaining garlic powder; cook and stir 1 minute. Whisk in cream; cook and stir 4-6 minutes or until thickened.

3. Return pork chops and juices to the skillet. Cover and cook 3-5 minutes or until meat reaches desired doneness (for medium-rare, a thermometer should read 145°; medium, 160°). Let stand 5 minutes before serving.

SWEET BARBECUED PORK CHOPS

I often prepare a double batch of these chops and freeze half to keep on hand. They're so easy and taste so fresh, family and friends never guess they were frozen!

—SUSAN HOLDERMAN FOSTORIA, OH

START TO FINISH: 25 MIN.
MAKES: 8 SERVINGS

- 2 tablespoons canola oil
- 8 boneless pork loin chops (¾ inch thick and 8 ounces each)
- ½ cup packed brown sugar
- ½ cup chopped sweet onion
- ½ cup each ketchup, barbecue sauce, French salad dressing and honey

1. In a large skillet, heat oil over medium heat. In batches, brown pork chops 2-3 minutes on each side. Return all to pan.

2. In a bowl, mix remaining ingredients; pour over chops. Bring to a boil. Reduce heat; simmer, covered, 4-5 minutes or until meat reaches desired doneness (for medium-rare, a thermometer should read 145°; medium, 160°). Let stand 5 minutes before serving.

FREEZE OPTION *Place pork chops in freezer containers; top with sauce. Cool and freeze. To use, partially thaw in refrigerator overnight. Heat through in a covered saucepan, gently stirring sauce and adding a little water if necessary.*

Cook to Cook

This is my first review. My family and I LOVED this. We changed it a little. Took out the chopped sweet onion and used Sweet Baby Ray's Sweet Vidalia Onion BBQ sauce and less ketchup. It was AMAZING. We are making the sauce again to cook up some chicken wings in the slow cooker. —YUM!JESLYN81

CINNAMON-APPLE PORK CHOPS

When I found this recipe online years ago, it quickly became a go-to standard. The ingredients are easy to keep on hand, and the one-pan cleanup is a bonus.

—CHRISTINA PRICE PITTSBURGH, PA

START TO FINISH: 25 MIN.
MAKES: 4 SERVINGS

- 4 boneless pork loin chops (4 ounces each)
- 2 tablespoons butter, divided
- 3 tablespoons brown sugar
- 1 teaspoon ground cinnamon
- ½ teaspoon ground nutmeg
- ¼ teaspoon salt
- 4 medium tart apples, thinly sliced
- 2 tablespoons chopped pecans

1. In a large skillet over medium heat, cook pork chops in 1 tablespoon butter 4-5 minutes on each side or until meat reaches desired doneness (for medium-rare, a thermometer should read 145°; medium, 160°).

2. Meanwhile, in a bowl, mix brown sugar, cinnamon, nutmeg and salt.

3. Remove chops and let stand 5 minutes before serving. Add the apples, pecans, brown sugar mixture and remaining butter to the pan; cook and stir until apples are tender. Serve with chops.

Cook to Cook

I made this with chicken breasts and it was delicious! Taking advice, I doubled the brown sugar mixture and was glad I did. I also seasoned the chicken with fresh ground pepper, garlic salt, cinnamon and brown sugar on one side and rubbed it in. Fantastic recipe and I will definitely make it again.
—JENNIFER KOPCZYK

NOTES

SPICED PORK MEDALLIONS WITH BOURBON SAUCE

I don't remember where I found this recipe, but it's become one of my standby entrees. I usually prepare it with a side of roasted vegetables.

—**KATHY KANTRUD** FENTON, MI

START TO FINISH: 25 MIN.
MAKES: 4 SERVINGS

- ½ **cup bourbon or reduced-sodium chicken broth**
- ¼ **cup packed dark brown sugar**
- 3 **tablespoons white vinegar**
- 3 **tablespoons reduced-sodium soy sauce**
- 2 **garlic cloves, minced**
- ½ **teaspoon pepper**
- ½ **teaspoon chili powder**
- ¼ **teaspoon ground cinnamon**
- ⅛ **teaspoon salt**
- ⅛ **teaspoon ground allspice**
- 1 **pork tenderloin (1 pound), cut into 12 slices**

1. In a small saucepan, combine the bourbon, brown sugar, vinegar, soy sauce, garlic and pepper. Bring to a boil; cook until liquid is reduced to about ½ cup, stirring occasionally.
2. Meanwhile, combine the chili powder, cinnamon, salt and allspice; rub over pork slices.
3. In a large skillet coated with cooking spray, cook pork over medium heat 2-4 minutes on each side or until tender. Serve with sauce.

PORK TENDERLOIN WITH ZESTY ITALIAN SAUCE

We like to serve this dish with garlic mashed potatoes and fresh green beans or buttery corn on the cob.

—JOE VINCE PORT HURON, MI

START TO FINISH: 25 MIN.
MAKES: 4 SERVINGS

- 1 pork tenderloin (1 pound), cut into 8 slices
- ½ teaspoon salt
- ¼ teaspoon pepper
- 1 tablespoon canola oil
- ½ cup white wine or chicken broth
- ½ cup zesty Italian salad dressing
- 1 tablespoon butter

1. Sprinkle pork with salt and pepper. In a large skillet, heat oil over medium-high heat. Brown pork, about 2 minutes on each side; remove from pan.

2. Add wine to pan, stirring to loosen browned bits from the bottom. Bring to a boil; cook until liquid is reduced by about half. Stir in dressing. Reduce heat; simmer, uncovered, 1-2 minutes or until slightly thickened.

3. Return pork to pan; simmer, covered, 3-5 minutes or until the meat reaches desired doneness (for medium-rare, a thermometer should read 145°; medium, 160°). Stir in butter. Let pork stand 5 minutes before serving.

Cook to Cook

I made this for New Year's Day dinner for my husband and me. It was so simple and tasted great. We even poured the sauce on our mashed potatoes. Thanks!
—JCV4

MAPLE PORK CHOPS

Tender pork chops are cooked in a maple glaze that makes every satisfying bite absolutely succulent.

—TASTE OF HOME TEST KITCHEN

START TO FINISH: 30 MIN.
MAKES: 4 SERVINGS

- 4 **boneless pork loin chops (1 inch thick and 6 ounces each)**
- 1 **teaspoon minced fresh thyme or ¼ teaspoon dried thyme**
- ½ **teaspoon salt**
- ½ **teaspoon pepper**
- 1 **tablespoon olive oil**
- ½ **cup brewed coffee**
- ¼ **cup maple syrup**
- 1 **tablespoon Dijon mustard**
- 2 **teaspoons Worcestershire sauce**

1. Sprinkle pork chops with thyme, salt and pepper. In a large skillet, brown the chops in oil. Remove and keep warm.

2. Add remaining ingredients to skillet. Bring to a boil; cook until liquid is reduced by half.

3. Return pork chops to skillet. Reduce heat; cover and simmer 10-12 minutes or until meat reaches desired doneness (for medium-rare, a thermometer should read 145°; medium, 160°). Let stand 5 minutes before serving. Serve with sauce.

SKILLET
SENSATIONS

MUFFULETTA PASTA

A friend gave me this recipe when she learned that I love muffuletta sandwiches. Very rich and filling, this easy skillet supper goes together quickly on a busy weeknight. Serve it with some cheesy garlic bread.

—**JAN HOLLINGSWORTH** HOUSTON, MS

START TO FINISH: 25 MIN.
MAKES: 8 SERVINGS

- 1 **package (16 ounces) bow tie pasta**
- 1 **bunch green onions, chopped**
- 2 **teaspoons plus ¼ cup butter, divided**
- 1 **tablespoon minced garlic**
- 1 **package (16 ounces) cubed fully cooked ham**
- 1 **jar (12.36 ounces) tapenade or ripe olive bruschetta topping, drained**
- 1 **package (3½ ounces) sliced pepperoni**
- 1 **cup heavy whipping cream**
- 2 **cups (8 ounces) shredded Italian cheese blend**

1. Cook pasta according to package directions. Meanwhile, in a large skillet, saute onions in 2 teaspoons butter until tender. Add garlic; cook 1 minute longer. Add ham, tapenade and pepperoni; saute 2 minutes longer.

2. Cube remaining butter; stir butter and cream into skillet. Bring to a boil over medium heat. Reduce heat; simmer, uncovered, 3 minutes.

3. Drain pasta; toss with ham mixture. Sprinkle with cheese.

Cook to Cook

Really good pasta. My husband loved it. Tasted like a muffuletta, definitely will be making it again. This recipe also is easy to halve. —DANIELLEYLEE

BACON &
ROSEMARY CHICKEN

Simple ingredients add up to simply fantastic flavor in this fast main dish everyone will rave about. It's likely to become a new family favorite at your house.

—**YVONNE STARLIN** HERMITAGE, TN

START TO FINISH: 30 MIN.
MAKES: 4 SERVINGS

- 4 **boneless skinless chicken breast halves (5 ounces each)**
- ½ **teaspoon salt**
- ¼ **teaspoon pepper**
- ¼ **cup all-purpose flour**
- 5 **bacon strips, chopped**
- 1 **tablespoon butter**
- 4 **garlic cloves, thinly sliced**
- 1 **tablespoon minced fresh rosemary or 1 teaspoon dried rosemary, crushed**
- ⅛ **teaspoon crushed red pepper flakes**
- 1 **cup reduced-sodium chicken broth**
- 2 **tablespoons lemon juice**

1. Pound chicken breasts slightly with a meat mallet to uniform thickness; sprinkle with salt and pepper. Place flour in a shallow bowl. Dip chicken in flour to coat both sides; shake off excess.

2. In a large skillet, cook bacon over medium heat until crisp, stirring occasionally. Remove with a slotted spoon; drain on paper towels. Discard drippings, reserving 2 tablespoons in pan. Cook chicken in butter and reserved drippings 4-6 minutes on each side or until a thermometer reads 165°. Remove and keep warm.

3. Add garlic, rosemary and pepper flakes to skillet; cook and stir 1 minute. Add broth and lemon juice; bring to a boil. Cook until liquid is reduced by half. Return chicken and bacon to skillet; heat through.

NOTES

_____
_____
_____
_____
_____
_____

**SKILLET
SENSATIONS**

BALSAMIC CHICKEN BREASTS

This no-fuss savory chicken is often requested by my crowd. It's easy, healthy and satisfying. Paired with a salad and whole wheat roll, it's a lovely meal that I feel good about serving!

—DENISE JOHANOWICZ MADISON, WI

PREP: 15 MIN. **COOK:** 20 MIN.
MAKES: 4 SERVINGS

- ¼ cup all-purpose flour
- ½ teaspoon pepper
- ⅛ teaspoon salt
- 4 boneless skinless chicken breast halves (4 ounces each)
- 1 tablespoon canola oil
- 1 small onion, thinly sliced
- ¼ cup water
- 2 tablespoons balsamic vinegar
- ½ teaspoon dried thyme
- ⅛ teaspoon dried rosemary, crushed

1. In a large resealable plastic bag, combine the flour, pepper and salt. Add the chicken, one piece at a time, and shake to coat.

2. In a large nonstick skillet coated with cooking spray, cook chicken in oil over medium heat 4-5 minutes on each side or until juices run clear. Remove and keep warm.

3. In the same pan, cook onion until tender. Add water, stirring to loosen browned bits. Add vinegar, thyme and rosemary; cook and stir 3-4 minutes or until sauce is slightly thickened. Serve with chicken.

SPINACH-STUFFED CHICKEN POCKETS

With their creamy filling and delightful crispy crust, these elegant entrees are easy enough for weeknights, yet special enough for guests, too.

—TASTE OF HOME TEST KITCHEN

START TO FINISH: 30 MIN.
MAKES: 4 SERVINGS

- 4 **cups fresh baby spinach**
- 2 **teaspoons plus ¼ cup olive oil, divided**
- 1 **garlic clove, minced**
- ½ **cup garlic-herb spreadable cheese**
- ⅔ **cup plus ¼ cup seasoned bread crumbs, divided**
- ½ **teaspoon salt, divided**
- 4 **boneless skinless chicken breast halves (6 ounces each)**
- 1 **egg, lightly beaten**
- ¼ **teaspoon pepper**

1. In a large skillet, saute spinach in 2 teaspoons oil until spinach is wilted. Add garlic; cook 1 minute longer. Remove from heat. Stir in spreadable cheese, ⅔ cup bread crumbs and ¼ teaspoon salt. Cut a pocket in the thickest part of each chicken breast; fill with spinach mixture. Secure with toothpicks.

2. Place egg in a shallow bowl. In another shallow bowl, combine the pepper and remaining bread crumbs and salt. Dip chicken in egg, then coat with bread crumb mixture.

3. In a large skillet over medium heat, cook chicken in remaining oil 8-10 minutes on each side or until a thermometer reads 165°. Discard toothpicks before serving.

Cook to Cook

I used mozzarella garlic cheese spread and put a little herb and garlic seasoning into the mix. —SMICHELICH

BUFFALO CHICKEN

Topped with gooey cheese and zesty Buffalo wing sauce, these chicken breasts have an unforgettable flavor.

—**JEANNE COLLINS** CARY, NC

START TO FINISH: 30 MIN.
MAKES: 4 SERVINGS

- 4 **boneless skinless chicken breast halves (5 ounces each)**
- ¼ **teaspoon salt**
- ¼ **teaspoon pepper**
- 2 **eggs**
- ½ **cup seasoned bread crumbs**

- 3 **tablespoons canola oil**
- ¼ **cup Buffalo wing sauce**
- ¼ **cup shredded provolone cheese**
- ¼ **cup shredded part-skim mozzarella cheese**

1. Flatten chicken to ½-in. thickness. Sprinkle with salt and pepper. In a shallow bowl, whisk eggs. Place bread crumbs in another shallow bowl. Dip the chicken in eggs, then coat with bread crumbs.

2. In a large skillet over medium heat, cook chicken in oil 7-10 minutes on each side or until chicken juices run clear, adding wing sauce during the last 2 minutes. Turn to coat chicken. Sprinkle with cheeses. Cover and cook until cheese is melted.

Cook to Cook

A new favorite for my husband and me. I make a couple of servings at the beginning of the week and then cut them up for sandwiches to bring to work. Just add some lettuce and tomato. So easy and very good!
—**LAURAMARIELAWSON**

APPLE-MUSTARD CHICKEN TENDERS

My husband says this chicken is sweet and a little bit sassy, just like me. I like to use Granny Smith apples for a bit of tartness. Winesaps are great for this dish, too.

—LINDA CIFUENTES MAHOMET, IL

START TO FINISH: 30 MIN.
MAKES: 6 SERVINGS

- 1½ pounds chicken tenderloins
- ½ teaspoon salt
- ¼ teaspoon pepper
- 3 tablespoons butter
- 2 small Granny Smith apples, thinly sliced
- ½ cup packed brown sugar
- ¼ cup stone-ground mustard

1. Sprinkle chicken with salt and pepper. In a large skillet, heat butter over medium heat. Add chicken; cook 4-6 minutes on each side or until no longer pink. Remove from pan.
2. Add apples, brown sugar and mustard to same pan; toss to combine. Cook, covered, over medium heat 3-4 minutes or until apples are tender. Stir in chicken; heat through.

NOTES

_____

_____

_____

_____

_____

_____

CHICKEN MARSALA WITH GORGONZOLA

We live near the Faribault, Minnesota, caves that are used to age the lovely AmaBlu cheese. Chicken topped with pungent Gorgonzola is simple enough for weeknights, but also elegant enough for a dinner party.

—**JILL ANDERSON** SLEEPY EYE, MN

PREP: 10 MIN. **COOK:** 30 MIN.
MAKES: 4 SERVINGS

- 4 boneless skinless chicken breast halves (6 ounces each)
- ¼ teaspoon plus ⅛ teaspoon salt, divided
- ¼ teaspoon pepper
- 3 tablespoons olive oil, divided
- ½ pound sliced baby portobello mushrooms
- 2 garlic cloves, minced
- 1 cup Marsala wine
- ⅔ cup heavy whipping cream
- ½ cup crumbled Gorgonzola cheese, divided
- 2 tablespoons minced fresh parsley

1. Sprinkle chicken with ¼ teaspoon salt and pepper. In a large skillet, cook chicken in 2 tablespoons oil over medium heat 6-8 minutes on each side or until a thermometer reads 165°. Remove and keep warm.

2. In same skillet, saute mushrooms in remaining oil until tender. Add garlic; cook 1 minute.

3. Add wine, stirring to loosen browned bits from pan. Bring to a boil; cook until liquid is reduced by a third. Stir in cream and remaining salt. Return to a boil; cook until slightly thickened.

4. Return chicken to pan; add ⅓ cup cheese. Cook until cheese is melted. Sprinkle with remaining cheese; garnish with parsley.

DIJON-CRUSTED CHICKEN BREASTS

If you're craving fried chicken, this recipe will hit the spot! A crisp and flavorful coating makes the easy entree feel special and indulgent.

—JACQUELINE CORREA LANDING, NJ

START TO FINISH: 25 MIN.
MAKES: 4 SERVINGS

- ⅓ cup dry bread crumbs
- 1 tablespoon grated Parmesan cheese
- 1 teaspoon Italian seasoning
- ½ teaspoon dried thyme
- ¼ teaspoon salt
- ¼ teaspoon pepper
- 4 boneless skinless chicken breast halves (4 ounces each)
- 2 tablespoons Dijon mustard
- 1 teaspoon olive oil
- 1 teaspoon reduced-fat margarine

1. Place the first six ingredients in a shallow bowl. Brush chicken with mustard; roll in crumb mixture.

2. In a large nonstick skillet, cook chicken in oil and margarine over medium heat 5-6 minutes on each side or until a thermometer reads 165°.

NOTE *This recipe was tested with Parkay Light stick margarine.*

Cook to Cook

My husband I both enjoyed this chicken dish. It is quick to make. The only change I made was that I pounded the chicken to about ¼ inch thick so it would cook faster. —**SALLY MINER**

CHICKEN WITH CREAMY JALAPENO SAUCE

My sister Amy created this entree that does a great job of making boring chicken breasts a lot more exciting. My husband and I just love the wonderful sauce!

—MOLLY CAPPONE LEWIS CENTER, OH

START TO FINISH: 25 MIN.
MAKES: 4 SERVINGS (2 CUPS SAUCE)

- 4 **boneless skinless chicken breast halves (4 ounces each)**
- ¼ **teaspoon salt**
- 1 **tablespoon canola oil**
- 2 **medium onions, chopped**
- ½ **cup reduced-sodium chicken broth**
- 2 **jalapeno peppers, seeded and minced**
- 2 **teaspoons ground cumin**
- 3 **ounces reduced-fat cream cheese, cubed**
- ¼ **cup reduced-fat sour cream**
- 3 **plum tomatoes, seeded and chopped**
- 2 **cups hot cooked rice**

1. Sprinkle chicken with salt. In a large nonstick skillet over medium-high heat, brown chicken in oil on both sides.
2. Add onions, broth, jalapenos and cumin. Bring to a boil. Reduce heat; cover and simmer 5-7 minutes or until a thermometer reads 165°. Remove chicken and keep warm.

3. Stir cream cheese and sour cream into onion mixture until blended. Stir in tomatoes; heat through. Serve with chicken and rice.

NOTE *Wear disposable gloves when cutting hot peppers; the oils can burn skin. Avoid touching your face.*

Cook to Cook

My family can't take a lot of heat (spicy heat), so I used fire-roasted poblano pepper instead of jalapenos. The pepper added good chili taste as well as a little smoky flavor to the dish, and it was fantastic. **—INDYHANNAH1**

SOUTHWEST BEAN AND CHICKEN PASTA

My wife, Jennie, is a great cook who's generally skeptical about my kitchen experiments. But she likes this recipe well enough to give me temporary kitchen privileges. If you can't find the soup called for here, cheese soup can be substituted.

—**MIKE KIRSCHBAUM** CARY, NC

START TO FINISH: 25 MIN.
MAKES: 6 SERVINGS

- 3 cups uncooked mostaccioli
- ¼ cup chopped onion
- ¼ cup chopped sweet red pepper
- 1 tablespoon canola oil
- ½ teaspoon minced garlic
- 1 can (10¾ ounces) condensed nacho cheese soup, undiluted
- 1 package (9 ounces) ready-to-use Southwestern chicken strips
- ¾ cup water
- 1 can (15 ounces) black beans, rinsed and drained
- ¼ cup shredded Monterey Jack cheese, optional

1. Cook mostaccioli according to package directions.
2. Meanwhile, in a large skillet, saute onion and red pepper in oil until tender. Add garlic; cook 1 minute longer. Stir in the soup, chicken and water. Bring to a boil. Reduce heat; cover and simmer 8 minutes.
3. Stir in beans; heat through. Drain mostaccioli; transfer to a serving bowl; top with chicken mixture. Sprinkle with cheese if desired.

NOTES

EASY MEDITERRANEAN CHICKEN

Friends and family love this special chicken recipe. I changed a few things to make it healthier, but it tastes just as good.

—KARA ZILIS OAK FOREST, IL

START TO FINISH: 30 MIN.
MAKES: 4 SERVINGS

- 4 boneless skinless chicken breast halves (4 ounces each)
- 1 tablespoon olive oil
- 1 can (14½ ounces) no-salt-added stewed tomatoes
- 1 can (14½ ounces) cut green beans, drained
- 1 cup water
- 1 teaspoon dried oregano
- ¼ teaspoon garlic powder
- 1½ cups instant brown rice
- 12 pitted Greek olives, halved
- ½ cup crumbled feta cheese

1. In a large nonstick skillet, brown chicken in oil on each side. Stir in the tomatoes, green beans, water, oregano and garlic powder. Bring to a boil; reduce heat. Cover and simmer for 10 minutes.

2. Stir in rice. Return to a boil. Cover and simmer 8-10 minutes longer or until a thermometer inserted in chicken reads 165° and rice is tender. Stir in olives; sprinkle with cheese.

Cook to Cook

This is a GREAT recipe— have made it several times. I dip the strips in ranch dressing. —**6FOREVERPAWS**

SOUTHERN FRIED CHICKEN STRIPS

What's not to love with these crowd-pleasing golden fried chicken strips? A hint of garlic makes them irresistible!

—**GENISE KRAUSE** STURGEON BAY, WI

PREP: 30 MIN. • **COOK:** 5 MIN./BATCH
MAKES: 6 SERVINGS

- 1 **egg**
- ½ **cup buttermilk**
- 1 **cup all-purpose flour**
- 1½ **teaspoons garlic powder**
- 1½ **teaspoons pepper**
- ½ **teaspoon salt**
- ½ **teaspoon paprika**
- 2 **pounds chicken tenderloins**
  Oil for deep-fat frying
- 2 **tablespoons grated Parmesan cheese**

1. In a shallow bowl, whisk egg and buttermilk. In a separate shallow bowl, combine the flour, garlic powder, pepper, salt and paprika. Dip chicken in egg mixture, then flour mixture.

2. In an electric skillet, heat oil to 375°. Fry chicken, a few pieces at a time, 2-3 minutes on each side or until no longer pink. Drain on paper towels. Sprinkle with cheese.

TURKEY CLUB ROULADES

Weeknights turn chic when these short-prep roulades with familiar ingredients are on the menu. Not a fan of turkey? Substitute lightly pounded chicken breasts.

—TASTE OF HOME TEST KITCHEN

PREP: 20 MIN. **COOK:** 15 MIN.
MAKES: 8 SERVINGS

- ¾ **pound fresh asparagus, trimmed**
- 8 **turkey breast cutlets (about 1 pound)**
- 1 **tablespoon Dijon-mayonnaise blend**
- 8 **slices deli ham**
- 8 **slices provolone cheese**
- ½ **teaspoon poultry seasoning**
- ½ **teaspoon pepper**
- 8 **bacon strips**

SAUCE
- ⅔ **cup Dijon-mayonnaise blend**
- 4 **teaspoons 2% milk**
- ¼ **teaspoon poultry seasoning**

1. Bring 4 cups water to a boil in a large saucepan. Add asparagus; cook, uncovered, 3 minutes or until crisp-tender. Drain and immediately place asparagus in ice water. Drain and pat dry. Set aside.

2. Spread the turkey with Dijon-mayonnaise. Layer with ham, cheese and asparagus. Sprinkle with poultry seasoning and pepper. Roll up tightly and wrap with bacon.

3. Cook roulades in a large skillet over medium-high heat 12-15 minutes, turning occasionally, or until bacon is crisp and turkey is no longer pink. Combine sauce ingredients; serve with the roulades.

Cook to Cook

My family loved this recipe. I made white rice and a small salad—called it dinner. I could not find the Dijon-mayo blend, so just made my own. The turkey breast cutlets were a little expensive—I will use pounded chicken breasts next time. Reminded me a little of Chicken Cordon Bleu. **—COLLEENAG**

PEANUT CHICKEN STIR-FRY

Peanut butter is one of my husband's favorite foods. I'm pleased—and so is he—that I can use it to make a delicious meal.

—DIANE KELLY PUYALLUP, WA

START TO FINISH: 30 MIN.
MAKES: 4 SERVINGS

- ½ **cup plus 1 tablespoon water, divided**
- ¼ **cup peanut butter**
- 3 **tablespoons soy sauce**
- 1 **tablespoon brown sugar**
- 2 **to 3 garlic cloves, minced**
- 2 **tablespoons canola oil**
- 1 **pound boneless skinless chicken breasts, cubed**
- 3 **cups fresh broccoli florets**
- 1 **tablespoon cornstarch**
  Hot cooked rice or noodles

1. In a small bowl, combine ½ cup water, peanut butter, soy sauce and brown sugar until smooth; set aside. In a skillet or wok, stir-fry garlic in oil 30 seconds. Add the chicken; stir-fry 5 minutes or until no longer pink. Add the broccoli; stir-fry 5 minutes.
2. Stir in peanut butter mixture; cook and stir 2-3 minutes or until sauce is smooth and broccoli is crisp-tender.
3. Combine cornstarch and remaining water until smooth; gradually add to skillet. Bring to a boil; cook and stir for 2 minutes or until thickened. Serve with rice or noodles.

NOTE *Reduced-fat peanut butter is not recommended for this recipe.*

SPICY SAUSAGE AND PENNE

I got the inspiration for this recipe from a dish at a local restaurant. It's a quick meal-in-one dish that I fix often. Substitute whatever pasta or veggies you have on hand for this versatile skillet supper.

—**BRIAN ALBRIGHT** SEWARD, NE

PREP: 10 MIN. **COOK:** 25 MIN.
MAKES: 4 SERVINGS

- 1 cup uncooked penne pasta
- 1 cup frozen mixed vegetables
- ½ pound smoked turkey sausage, cut into ¼-inch slices
- 2 tablespoons all-purpose flour
- ¼ teaspoon garlic powder
- ¼ teaspoon ground mustard
- ¼ teaspoon crushed red pepper flakes
- 1¼ cups fat-free milk
- ⅓ cup shredded part-skim mozzarella cheese

1. Cook pasta in a large saucepan according to package directions, adding the vegetables during the last 6 minutes of cooking.

2. Meanwhile, in a large nonstick skillet coated with cooking spray, brown sausage; remove from skillet and keep warm.

3. In a small bowl, combine the flour, garlic powder, mustard and pepper flakes; gradually whisk in milk until smooth. Add milk mixture to the skillet, stirring to loosen browned bits from pan. Bring to a boil; cook and stir 1-2 minutes or until thickened.

4. Drain pasta and vegetables; stir into pan. Add cheese and reserved sausage; cook and stir until cheese is melted.

Cook to Cook

This was a wonderful surprise! I didn't have the mixed veggies, so I used frozen peas and corn. Only thing I did different was to add a little shredded sharp cheddar. My hubby, who never gives high praise, went back for seconds, so in my book this is a keeper. —**REC-CHEF**

BALSAMIC CHICKEN SALAD

This is an easy, stylish and tasty alternative to frozen dinners. My husband gave it high marks the first time I served it, and he regularly requests that I make it.

—**REBECCA LINDAMOOD** BELFAST, NY

START TO FINISH: 20 MIN.
MAKES: 6 SERVINGS

- 6 **boneless skinless chicken breast halves (4 ounces each), cut into 3-inch strips**
- 4 **tablespoons olive oil, divided**
- ½ **teaspoon minced garlic**
- ¼ **cup balsamic vinegar**
- 1½ **cups halved cherry tomatoes**
- 1 **tablespoon minced fresh basil or 1 teaspoon dried basil**
- ¼ **teaspoon salt**
- ⅛ **teaspoon pepper**
- 6 **cups torn mixed salad greens**

1. In a large skillet, saute chicken in 1 tablespoon of oil until no longer pink. Add garlic; cook 1 minute longer. Remove from pan.

2. In the same skillet, bring vinegar to a boil. Add the chicken, tomatoes, basil, salt, pepper and remaining oil; cook and stir until heated through. Divide salad greens among six plates; top with chicken mixture.

NOTES

SAUSAGE & VEGETABLE SKILLET DINNER

I threw this together one night trying to use up produce before going out of town. Who knew it was going to be such a hit! Now it's a go-to recipe when I don't have much time to cook or wash dishes.

—ELIZABETH KELLEY CHICAGO, IL

START TO FINISH: 30 MIN.
MAKES: 4 SERVINGS

- 1 tablespoon olive oil
- 1 package (12 ounces) fully cooked Italian chicken sausage links, cut into 1-inch pieces
- 1 large onion, chopped
- 3 garlic cloves, minced
- ¼ teaspoon crushed red pepper flakes
- 8 medium red potatoes (about 2 pounds), thinly sliced
- 1 package (10 ounces) frozen corn
- 1¼ cups vegetable broth
- ¼ teaspoon pepper
- 2 cups fresh baby spinach

1. In a 12-in. skillet, heat oil over medium-high heat. Add sausage and onion; cook and stir until sausage is browned and onion is tender. Add garlic and pepper flakes; cook 1 minute.
2. Add the potatoes, corn, broth and pepper; bring to a boil. Reduce heat; simmer, covered, 12-15 minutes or until potatoes are tender. Add spinach; cook just until wilted.

Cook to Cook

I made this for my hungry family after football practice, as I was needing something quick and had to use up some leftover cheddar brats. My family loved this from the start. We added shredded Romano cheese, and some of us used shredded cheddar. It's whatever you prefer. Next time, I will add fresh mushrooms. This is now a mainstay at my house! **—JBLUNT4**

PEKING SHRIMP

In the summer, we spend as much time as possible at our vacation home in a beach town. I prepare lots of seafood because it's so fresh and readily available there, but this main dish is a year-round favorite.

—**JANET EDWARDS** BEAVERTON, OR

START TO FINISH: 25 MIN.
MAKES: 4 SERVINGS

- 1 **tablespoon cornstarch**
- ¼ **cup cold water**
- ¼ **cup corn syrup**
- 2 **tablespoons reduced-sodium soy sauce**
- 2 **tablespoons sherry or chicken broth**
- 1 **garlic clove, minced**
- ¼ **teaspoon ground ginger**
- 1 **small green pepper, cut into 1-inch pieces**
- 2 **tablespoons canola oil**
- 1 **pound uncooked medium shrimp, peeled and deveined**
- 1 **medium tomato, cut into wedges Hot cooked rice, optional**

1. In a bowl, mix cornstarch and water until smooth. Stir in corn syrup, soy sauce, sherry, garlic and ginger; set aside.

2. In a nonstick skillet or wok, stir-fry green pepper in oil 3 minutes. Add shrimp; stir-fry 3 minutes longer or until shrimp turn pink.

3. Stir cornstarch mixture and add to the pan. Bring to a boil; cook and stir 2 minutes or until thickened. Add the tomato; heat through. Serve with rice if desired.

CAJUN SHRIMP AND RICE

I have a friend with celiac disease and I serve this when she comes over for lunch. It allows her to have something besides meat and potatoes.

—**RUTH MILLER** BOYERTOWN, PA

START TO FINISH: 15 MIN.
MAKES: 4 SERVINGS

- 1 package (8.8 ounces) ready-to-serve long grain rice
- 1 pound uncooked medium shrimp, peeled and deveined
- 2 teaspoons Cajun seasoning
- 1 tablespoon olive oil
- 1 tablespoon butter
- 1½ teaspoons minced garlic
- 1 package (6 ounces) frozen snow peas

1. Cook rice according to package directions.

2. Meanwhile, in a large skillet, saute shrimp and Cajun seasoning in oil and butter until shrimp turn pink. Add garlic; cook 1 minute. Add peas and rice. Cook 2-3 minutes or until heated through.

WALNUT-CRUSTED ORANGE ROUGHY

A crispy, crunchy crust and moist, tender fish make this recipe a winner. The dipping sauce is salty-sweet and pairs beautifully with walnuts.

—TASTE OF HOME TEST KITCHEN

START TO FINISH: 25 MIN.
MAKES: 4 SERVINGS

- 4 **orange roughy fillets (5 ounces each)**
- ½ **teaspoon salt**
- ¼ **teaspoon pepper**
- ¼ **cup all-purpose flour**
- 1 **egg, lightly beaten**
- 1 **cup finely chopped walnuts**
- 3 **tablespoons seasoned bread crumbs**
- 1 **tablespoon sesame seeds**
- 1 **tablespoon dried parsley flakes**
- 2 **tablespoons butter**
- ¼ **cup honey**
- 1½ **teaspoons soy sauce**

1. Sprinkle fillets with salt and pepper. Place flour and egg in separate shallow bowls. In another shallow bowl, combine the walnuts, bread crumbs, sesame seeds and parsley. Dip fish in flour, egg, then walnut mixture.

2. In a large skillet over medium heat, cook fish in butter in batches for 2-3 minutes on each side or until fish flakes easily with a fork. In a small bowl, whisk the honey and soy sauce; serve with fish.

Cook to Cook

My husband is allergic to walnuts, so I used peanuts instead. I also used the flounder I had in my freezer, but other than that I followed the recipe and my family really liked it. My son was the only exception; he liked the fish without the crusty topping. I will definitely make this again. Very easy and quick. —TOOTGIRL

NOTES

SHRIMP FRIED RICE

My delectable shrimp dish is filled with color and taste that make it vanish quickly. Our family of four can't get enough of it. Bacon adds crispness and heartiness. Consider this recipe when you need a different entree or brunch item.

—SANDRA THOMPSON WHITE HALL, AR

START TO FINISH: 20 MIN.
MAKES: 8 SERVINGS

- 4 **tablespoons butter, divided**
- 4 **eggs, lightly beaten**
- 3 **cups cold cooked rice**
- 1 **package (16 ounces) frozen mixed vegetables**
- 1 **pound uncooked medium shrimp, peeled and deveined**
- ½ **teaspoon salt**
- ¼ **teaspoon pepper**
- 8 **bacon strips, cooked and crumbled, optional**

1. In a large skillet, melt 1 tablespoon butter over medium-high heat. Pour eggs into skillet. As eggs set, lift edges, letting uncooked portion flow underneath. Remove the eggs and keep warm.

2. Melt remaining butter in skillet. Add rice, vegetables and shrimp; cook and stir 5 minutes or until shrimp turn pink. Meanwhile, chop eggs into small pieces. Return eggs to the pan; sprinkle with salt and pepper. Cook until heated through, stirring occasionally. Sprinkle with bacon if desired.

NOTES

_____
_____
_____
_____
_____
_____

MEDITERRANEAN MAHI MAHI

I created this entree when a friend gave me some fresh-caught mahi mahi. Shortly after, I entered the recipe in a contest and won! I think you'll agree it's a keeper.

—VIRGINIA ANTHONY JACKSONVILLE, FL

PREP: 30 MIN. • **BAKE:** 10 MIN.
MAKES: 4 SERVINGS

- 1 **medium onion, chopped**
- 1 **medium green pepper, chopped**
- 4½ **teaspoons olive oil, divided**
- 1 **garlic clove, minced**
- ¾ **cup salsa**
- ½ **cup white wine or chicken broth**
- ¼ **cup halved Greek olives**
- ½ **teaspoon Greek seasoning**
- 4 **mahi mahi fillets (6 ounces each)**
- ¼ **teaspoon salt**
- ¼ **teaspoon pepper**
- ¼ **cup crumbled tomato and basil feta cheese**

1. Preheat oven to 425°. In a large ovenproof skillet, saute onion and green pepper in 1½ teaspoons oil until tender. Add garlic; saute 1 minute.

2. Stir in the salsa, wine, olives and Greek seasoning. Bring to a boil. Reduce heat; simmer, uncovered, 5 minutes or until slightly thickened.

Transfer to a bowl; set aside.

3. Sprinkle mahi mahi with salt and pepper. In same skillet, lightly brown fillets in the remaining oil 2 minutes on each side. Spoon salsa mixture over fillets.

4. Bake, uncovered, 6 minutes. Sprinkle with cheese; bake 2-3 minutes longer or until fish just turns opaque.

Cook to Cook

Really flavorful. If you don't want it spicy, just add a can of diced tomatoes. I added more olives and a little bit of lemon juice. Served with boiled baby potatoes—so good! —COOPGIRL703

CRUNCHY-COATED WALLEYE

Potato flakes make a golden coating for these fish fillets, which are a breeze to fry on the stovetop.

—SONDRA OSTHEIMER BOSCOBEL, WI

START TO FINISH: 20 MIN.
MAKES: 4 SERVINGS

- ⅓ cup all-purpose flour
- 1 teaspoon paprika
- ½ teaspoon salt
- ¼ teaspoon pepper
- ¼ teaspoon onion powder
- ¼ teaspoon garlic powder
- 2 eggs
- 2¼ pounds walleye, perch or pike fillets
- 1½ cups mashed potato flakes
- ⅓ cup canola oil
  Tartar sauce and lemon wedges, optional

1. In a shallow bowl, combine flour, paprika, salt, pepper, onion powder and garlic powder. In another bowl, beat the eggs. Dip both sides of fillets in flour mixture and eggs, then coat with potato flakes.

2. In a large skillet, fry fillets in oil for 5 minutes on each side or until fish flakes easily with a fork. Serve with tartar sauce and lemon if desired.

SALMON WITH VEGETABLE SALSA

This salsa recipe is great with not only salmon, but also grilled chicken breasts and barbecued shrimp kabobs. The only fresh ingredient not available in my son's garden was the avocado!

—MRS. PRISCILLA GILBERT

INDIAN HARBOUR BEACH, FL

START TO FINISH: 30 MIN.
MAKES: 4 SERVINGS

1½ cups grape tomatoes, halved
1½ cups chopped peeled cucumber
1 medium ripe avocado, peeled and cubed
1 small red onion, chopped
2 tablespoons minced fresh cilantro
1 jalapeno pepper, seeded and minced
2 tablespoons lime juice
½ teaspoon salt

FISH
4 salmon fillets (6 ounces each)
1 tablespoon lime juice
½ teaspoon salt
¼ teaspoon cayenne pepper
1 tablespoon butter

1. In a large bowl, combine tomatoes, cucumber, avocado, onion, cilantro, jalapeno, lime juice and salt; set aside.
2. Drizzle salmon with lime juice. Sprinkle with salt and cayenne pepper. In a large skillet, cook fillets in butter 3-4 minutes on each side or until fish flakes easily with a fork. Serve with the salsa.

NOTE *Wear disposable gloves when cutting hot peppers; the oils can burn skin. Avoid touching your face.*

MUSHROOM BURGERS

Ready to turn over a new burger? I guarantee that no one will be missing the beef after they've tasted these fantastic vegetarian burgers. They're hearty, moist, tender and full of flavor.

—**DENISE HOLLEBEKE** PENHOLD, AB

START TO FINISH: 30 MIN.
MAKES: 4 SERVINGS

- 2 **eggs, lightly beaten**
- 2 **cups finely chopped fresh mushrooms**
- ½ **cup dry bread crumbs**
- ½ **cup shredded cheddar cheese**
- ½ **cup finely chopped onion**
- ¼ **cup all-purpose flour**
- ½ **teaspoon salt**
- ¼ **teaspoon dried thyme**
- ¼ **teaspoon pepper**
- 1 **tablespoon canola oil**
- 4 **whole wheat hamburger buns, split**

1. In a large bowl, combine first nine ingredients. Shape into four patties.
2. In a large skillet, cook patties in oil over medium heat 3 minutes on each side or until crisp and lightly browned. Serve on buns.

Cook to Cook

I was surprised at how much my family loved this recipe, since we are not vegetarians. It's a fast and light dish perfect for weekday dinners. I substituted oatmeal, which I have on hand, for the bread crumbs and they were great. Mushroom burgers have become a new family favorite!
—JKNIGHT0012

SWEET POTATO & BEAN QUESADILLAS

Sweet potatoes and black beans roll up together for a quesadilla that's easy, fast, fun and delicious.

— BRITTANY HUBBARD GERING, NE

START TO FINISH: 30 MIN.
MAKES: 4 SERVINGS

- 2 **medium sweet potatoes**
- 4 **whole wheat tortillas (8 inches)**
- ¾ **cup canned black beans, rinsed and drained**
- ½ **cup shredded pepper jack cheese**
- ¾ **cup salsa**

1. Scrub sweet potatoes; pierce several times with a fork. Place on a microwave-safe plate. Microwave, uncovered, on high 7-9 minutes or until very tender, turning once.

2. When cool enough to handle, cut each potato lengthwise in half. Scoop out pulp. Spread onto one half of each tortilla; top with beans and cheese. Fold other half of tortilla over filling.

3. Heat a griddle or skillet over medium heat. Cook quesadillas for 2-3 minutes on each side or until golden brown and cheese is melted. Serve with salsa.

NOTE *This recipe was tested in a 1,100-watt microwave.*

NOTES

_____
_____
_____
_____
_____
_____
_____
_____
_____

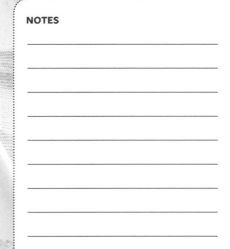

Cook to Cook

I'll make this again—a nice change from standard American cheese. I didn't have my multigrain bread so used the whole grain white. Next time I'll chop my basil leaves so a whole leaf doesn't come out when taking a bite. —**BASILANDTHYME**

BEST-EVER GRILLED CHEESE SANDWICHES

For a classic grilled sandwich, this recipe is the best. You can also use your imagination for other fillings, such as a sprinkle of Parmesan cheese, Italian seasoning, chives or even a tiny spoonful of salsa.
—**EDIE DESPAIN** LOGAN, UT

START TO FINISH: 20 MIN.
MAKES: 2 SERVINGS

- 2 tablespoons mayonnaise
- 1 teaspoon Dijon mustard
- 4 slices sourdough bread
- 2 slices Swiss cheese
- 2 slices cheddar cheese
- 2 slices sweet onion
- 1 medium tomato, sliced
- 6 cooked bacon strips
- 2 tablespoons butter, softened

1. Combine mayonnaise and mustard; spread over two bread slices. Layer with cheeses, onion, tomato and bacon; top with remaining bread. Spread outsides of sandwiches with butter.

2. In a small skillet over medium heat, toast sandwiches 2-3 minutes on each side or until cheese is melted.

4

SIZZLE & SEAR ENTREES

Fire up the grill or broiler for juicy meats, poultry and seafood.

SIZZLE & SEAR ENTREES INDEX

Cook to Cook

Look for
THESE boxes
for helpful tidbits!

BALSAMIC-GLAZED BEEF SKEWERS

With only five easy-to-double ingredients, these mouthwatering kabobs are one of our favorite recipes. To prevent wooden skewers from burning, soak them in water for 30 minutes before threading the meat on them. We like these skewers with hot cooked rice and a tossed salad.

—CAROLE FRASER TORONTO, ON

START TO FINISH: 25 MIN.
MAKES: 4 SERVINGS

- ¼ **cup balsamic vinaigrette**
- ¼ **cup barbecue sauce**
- 1 **teaspoon Dijon mustard**
- 1 **beef top sirloin steak (1 pound),**
  cut into 1-inch cubes
- 2 **cups cherry tomatoes**

1. In a large bowl, whisk vinaigrette, barbecue sauce and mustard until blended. Reserve ¼ cup marinade for basting. Add beef to the remaining marinade; toss to coat.

2. Alternately thread beef and tomatoes on four metal or soaked wooden skewers. Moisten a paper towel with cooking oil; using long-handled tongs, rub on grill rack to coat lightly.

3. Grill skewers, covered, over medium heat or broil 4 in. from heat 6-9 minutes or until beef reaches desired doneness, turning occasionally and basting frequently with reserved marinade during the last 3 minutes.

PAUL BUNYAN BURGERS

This is one of my go-to grilling recipes. To make these burgers even faster, substitute canned mushrooms and bacon bits.

—JO REED CRAIG, CO

START TO FINISH: 30 MIN.
MAKES: 3 SERVINGS

- 6   **bacon strips, diced**
- 1   **cup sliced fresh mushrooms**
- 3   **thin onion slices**
- 1   **egg, lightly beaten**
- 1   **tablespoon Worcestershire sauce**
- ½   **teaspoon seasoned salt**
- ½   **teaspoon salt**
- ½   **teaspoon pepper**
- ½   **teaspoon prepared horseradish**
- 1   **pound ground beef**
- 3   **slices process American cheese**
- 3   **hamburger buns, split**

1. In a large skillet, cook bacon over medium heat until crisp. Remove with a slotted spoon to paper towels. In the drippings, saute mushrooms and onion until tender. Transfer to a large bowl with a slotted spoon; add bacon.

2. In another bowl, combine the egg, Worcestershire sauce, seasoned salt, salt, pepper and horseradish; sprinkle beef over mixture and mix well. Shape into six ¼-in.-thick patties.

3. Divide bacon mixture among three patties. Top with a cheese slice; fold in corners of cheese. Top with remaining patties; seal edges.

4. Grill, uncovered, over medium-hot heat 5-6 minutes a side or until a thermometer reads 160° and meat juices run clear. Serve on buns.

Cook to Cook

We thought this was especially good! I added a little garlic powder and garlic salt instead of plain salt. A treat! I also spread some BBQ sauce on top as I was grilling. — KSHEA

STEAKS WITH MUSHROOM CREAM SAUCE

A versatile sauce tops these sirloin steaks and enhances their beefy flavor. The delicious sauce would also taste great over grilled chicken or pork.

—LADONNA REED PONCA CITY, OK

START TO FINISH: 25 MIN.
MAKES: 4 SERVINGS

- 4 beef top sirloin steaks (6 ounces each)
- ¼ teaspoon salt
- ¼ teaspoon pepper

SAUCE

- 1 jar (4½ ounces) sliced mushrooms, drained
- 1 teaspoon minced garlic
- 1 teaspoon canola oil
- ½ cup French onion dip
- 2 tablespoons half-and-half cream
- ½ teaspoon minced chives
- ¼ teaspoon pepper

1. Sprinkle steaks with salt and pepper. Grill steaks, covered, over medium heat or broil 4 in. from heat 5-7 minutes on each side or until meat reaches desired doneness (for medium-rare, a thermometer should read 145°; medium, 160°; well-done, 170°).

2. In a large skillet, saute mushrooms and garlic in oil 3 minutes. Stir in onion dip, cream, chives and pepper. Bring to a gentle boil. Reduce heat; simmer, uncovered, 2-3 minutes or until heated through. Serve with steaks.

NOTES

LOADED FLANK STEAK

For a scrumptious steak dinner, try this recipe. The stuffing makes it elegant enough to serve to guests.

—TAMMY THOMAS MUSTANG, OK

START TO FINISH: 25 MIN.
MAKES: 6 SERVINGS

- ½ **cup butter, softened**
- 6 **bacon strips, cooked and crumbled**
- 3 **green onions, chopped**
- 2 **tablespoons ranch salad dressing mix**
- ½ **teaspoon pepper**
- 1 **beef flank steak (1½ to 2 pounds)**

1. In a small bowl, beat the first five ingredients. Cut a pocket horizontally in steak; fill with butter mixture.

2. Grill steak, covered, over medium heat or broil 4 in. from heat 5-7 minutes on each side or until meat reaches desired doneness (for medium-rare, a thermometer should read 145°; medium, 160°; well-done, 170°). Let stand 5 minutes before serving. To serve, slice across the grain.

Cook to Cook

These are fantastic! I added an egg and some bread crumbs, and they were delicious. The sauce is a must-try.
—**COOKINGAT#8**

BBQ BACON BURGERS

With a slice of bacon inside and a tasty barbecue-mayo sauce on top, these are definitely not ordinary burgers. We think you'll agree.

—**JOAN SCHOENHERR** EASTPOINTE, MI

START TO FINISH: 30 MIN.
MAKES: 4 SERVINGS

- ¼ cup mayonnaise
- ¼ cup barbecue sauce
- 4 bacon strips, cooked and crumbled
- 1½ teaspoons dried minced onion
- 1½ teaspoons steak seasoning
- 1 pound ground beef
- 4 slices Swiss cheese
- 4 hamburger buns, split
  Lettuce leaves and tomato slices

1. In a small bowl, mix mayonnaise and barbecue sauce. In another bowl, combine the bacon, 2 tablespoons mayonnaise mixture, onion and steak seasoning; crumble beef over mixture and mix well. Shape into four patties.

2. Grill burgers, covered, over medium heat 5-7 minutes on each side or until a thermometer reads 160° and juices run clear.

3. Top with cheese. Cover and cook 1-2 minutes longer or until cheese is melted. Spread remaining mayonnaise mixture over buns; top each with a burger, lettuce and tomato.

GRILLED STEAK SALAD

With plenty of sliced steak and veggies, my main dish salad will please even the biggest appetites. It's a terrific dinner on a summer day or any time you feel like grilling.

—**MILDRED SHERRER** FORT WORTH, TX

START TO FINISH: 30 MIN.
MAKES: 4 SERVINGS

- ½ **teaspoon salt**
- ½ **teaspoon garlic powder**
- ½ **teaspoon pepper**
- 1 **beef flank steak (1 pound)**
- 1 **large sweet onion, sliced**
- 1 **package (5 ounces) spring mix salad greens**
- 1 **can (16 ounces) kidney beans, rinsed and drained**
- 1 **jar (7 ounces) roasted sweet red peppers, drained and sliced**
- ⅓ **cup balsamic vinegar**
- 2 **tablespoons minced fresh basil or 2 teaspoons dried basil**
- 2 **tablespoons olive oil**
- 1 **teaspoon Dijon mustard**

1. Combine the salt, garlic powder and pepper; rub over steak. Moisten a paper towel with cooking oil; using long-handled tongs, rub on grill rack to coat lightly.

2. Grill the steak, covered, over medium heat 6-8 minutes on each side or until meat reaches desired doneness (for medium-rare, a thermometer should read 145°; medium, 160°; well-done, 170°).

3. Place onion slices on a double thickness of heavy-duty foil (about 12 in. square). Fold foil around onion; seal tightly. Add to grill with steak. Grill, covered, over medium heat 16-20 minutes or until tender. Open foil carefully to allow steam to escape.

4. Let the steak stand 5 minutes before slicing.

5. Meanwhile, in a large bowl, combine the greens, beans, red peppers and grilled onion.

6. In a small bowl, whisk the vinegar, basil, oil and mustard. Pour ¼ cup over salad; toss to coat. Divide among four salad plates. Slice flank steak across the grain; arrange over salads. Drizzle with remaining dressing.

NOTES

GRILLED STEAKS WITH MUSHROOM SAUCE

When busy midweek days call for something special, this steak entree with its savory sauce will fit the bill beautifully.

—TASTE OF HOME TEST KITCHEN

START TO FINISH: 20 MIN.
MAKES: 4 SERVINGS

- 1 **beef top sirloin steak (1½ pounds)**
- ½ **teaspoon steak seasoning**
- 1 **pound small fresh mushrooms**
- ¼ **cup butter, cubed**
- ½ **cup beef broth**
- 1 **tablespoon Dijon mustard**
- ½ **teaspoon dried rosemary, crushed**
- ½ **teaspoon dried thyme**

1. Cut steak into four pieces; sprinkle with steak seasoning. Grill steaks, covered, over medium heat or broil 4 in. from heat 5-7 minutes on each side or until meat reaches desired doneness (for medium-rare, a thermometer should read 145°; medium, 160°; well-done, 170°).

2. Meanwhile, in a large skillet, saute mushrooms in butter until tender. Stir in the remaining ingredients. Bring to a boil; cook until liquid is reduced by about half. Serve with the steaks.

Cook to Cook

I always keep a jar of minced garlic in my refrigerator, so I added a teaspoon to the mushrooms. But I totally enjoyed this recipe! It was quick and delicious.
—CHINADOLL2008

STEAK & NEW POTATO TOSS

I usually use leftover barbecued steak to make this fabulous main dish salad. It's pretty, too, with the red pepper, green broccoli and white potatoes.

—DEYANNE DAVIES ROSSLAND, BC

START TO FINISH: 30 MIN.
MAKES: 4 SERVINGS

- 1 **pound small red potatoes, scrubbed and cut into wedges**
- 1¼ **pounds beef top sirloin steak**
- 3 **cups fresh broccoli florets**
- ¼ **cup olive oil**
- 2 **tablespoons cider vinegar**
- 2 **green onions, thinly sliced**
- 2 **garlic cloves, minced**
- ½ **teaspoon ground mustard**
- ½ **teaspoon paprika**
- ¼ **teaspoon pepper**
- 1 **medium sweet red pepper, chopped**

1. Place potatoes in a large saucepan and cover with water. Bring to a boil. Reduce heat; cover and cook 10-15 minutes or until tender.

2. Meanwhile, grill steak, covered, over medium heat 8-11 minutes on each side or until meat reaches desired doneness (for medium-rare, a thermometer should read 145°; medium, 160°; well-done, 170°). Let stand 10 minutes before thinly slicing across the grain.

3. Place broccoli florets in a steamer basket. Place in a saucepan over 1 in. of water. Bring to a boil. Cover and steam for 2-3 minutes or until crisp-tender.

4. In a small bowl, combine the oil, vinegar, green onions, garlic, mustard, paprika and pepper.

5. Drain broccoli and potatoes; place in a large bowl. Add beef and red pepper; drizzle with vinaigrette and toss to coat. Serve warm or cold.

Cook to Cook

This dish has become a staple in our home. I have altered it by adding a tablespoon of Crab Boil to the potato water. I then toss the parboiled potatoes in some olive oil and toss them in grated Parmesan before placing them in a basket on the grill with the meat. —ON_KP_AGAIN

STEAK SANDWICH KABOBS

Seasoned steak skewers are grilled with bread and veggies, then topped with provolone cheese for a fantastic meal. Coleslaw, spruced up with chopped walnuts, is a great side for the kabobs.

—TASTE OF HOME TEST KITCHEN

START TO FINISH: 25 MIN.
MAKES: 4 SERVINGS

- 1 **pound beef top sirloin steak, cut into 1-inch cubes**
- 1 **teaspoon steak seasoning**
- 1 **medium sweet red pepper, cut into 1-inch chunks**
- 6 **ounces focaccia bread, cut into 1-inch cubes**
- 1 **medium onion, cut into 1-inch chunks**
- 1 **tablespoon olive oil**
- 3 **slices provolone cheese, cut into strips**
- 2 **cups deli coleslaw**
- ½ **cup chopped walnuts**

1. Sprinkle beef with steak seasoning. Alternately thread the beef, red pepper, bread cubes and onion onto four metal or soaked wooden skewers; brush with oil.

2. Grill, covered, over medium heat 8-10 minutes or until meat reaches desired doneness, turning occasionally. Top with cheese; grill 1-2 minutes longer or until cheese is melted.

3. In a small bowl, combine coleslaw and walnuts. Serve with kabobs. .

NOTES

CHILI-APRICOT PORK CHOPS

With a slightly spicy-sweet glaze created with just four ingredients, these chops are not only tasty—they're super-easy, too.

—**LILY JULOW** LAWRENCEVILLE, GA

START TO FINISH: 20 MIN.
MAKES: 4 SERVINGS

- ¼ **cup apricot preserves**
- ¼ **cup chili sauce**
- 1 **tablespoon spicy brown mustard**
- 1 **tablespoon water**
- 4 **bone-in pork loin chops (7 ounces each)**
- ¼ **teaspoon salt**
- ¼ **teaspoon pepper**

1. In a small bowl, combine the preserves, chili sauce, mustard and water. Sprinkle pork chops with salt and pepper. Spoon glaze over both sides of pork.

2. Broil 4-5 in. from heat for 4-5 minutes on each side or until meat reaches desired doneness (for medium-rare, a thermometer should read 145°; medium, 160°). Let stand 5 minutes before serving.

Cook to Cook

These were great! I used sugar-free preserves and boneless chops, so I kept them a little farther from the heat and monitored them with a meat thermometer. They ended up so juicy, with the preserves being a little crispy.

—**GRETCHEEPOO**

CHIPOTLE BBQ PORK SANDWICHES

I first made these for a summer barbecue with guests who love traditional BBQ pork sandwiches but wanted something lighter. They loved these and didn't miss the extra calories one bit. Crunchy coleslaw tames the heat!

—PRISCILLA YEE CONCORD, CA

PREP: 20 MIN. • **GRILL:** 20 MIN.
MAKES: 4 SERVINGS

- ½ cup barbecue sauce
- 1 tablespoon honey
- 2 chipotle peppers in adobo sauce, chopped
- 1 pork tenderloin (1 pound)
- 1½ cups coleslaw mix
- 2 tablespoons reduced-fat sour cream
- 2 tablespoons Miracle Whip Light
- 1 tablespoon Dijon mustard
- 4 hamburger buns, split

1. In a small bowl, combine the barbecue sauce, honey and peppers. Set aside ¼ cup until serving.

2. Moisten a paper towel with cooking oil; using long-handled tongs, rub on grill rack to coat lightly. Prepare grill for indirect heat, using a drip pan.

3. Place pork over drip pan. Grill, covered, over indirect medium-hot heat for 20-25 minutes or until the meat reaches desired doneness (for medium-rare, a thermometer should read 145°; medium, 160°), basting occasionally with the remaining barbecue sauce. Let stand 5 minutes before slicing.

4. Meanwhile, combine coleslaw mix, sour cream, Miracle Whip Light and mustard. Brush cut sides of buns with reserved barbecue sauce. Cut pork into ¼-in. slices; place on bun bottoms. Top with coleslaw and bun tops.

GRILLED PORK CHOPS

This marinade is so simple that I use it on all kinds of meat. For a more robust flavor, let the meat marinate overnight.

—LORI DANIELS BEVERLY, WV

PREP: 10 MIN. + MARINATING
GRILL: 10 MIN. • **MAKES:** 4 SERVINGS

- ½ cup packed brown sugar
- ½ cup soy sauce
- 2 garlic cloves, minced
- ¼ teaspoon pepper
- 4 bone-in pork loin chops
  (1 inch thick and 8 ounces each)

1. In a small bowl, combine the brown sugar, soy sauce, garlic and pepper. Pour marinade into a large resealable plastic bag. Add pork chops; seal bag and turn to coat. Refrigerate 8 hours or overnight.

2. Drain chops and discard marinade. Moisten a paper towel with cooking oil; using long-handled tongs, rub on grill rack to coat lightly.

3. Grill chops, covered, over medium heat or broil 4-5 in. from heat for 4-5 minutes on each side or until meat reaches desired doneness (for medium-rare, a thermometer should read 145°; medium, 160°). Let stand 5 minutes before serving.

Cook to Cook

A nice marinade; for a variation, I often add a 6 oz. can of pineapple juice.
—DSICARD

HAM WITH PINEAPPLE SALSA

A dear friend shared this recipe when she moved from Hawaii to Colorado. Now it's one of my favorite ways to eat ham. I get lots of requests for the recipe whenever I make it for guests.

—DAWN WILSON BUENA VISTA, CO

START TO FINISH: 25 MIN.
MAKES: 4 SERVINGS

- 1 **can (8 ounces) crushed pineapple, drained**
- 2 **tablespoons orange marmalade**
- 1 **tablespoon minced fresh cilantro**
- 2 **teaspoons lime juice**
- 2 **teaspoons chopped jalapeno pepper**
- ¼ **teaspoon salt**
- 1 **bone-in fully cooked ham steak (1½ pounds)**

1. For salsa, in a small bowl, combine the first six ingredients; set aside.
2. Place ham steak on an ungreased rack in a broiler pan. Broil 4-6 in. from heat 4-5 minutes on each side or until a thermometer reads 140°. Cut into serving-size pieces; serve with salsa.

NOTE *Wear disposable gloves when cutting hot peppers; the oils can burn skin. Avoid touching your face.*

NOTES

_____
_____
_____
_____
_____
_____
_____
_____
_____

GRILLED PORK TENDERLOIN SATAY

My dad used to make this often, pairing peanut butter and soy sauce for a great Asian-style entree. I like to serve it with roasted veggies and yellow rice.

—GAYLE JEFFERSON LAS VEGAS, NV

PREP: 25 MIN. • **GRILL:** 10 MIN.
MAKES: 8 SKEWERS (½ CUP SAUCE)

- 1 **small onion, chopped**
- ¼ **cup packed brown sugar**
- ¼ **cup water**
- 3 **tablespoons reduced-sodium soy sauce**
- 2 **tablespoons reduced-fat creamy peanut butter**
- 4½ **teaspoons canola oil**
- 2 **garlic cloves, minced**
- ¼ **teaspoon ground ginger**
- 1 **pork tenderloin (1 pound)**

1. In a small saucepan, bring the first eight ingredients to a boil. Reduce heat; simmer, uncovered, 10-12 minutes or until thickened. Set aside ½ cup of mixture for sauce.

2. Cut pork in half widthwise; cut each half into thin strips. Thread pork strips onto eight metal or soaked wooden skewers. Grill, uncovered, over medium-hot heat 2-3 minutes on each side or until no longer pink, basting occasionally with remaining mixture. Serve with reserved sauce.

PORK CHOPS WITH BLUE CHEESE SAUCE

These wonderful chops have a unique kick. This recipe makes a decadent, but quick and easy weeknight meal. Even if you aren't a blue cheese fan, you'll enjoy this mild-tasting sauce.

—KATHLEEN SPECHT CLINTON, MT

START TO FINISH: 25 MIN.
MAKES: 4 SERVINGS

- 4 **bone-in pork loin chops (7 ounces each)**
- 1 **teaspoon coarsely ground pepper**
- 1 **teaspoon butter**
- 1 **green onion, finely chopped**
- 1 **garlic clove, minced**
- 1 **tablespoon all-purpose flour**
- ⅔ **cup fat-free milk**
- 3 **tablespoons crumbled blue cheese**
- 1 **tablespoon white wine or reduced-sodium chicken broth**

1. Preheat broiler. Sprinkle pork chops on both sides with pepper; place on a broiler pan coated with cooking spray. Broil 4-5 in. from heat 4-5 minutes on each side or until meat reaches desired doneness (for medium-rare, a thermometer should read 145°; medium, 160°). Let stand 5 minutes before serving.

2. Meanwhile, in a small saucepan, heat butter over medium-high heat. Add green onion and garlic; cook and stir until tender. Stir in flour until blended; gradually whisk in milk. Bring to a boil, stirring constantly; cook and stir 1-2 minutes or until thickened. Add cheese and wine; heat through. Serve chops with sauce.

Cook to Cook

I made this last night, and let me tell you how yummy it was! I made the sauce exactly as the recipe states, and it was so flavorful and creamy. I can see using it on filet mignon or as a burger topping, too. Personally, I don't like bone-in pork chops, so I used a pork loin that I cut into medallions and sauteed with salt, pepper and dried marjoram (for fun). Love, love, loved it!
—DMWILMOTH

SPICE-RUBBED RIBS

For grilling, here's the rub I recommend. It's made with a wonderful blend of spices. If you have some left after making ribs, put it in a shaker and use it another day on pork or beef roasts, tenderloins, steaks and more. It's great alone or under a sauce.

—CHERYL EWING ELLWOOD CITY, PA

PREP: 10 MIN. • **GRILL:** 1 HOUR
MAKES: 10 SERVINGS

- 3 tablespoons paprika
- 2 tablespoons plus 1 teaspoon salt
- 2 tablespoons plus 1 teaspoon garlic powder
- 2 tablespoons cayenne pepper
- 4 teaspoons onion powder
- 4 teaspoons dried oregano
- 4 teaspoons dried thyme
- 4 teaspoons pepper
- 10 pounds pork baby back ribs

1. In a small bowl, combine the seasonings; rub over ribs.

2. Prepare grill for indirect heat, using a drip pan. Grill ribs, covered, over indirect medium heat 1 hour or until meat is tender, turning occasionally.

Cook to Cook

I have searched through SO many rub recipes, and this one is wonderful. Simple but with LOTS of flavor. I even get requests to not add BBQ sauce over the rub on ribs and chicken; people prefer just the rub!
—HONORTHEMOSTHIGH

PORK CHOPS WITH BLACKBERRY SAUCE

Quick, easy and oh-so-good describes these chops! Try them any busy weeknight or weekend.

—**MRS. PRISCILLA GILBERT**
INDIAN HARBOUR BEACH, FL

START TO FINISH: 20 MIN.
MAKES: 4 SERVINGS

- 4 **bone-in pork loin chops (7 ounces each)**
- ¼ **cup seedless blackberry spreadable fruit**
- 3 **tablespoons ketchup**
- ¼ **teaspoon minced garlic**
- ¼ **teaspoon prepared mustard**
- ¼ **teaspoon cornstarch**
- 1 **tablespoon A.1. steak sauce**

1. Broil chops 4-5 in. from heat 4-5 minutes on each side or until meat reaches desired doneness (for medium-rare, a thermometer should read 145°; medium, 160°). Let stand 5 minutes before serving.

2. Meanwhile, in a small saucepan, combine the spreadable fruit, ketchup, garlic and mustard. Bring to a boil. Combine cornstarch and steak sauce until smooth. Gradually stir into pan. Bring to a boil; cook and stir 2 minutes or until thickened. Serve with the pork chops.

NOTES

HERBTASTIC PORK CHOPS

Pork chops can be prepared numerous ways, but there's no easier preparation than smothering them with fresh herbs straight from the garden and firing up the grill. Add sliced summer squash to round out the meal.

—JENN TIDWELL FAIR OAKS, CA

START TO FINISH: 30 MIN.
MAKES: 4 SERVINGS

- ⅔ cup olive oil
- ¼ cup minced fresh sage
- ¼ cup minced fresh parsley
- 8 garlic cloves, minced
- 2 tablespoons minced fresh thyme
- 1 tablespoon minced fresh rosemary
- ¼ teaspoon salt
- ¼ teaspoon pepper
- 2 yellow summer squash, sliced lengthwise
- 4 bone-in pork loin chops (¾ inch thick)

1. In a small bowl, combine the first eight ingredients; reserve ⅓ cup for serving. Rub both sides of squash and pork chops with remaining mixture.

2. Grill, covered, over medium heat 4-5 minutes on each side or until meat reaches desired doneness (for medium-rare, a thermometer should read 145°; medium, 160°) and squash is tender. Let pork stand 5 minutes before serving. Serve pork and squash with reserved herb mixture.

Cook to Cook

This recipe came out great and was so easy to cook. I had all the herbs growing in my garden and added a little basil. I will try this herb mixture on other foods. —AGNEW46

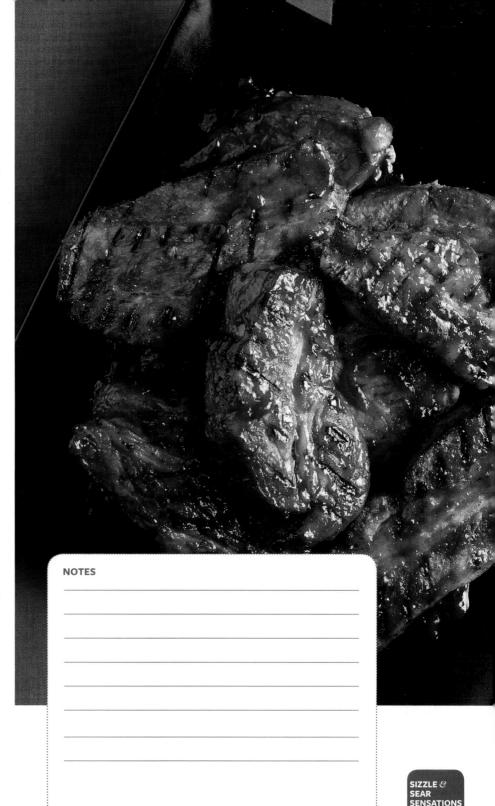

CHINESE COUNTRY-STYLE PORK RIBS

Here's a recipe that makes ribs tangy and tender. The Chinese-style glaze gives them a uniquely different flavor that we love.

—JAMIE WETTER BOSCOBEL, WI

PREP: 25 MIN. • **GRILL:** 10 MIN.
MAKES: 8 SERVINGS

- 4 **pounds bone-in country-style pork ribs**
- ½ **cup water**
- 1 **tablespoon liquid smoke, optional**
- ½ **teaspoon onion powder**
- ½ **cup chili sauce**
- ¼ **cup hoisin sauce**
- 2 **tablespoons honey**
- ⅛ **teaspoon cayenne pepper**

1. Cut ribs into serving-size pieces; place in a 3-qt. microwave-safe dish with water, liquid smoke if desired, and onion powder. Cover and microwave on high 15-20 minutes or until tender.

2. Meanwhile, in a small saucepan, mix remaining ingredients. Bring to a boil. Reduce heat; simmer, uncovered, 5-8 minutes or until slightly thickened, stirring occasionally.

3. Drain ribs. Moisten a paper towel with cooking oil; using long-handled tongs, rub on grill rack to coat lightly. Grill ribs, covered, over medium heat 8-10 minutes or until browned, turning occasionally and basting with sauce.

FREEZE OPTION *Place cooled ribs in a resealable freezer bag and freeze up to 3 months. To use, thaw in refrigerator overnight. Preheat oven to 325°. Place ribs in a baking pan; cover and bake 35-40 minutes or until heated through.*

NOTE *This recipe was tested in a 1,100-watt microwave.*

NOTES

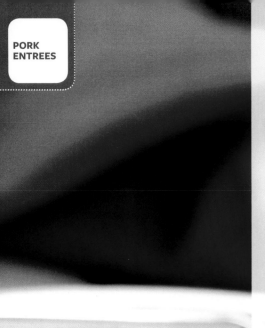

QUICK APPLE-GLAZED PORK CHOPS

You probably have all of the spices you need for these succulent pork chops in your pantry or spice rack. This versatile rub is also delicious on chicken or fish.

—TASTE OF HOME TEST KITCHEN

START TO FINISH: 20 MIN.
MAKES: 4 SERVINGS

- 2 **tablespoons brown sugar**
- 2 **teaspoons paprika**
- 1 **teaspoon salt**
- 1 **teaspoon onion powder**
- 1 **teaspoon garlic powder**
- 1 **teaspoon ground mustard**
- 1 **teaspoon dried thyme**
- ½ **teaspoon pepper**
- 4 **boneless pork loin chops
  (1 inch thick and 6 ounces each)**
- 2 **tablespoons apple jelly**

1. Combine the first eight ingredients; rub over both sides of pork chops.

2. Cook in batches on an indoor grill coated with cooking spray 3-4 minutes on each side or until meat reaches desired doneness (for medium-rare, a thermometer should read 145°; medium, 160°). Let the pork stand 5 minutes before serving.

3. In a microwave-safe bowl, heat jelly until warmed; brush over pork chops.

MEXICALI CHICKEN

I've been making this dish for years—to the delight of my family. It's great served with Spanish rice and refried beans. Add cilantro to the salsa, if desired.

—AVANELL HEWITT
NORTH RICHLAND HILLS, TX

START TO FINISH: 30 MIN.
MAKES: 4 SERVINGS

- 1 **medium tomato, finely chopped**
- 1 **small onion, finely chopped**
- 2 **jalapeno peppers, seeded and chopped**
- 2 **tablespoons lime juice**
- 1 **garlic clove, minced**
- ¼ **teaspoon salt**
- ⅛ **teaspoon pepper**
- 4 **boneless skinless chicken breast halves (4 ounces each)**
- 1 **to 2 teaspoons reduced-sodium taco seasoning**
- 4 **bacon strips, halved**
- 4 **slices reduced-fat provolone cheese**
- 1 **medium lime, cut into four wedges**

1. In a small bowl, combine the tomato, onion, jalapenos, lime juice, garlic, salt and pepper. Chill until serving.

2. Sprinkle chicken with taco seasoning; set aside. In a large skillet, cook bacon over medium heat until crisp. Remove to paper towels; drain.

3. If grilling the chicken, moisten a paper towel with cooking oil; using long-handled tongs, rub on grill rack to coat lightly. Grill chicken, covered, over medium heat or broil 4 in. from heat for 4-7 minutes on each side or until a thermometer reads 165°.

4. Top with bacon and cheese; cook 1 minute longer or until cheese is melted. Serve with salsa; squeeze lime wedges over top.

NOTE *Wear disposable gloves when cutting hot peppers; the oils can burn skin. Avoid touching your face.*

Cook to Cook

Awesome chicken dish! I was actually quite disappointed to be full! With a little extra tomato and lime juice, as well as cilantro, the salsa gives a surprisingly spicy kick. Great recipe, can't wait to try it again. **—JMHAGER**

GRILLED PEPPER JACK CHICKEN SANDWICHES

Zesty cheese, yummy bacon and grilled flavor will have you thinking this sandwich came from a restaurant. Use a broiler if you don't want to venture outside.

—**LINDA FOREMAN** LOCUST GROVE, OK

START TO FINISH: 25 MIN.
MAKES: 2 SERVINGS

- 2 **boneless skinless chicken breast halves (4 ounces each)**
- 1 **teaspoon poultry seasoning**
- 2 **center-cut bacon strips, cooked and halved**
- 2 **slices (½ ounce each) pepper jack cheese**
- 2 **hamburger buns, split**
- 2 **lettuce leaves**
- 1 **slice onion, separated into rings**
- 2 **slices tomato**
  Dill pickle slices, optional

1. Sprinkle chicken with poultry seasoning. Moisten a paper towel with cooking oil; using long-handled tongs, rub on grill rack to coat lightly.

2. Grill chicken, covered, over medium heat or broil 4 in. from heat 4-7 minutes on each side or until a thermometer reads 165°.

3. Top with bacon and cheese; cover and cook 1-2 minutes longer or until cheese is melted.

4. Serve on buns with lettuce, onion, tomato and pickles if desired.

Cook to Cook

I didn't use poultry seasoning because I didn't have it. I just seasoned with salt, pepper and garlic powder. We also omitted the bacon and used whole wheat buns (to cut some calories/fat). Overall it was great! We eat chicken a LOT, and sometimes I forget about these classic ways to make it tasty! Thanks! —**LACICHADD**

NOTES

_____

_____

_____

_____

_____

_____

SPICY BARBECUED CHICKEN

My grown children still beg for my chicken. They like the savory barbecue sauce so much, they've been known to hover over me to snitch a spoonful behind my back!

—**PATRICIA PARKER** CONNELLY SPRINGS, NC

PREP: 25 MIN. • **GRILL:** 45 MIN.
MAKES: 8 SERVINGS

- 1½ cups sugar
- 1½ cups ketchup
- ½ cup water
- ¼ cup lemon juice
- ¼ cup cider vinegar
- ¼ cup Worcestershire sauce
- 2 tablespoons plus 2 teaspoons chili powder
- 2 tablespoons plus 2 teaspoons prepared mustard
- 1 teaspoon salt
- ½ teaspoon crushed red pepper flakes
- 2 broiler/fryer chickens (3½ to 4 pounds each), cut up

1. In a large saucepan, combine the first 10 ingredients; bring to a boil. Reduce heat; simmer, uncovered, 15 minutes.

2. Grill chicken, covered, over medium heat 40 minutes, turning several times. Set half of the barbecue sauce aside. Baste chicken with remaining sauce; grill 5-10 minutes longer or until juices run clear. Serve with reserved sauce.

CRISPY GARLIC-BROILED CHICKEN THIGHS

These easy garlicky chicken thighs are also great on the grill.

—KELLEY FRENCH COLCHESTER, VT

START TO FINISH: 25 MIN.
MAKES: 4 SERVINGS

- ⅓ cup butter, melted
- ¼ cup reduced-sodium soy sauce
- 7 garlic cloves, minced
- ½ teaspoon pepper
- 8 bone-in chicken thighs (about 3 pounds)

1. In a large bowl, mix the butter, soy sauce, garlic and pepper. Reserve ¼ cup soy mixture for basting. Add chicken to remaining soy mixture; turn to coat.

2. Place chicken on a broiler pan, skin side down. Broil 4-6 in. from heat for 10-15 minutes on each side or until a thermometer reads 170°-175°. Brush occasionally with reserved soy mixture during the last 10 minutes of cooking.

Cook to Cook

This was super good! My whole family loved it, and this will definitely be a monthly meal. I served with Parmesan noodles. **—SHORTSANDSCOOTER**

ORANGE-MAPLE GLAZED CHICKEN

Use a fresh orange for the zest and juice in this tasty recipe that combines citrus with maple syrup and balsamic vinegar.

—LILY JULOW LAWRENCEVILLE, GA

PREP: 25 MIN. • **GRILL:** 10 MIN.
MAKES: 6 SERVINGS

- ⅓ cup orange juice
- ⅓ cup maple syrup
- 2 tablespoons balsamic vinegar
- 1½ teaspoons Dijon mustard
- 1 teaspoon salt, divided
- ¾ teaspoon pepper, divided
- 1 tablespoon minced fresh basil or 1 teaspoon dried basil
- ½ teaspoon grated orange peel
- 6 boneless skinless chicken breast halves (6 ounces each)

1. In a small saucepan, combine the orange juice, syrup, vinegar, mustard, ½ teaspoon salt and ¼ teaspoon pepper. Bring to a boil; cook until liquid is reduced to ½ cup, about 5 minutes. Stir in basil and orange peel. Remove from heat; set aside.

2. Sprinkle chicken with remaining salt and pepper. Grill chicken, covered, over medium heat 5-7 minutes on each side or until a thermometer reads 165°, basting frequently with the orange juice mixture.

NOTES

_____
_____
_____
_____
_____
_____
_____
_____
_____
_____

GARDEN TURKEY BURGERS

These juicy burgers get plenty of color and flavor from onion, zucchini and red pepper. I often make the mixture ahead of time and put it in the refrigerator. Later, I can put the burgers on the grill and then whip up a salad or side dish.

—SANDY KITZMILLER UNITYVILLE, PA

START TO FINISH: 25 MIN.
MAKES: 6 SERVINGS

- 1 **cup old-fashioned oats**
- ¾ **cup chopped onion**
- ¾ **cup finely chopped sweet red or green pepper**
- ½ **cup shredded zucchini**
- ¼ **cup ketchup**
- 2 **garlic cloves, minced**
- ¼ **teaspoon salt, optional**
- 1 **pound ground turkey**
- 6 **whole wheat hamburger buns, split and toasted**

1. In a large bowl, combine the first seven ingredients. Crumble turkey over mixture and mix well. Shape into six ½-in.-thick patties.

2. Moisten a paper towel with cooking oil; using long-handled tongs, rub on grill rack to coat lightly.

3. Grill burgers, covered, over medium heat or broil 4 in. from heat 4-6 minutes on each side or until a thermometer reads 165° and the juices run clear. Serve on buns.

POTATO-SAUSAGE FOIL PACKS

We had these satisfying campfire bundles at a friend's house for dinner and loved the simplicity of this great summer meal.

—**ALISSA KEITH** LYNCHBURG, VA

PREP: 20 MIN. • **GRILL:** 30 MIN.
MAKES: 4 SERVINGS

- 1 **package (14 ounces) smoked turkey kielbasa, sliced**
- 2 **large potatoes, cut into wedges**
- 1 **each medium green, sweet red and yellow peppers, cut into 1-inch pieces**
- 1 **medium onion, chopped**
- 4 **teaspoons lemon juice**
- 4 **teaspoons olive oil**
- ½ **teaspoon garlic powder**
- ½ **teaspoon pepper**
- ¼ **teaspoon salt**

1. Divide the kielbasa, potatoes, peppers and onion among four double thicknesses of heavy-duty foil (about 18x12 in.). Drizzle with lemon juice and oil; sprinkle with garlic powder, pepper and salt.

2. Fold foil around kielbasa mixture and seal tightly. Grill, covered, over medium heat 30-35 minutes or until potatoes are tender. Open foil carefully to allow steam to escape.

Cook to Cook

I made this tonight for dinner, and my husband and 93-year-old dad loved it! We are not fond of cooked peppers, so I substituted about ½ lb. broccoli florets, microwaving them for about 2 minutes before adding them to the packets. This was a very tasty dish that I will definitely make again this summer. And cleanup was a breeze! Thanks for sharing.

—**MAR52TY**

HONEY-MUSTARD CHICKEN

If my family had their wish, I'd serve this chicken on the grill every night. The sweet and tangy glaze is an appealing alternative to traditional tomato-based sauces.

—**HEIDI HOLMES** RENTON, WA

PREP: 10 MIN. • **GRILL:** 50 MIN.
MAKES: 4 SERVINGS

- 1 **cup pineapple juice**
- ¾ **cup honey**
- ½ **cup Dijon mustard**
- 1 **teaspoon ground ginger**
- 2 **tablespoons cornstarch**
- ¼ **cup cold water**
- 1 **broiler/fryer chicken
  (3½ to 4 pounds), cut up**

1. In a small saucepan, combine the pineapple juice, honey, mustard and ginger; bring to a boil. Combine the cornstarch and water; gradually whisk into honey mixture. Cook and stir 2-3 minutes or until thickened. Reserve ¾ cup to serve with chicken if desired.

2. Baste chicken with remaining glaze. Grill, covered, over medium-low heat 30 minutes. Turn chicken; brush again with glaze. Grill, uncovered, 20 minutes or until juices run clear. Serve with reserved glaze if desired.

Cook to Cook

We LOVE this chicken recipe! I have made it several times and used ginger ale and Sierra Mist in place of the pineapple juice—and both turned out just as wonderful as the original.
—**SUPERSHEARS5**

COLESLAW CHICKEN WRAPS

This portable sandwich is perfect for outdoor dining in the summertime. We like the fun, fresh spin on regular coleslaw using pineapple and toasted almonds.

—**BARB AGNEW** MAHNOMEN, MN

PREP: 15 MIN. + MARINATING
GRILL: 15 MIN. • **MAKES:** 8 SERVINGS

- 1 bottle (16 ounces) reduced-fat poppy seed salad dressing, divided
- 2 pounds boneless skinless chicken breasts
- 1 can (20 ounces) unsweetened pineapple tidbits, drained
- 1 package (14 ounces) coleslaw mix
- 1 medium sweet red pepper, finely chopped
- 8 whole wheat tortillas (8 inches)
- ½ cup sliced almonds, toasted

1. Place 1 cup dressing in a large resealable plastic bag. Add chicken; seal bag and turn to coat. Refrigerate for 1 hour.

2. Drain chicken and discard marinade. Moisten a paper towel with cooking oil; using long-handled tongs, rub on grill rack to coat lightly.

3. Grill the chicken, covered, over medium heat or broil 4 in. from heat 6-8 minutes on each side or until a thermometer reads 165°. Let stand 5 minutes before slicing.

4. Meanwhile, in a large bowl, mix the pineapple, coleslaw mix, red pepper and remaining dressing; toss to coat. Divide among tortillas; top with the chicken and sprinkle with almonds. Roll up tightly; secure with toothpicks.

NOTES

SWEET AND SPICY GRILLED CHICKEN

This simple recipe has become my family's favorite way to eat chicken. The blend of sweet and spicy is perfect.

— **MELISSA BALL** PEARISBURG, VA

START TO FINISH: 20 MIN.
MAKES: 6 SERVINGS

- 2 **tablespoons brown sugar**
- 1 **tablespoon paprika**
- 2 **teaspoons onion powder**
- 1½ **teaspoons salt**
- 1 **teaspoon chili powder**
- 6 **boneless skinless chicken breast halves (6 ounces each)**

1. Combine the first five ingredients; rub over chicken.

2. Moisten a paper towel with cooking oil; using long-handled tongs, rub on grill rack to coat lightly.

3. Grill chicken, covered, over medium heat or broil 4 in. from heat 4-5 minutes on each side or until a thermometer reads 165°.

Cook to Cook

Very good. I added garlic, onion powder and cumin. Will definitely make again!
—**MISS ARLENE**

CHINESE TAKEOUT-ON-A-STICK

I like to serve this chicken and broccoli with rice, along with a side of pineapple or other fresh fruit. Leftovers (if there are any) are great the next day when used in a salad or wrapped in a flour tortilla with a little mayonnaise.

—BETHANY SEELEY WARWICK, RI

START TO FINISH: 30 MIN.
MAKES: 4 SERVINGS

- 3 tablespoons reduced-sodium soy sauce
- 3 tablespoons sesame oil
- 4 teaspoons brown sugar
- 4 teaspoons minced fresh gingerroot
- 2 garlic cloves, minced
- ½ teaspoon crushed red pepper flakes
- 1 pound boneless skinless chicken breasts, cut into 1-inch cubes
- 3 cups fresh broccoli florets

1. In a large bowl, combine the first six ingredients; remove and set aside 3 tablespoons for basting.

2. Add chicken to remaining soy sauce mixture; toss to coat. On four metal or soaked wooden skewers, alternately thread chicken and broccoli.

3. Moisten a paper towel with cooking oil; using long-handled tongs, rub onto grill rack to coat lightly.

4. Grill skewers, covered, over medium heat or broil 4 in. from heat 10-15 minutes or until chicken is no longer pink, turning occasionally; baste with reserved soy mixture during the last 4 minutes of cooking.

1-2-3 GRILLED SALMON

I love salmon, but my husband doesn't. So I combined flavors I knew he liked to create this entree, and now it's the only salmon recipe he will eat. It's so easy and only requires a handful of ingredients.

—NICOLE CLAYTON PRESCOTT, AZ

PREP: 10 MIN. + MARINATING
GRILL: 5 MIN. • **MAKES:** 6 SERVINGS

- ⅓ **cup olive oil**
- 3 **tablespoons reduced-sodium soy sauce**
- 2 **tablespoons Dijon mustard**
- ½ **teaspoon dried minced garlic**
- 6 **salmon fillets (5 ounces each)**

1. In a small bowl, combine the oil, soy sauce, mustard and garlic. Pour half of marinade into a large resealable plastic bag. Add the salmon; seal bag and turn to coat. Refrigerate 30 minutes. Refrigerate remaining marinade.
2. Drain fish and discard marinade. Moisten a paper towel with cooking oil; using long-handled tongs, rub onto grill rack to coat lightly.
3. Grill salmon, covered, over high heat 5-10 minutes or until fish flakes easily with a fork. Drizzle with the reserved marinade.

NOTES

_____
_____
_____
_____
_____
_____

GRILLED TILAPIA WITH LEMON BASIL VINAIGRETTE

We aren't big fish eaters, but a friend made this for us, and we couldn't believe how wonderful it was! I love making it for guests because it's simple, looks lovely and tastes restaurant-worthy.

—**BETH COOPER** COLUMBUS, OH

START TO FINISH: 25 MIN.
MAKES: 4 SERVINGS

- 3 **tablespoons lemon juice**
- 3 **tablespoons minced fresh basil, divided**
- 2 **tablespoons olive oil**
- 2 **garlic cloves, minced**
- 2 **teaspoons capers, drained**
- ½ **teaspoon grated lemon peel**
- 4 **tilapia fillets (6 ounces each)**
- ½ **teaspoon salt**
- ¼ **teaspoon pepper**

1. For vinaigrette, in a small bowl, whisk the lemon juice, 2 tablespoons basil, olive oil, garlic, capers and lemon peel; set aside 2 tablespoons for sauce. Sprinkle fillets with salt and pepper. Brush both sides of fillets with remaining vinaigrette.

2. Moisten a paper towel with cooking oil; using long-handled tongs, rub on grill rack to coat lightly.

3. Grill, covered, over medium heat or broil 4 in. from heat 3-4 minutes on each side or until fish flakes easily with a fork. Brush with reserved vinaigrette and sprinkle with remaining basil.

Cook to Cook

Super easy to make and very flavorful. I broiled versus grilled this, and it turned out great. Definitely a redo.
—**SUSAN'S KITCHEN**

PARMESAN-BROILED TILAPIA

Simple Parmesan cheese brings such richness to an otherwise mild-tasting fish. This is one dish where leftovers are never a problem!

— **TRACY LOCKEN** GILLETTE, WYOMING

START TO FINISH: 15 MIN.
MAKES: 4 SERVINGS

- ½ **cup grated Parmesan cheese**
- 3 **tablespoons butter, softened**
- 2 **tablespoons mayonnaise**
- ¼ **teaspoon dried basil**
- ¼ **teaspoon pepper**
- ⅛ **teaspoon onion powder**
- ⅛ **teaspoon celery salt**
- 4 **tilapia fillets (6 ounces each)**
- 4 **lemon wedges**

1. In a small bowl, mix the first seven ingredients. Arrange the 9 fillets in a 15x10x1-in. baking pan coated with cooking spray. Spread cheese mixture over fish.

2. Broil 4 in. from the heat 4-5 minutes or until topping is lightly browned and fish flakes easily with a fork, rotating pan halfway for more even browning. Serve with lemon wedges.

NOTES

_____

_____

_____

_____

_____

_____

_____

_____

BROILED GREEK FISH FILLETS

Olives, onion, dill and feta cheese combine in this tangy, Greek-inspired topping. It boosts the flavor of tilapia or your favorite whitefish. I usually serve the fish with rice.

—JENNIFER MASLOWSKI NEW YORK, NY

START TO FINISH: 25 MIN.
MAKES: 8 SERVINGS

- 8 **tilapia fillets (4 ounces each)**
- ¼ **teaspoon salt**
- ¼ **teaspoon pepper**
- ¼ **cup plain yogurt**
- 2 **tablespoons butter, softened**
- 1 **tablespoon lime juice**
- 1 **small red onion, finely chopped**
- ½ **cup pitted Greek olives**
- 1 **teaspoon dill weed**
- ½ **teaspoon paprika**
- ¼ **teaspoon garlic powder**
- ½ **cup crumbled feta cheese**

1. Sprinkle tilapia with salt and pepper. Place on a broiler pan coated with cooking spray.
2. In a small bowl, combine the yogurt, butter and lime juice. Stir in the onion, olives and seasonings. Spread down the middle of each fillet; sprinkle with feta cheese.
3. Broil 3-4 in. from heat 6-9 minutes or until fish flakes easily with a fork.

Cook to Cook

I made this for myself for lunch today. It was so good! Wonderful flavors, and so delicate and light, the toppings didn't overpower the fish at all. Oh, and that bit of salty crunch from the broiled feta on top was heavenly. I know what lunch tomorrow is going to be—maybe every day this week. :) **—POTROAST911**

SPICY SHRIMP KABOBS

Because these kabobs are so good, guests always think I labored over the preparation. But really, you can make them in no time.

—**MARCIA PILGERAM** SANDPOINT, ID

START TO FINISH: 30 MIN.
MAKES: 8 KABOBS

- ¼ **cup butter, cubed**
- 2 **tablespoons lemon juice**
- 1 **teaspoon ground coriander**
- 1 **teaspoon ground cumin**
- ½ **teaspoon paprika**
- ½ **teaspoon grated lemon peel**
- ¼ **teaspoon salt**
- 1 **pound uncooked large shrimp, peeled and deveined**

1. In a small saucepan, melt butter; add the lemon juice, spices, lemon peel and salt.
2. Thread shrimp onto eight metal or soaked wooden skewers. Place skewers in a greased 15x10x1-in. baking pan. Broil 3-4 in. from the heat 3-4 minutes on each side or until the shrimp turn pink, basting occasionally with the butter mixture.

Cook to Cook

My family liked this recipe, and it was easy and quick. The next time I make it, I will add Tony Chachere's or cayenne pepper for a little more kick. —**DORIS49**

5

LEAVE IT TO THE OVEN

A little prep is all these oven-baked dishes need.

LEAVE IT TO THE OVEN INDEX

Cook to Cook

Look for
THESE boxes
for helpful tidbits!

FREEZE IT

CAJUN BEEF CASSEROLE

Have little ones who won't eat veggies? They won't complain one bit when you bring this hearty dish with a corn bread crust to the table. For picky eaters, try using less Cajun seasoning.
—**TASTE OF HOME TEST KITCHEN**

PREP: 15 MIN. • **BAKE:** 25 MIN.
MAKES: 6 SERVINGS

- 1 package (8½ ounces) corn bread/ muffin mix
- 1 pound ground beef
- 2 cans (14½ ounces each) diced tomatoes, drained
- 2 cups frozen mixed vegetables, thawed
- 1 can (6 ounces) tomato paste
- 1 to 2 teaspoons Cajun seasoning
- 1 cup (4 ounces) shredded cheddar cheese
- 2 green onions, thinly sliced

1. Preheat oven to 350°. Prepare corn bread batter according to package directions. Spread into a greased 11x7-in. baking dish.
2. In a skillet, cook beef over medium heat until no longer pink; drain. Add tomatoes, vegetables, tomato paste and seasoning. Bring to a boil. Reduce heat; simmer, uncovered, 5 minutes. Pour over top. Sprinkle with cheese.
3. Bake, uncovered, 25-30 minutes or until golden brown. Top with onions.

FREEZE OPTION *Wrap individual portions of cooled casserole in plastic wrap and transfer to a resealable plastic bag. To use, partially thaw in refrigerator overnight. Remove from refrigerator 30 minutes before baking. Preheat oven to 350°. Unwrap casserole and transfer to a baking dish. Bake until a thermometer inserted in center reads 165°.*

LEAVE IT TO
THE OVEN

BEEF BRISKET WITH MOP SAUCE

This brisket roasts in a sauce that adds great flavor. When one of our sons lived in the South, I learned that "mop sauce" is traditionally prepared for Texas ranch-style barbecues in batches so large, they're brushed on the meat with a mop! You won't need that much for my recipe, but you'll still get the big-time taste.
—**DARLIS WILFER** WEST BEND, WI

PREP: 20 MIN. • **BAKE:** 2 HOURS
MAKES: 10-12 SERVINGS

- ½ cup water
- ¼ cup cider vinegar
- ¼ cup Worcestershire sauce
- ¼ cup ketchup
- ¼ cup dark corn syrup
- 2 tablespoons canola oil
- 2 tablespoons prepared mustard
- 1 fresh beef brisket (3 pounds)

1. Preheat oven to 350°. In a large saucepan, combine the first seven ingredients. Bring to a boil, stirring constantly. Reduce heat; simmer 5 minutes, stirring occasionally. Remove from the heat.

2. Place brisket in a shallow roasting pan; pour sauce over the top. Cover and bake 2 to 2½ hours or until meat is tender. Let stand 5 minutes. Thinly slice meat across the grain.

NOTE *This is a fresh beef brisket, not corned beef.*

Cook to Cook

Sauce is terrific, meat is tender, family loves it. Have made this 10+ times since learning the recipe, and am now in the process of copying the recipe onto my own files so it won't be lost.
—**SARAH IN PORTLAND**

_____

_____

_____

_____

_____

_____

FIRECRACKER CASSEROLE

Growing up, I couldn't get enough of this Southwestern casserole my mother frequently placed on the dinner table. Now I fix it for my husband and me. The casserole reminds us of enchiladas.

—TERESSA EASTMAN EL DORADO, KS

PREP: 15 MIN. • **BAKE:** 25 MIN.
MAKES: 8 SERVINGS

- 2 **pounds ground beef**
- 1 **medium onion, chopped**
- 1 **can (15 ounces) black beans, rinsed and drained**
- 1 **to 2 tablespoons chili powder**
- 2 **to 3 teaspoons ground cumin**
- ½ **teaspoon salt**
- 4 **flour tortillas (6 inches)**
- 1 **can (10¾ ounces) condensed cream of mushroom soup, undiluted**
- 1 **can (10 ounces) diced tomatoes and green chilies, undrained**
- 1 **cup (4 ounces) shredded cheddar cheese**

1. Preheat oven to 350°. In a large skillet, cook beef and onion until the meat is no longer pink; drain. Add the beans, chili powder, cumin and salt.
2. Transfer to a greased 13x9-in. baking dish. Arrange tortillas over the top. Combine soup and tomatoes; pour over tortillas. Sprinkle with cheese.
3. Bake, uncovered, 25-30 minutes or until heated through.

HAMBURGER NOODLE BAKE

I like to save time in the kitchen and this bake fits my needs. It makes two dinners... one for now and one to freeze for later.
—**PATRICIA TELLER** LEWISTON, ID

PREP: 20 MIN. • **BAKE:** 35 MIN.
MAKES: 2 CASSEROLES (4 SERVINGS EACH)

- 5 **cups uncooked egg noodles**
- 2 **pounds ground beef**
- 1 **cup chopped onion**
- ½ **cup chopped green pepper**
- 2 **cans (10¾ ounces each) condensed tomato soup, undiluted**
- 2 **cups (8 ounces) shredded cheddar cheese**
- 1½ **cups water**
- ½ **cup chili sauce**
- 1½ **cups soft bread crumbs**
- 3 **tablespoons butter, melted**

1. Preheat oven to 350°. Cook noodles according to package directions until al dente; drain.
2. Meanwhile, in a large skillet, cook beef, onion and green pepper over medium-high heat for 10-12 minutes or until meat is no longer pink; drain. Stir in noodles, soup, cheese, water and chili sauce. Transfer to two greased 8-in.-square baking dishes.
3. Toss bread crumbs and butter; sprinkle over casseroles. Bake, uncovered, 35-40 minutes or until bubbly and golden brown.

FREEZE OPTION *Cool unbaked casseroles; cover and freeze up to 3 months. To use, partially thaw in refrigerator overnight. Remove from refrigerator 30 minutes before baking. Preheat oven to 350°. Cover dish with foil; bake 45-50 minutes or until heated through and a thermometer inserted in center reads 165°. Uncover; bake 10-15 minutes longer or until topping is golden brown.*

BEEF SIRLOIN TIP ROAST

This meaty main course, served with a mouthwatering mushroom gravy, is a snap to assemble and pop in the oven. It is my husband's favorite.

—MRS. BURGESS MARSHBANKS
BUIES CREEK, NC

PREP: 10 MIN. • **BAKE:** 2½ HOURS
MAKES: 12 SERVINGS

- 1 beef sirloin tip roast (3 pounds)
- 1¼ cups water, divided
- 1 can (8 ounces) mushroom stems and pieces, drained
- 1 envelope onion soup mix
- 2 tablespoons cornstarch

1. Preheat oven to 350°. Place a large piece of heavy-duty foil (21x17 in.) in a shallow roasting pan. Place roast on foil. Pour 1 cup water and mushrooms over roast. Sprinkle with soup mix. Wrap foil around roast; seal tightly.

2. Bake 2½ to 3 hours or until the meat reaches desired doneness (for medium-rare, a thermometer should read 145°; medium, 160°; well-done, 170°).

3. Remove roast to a serving platter and keep warm. Pour drippings and mushrooms into a saucepan. Combine cornstarch and remaining water until smooth; gradually stir into drippings. Bring to a boil; cook and stir 2 minutes or until thickened. Serve with the sliced beef.

Cook to Cook

Great recipe! I substituted beef broth for water and used fresh mushrooms. Very tasty, with lots of gravy.
—DFREUTER415

LEAVE IT TO THE OVEN

BUSY-DAY MEAT LOAF

Here's a tender meat loaf that's delicious for any day. It's nice that you get two loaves from the recipe. Freeze the extra one for an easy dinner at a later date.

—SHIRLEY SNYDER PAYSON, AZ

PREP: 15 MIN. • **BAKE:** 55 MIN.
MAKES: 2 LOAVES (6 SERVINGS EACH)

- 1 egg, lightly beaten
- 1 cup beef broth
- ½ cup quick-cooking oats
- 1 tablespoon dried minced onion
- 2 teaspoons dried parsley flakes
- 1 teaspoon salt
- ½ teaspoon pepper
- 1½ pounds lean ground beef (90% lean)
- 1 pound bulk pork sausage
- 1 can (8 ounces) tomato sauce

1. Preheat oven to 350°. In a large bowl, combine first seven ingredients. Crumble the beef and sausage over mixture and mix well. Pat into two greased 8x4-in. loaf pans. Top with tomato sauce.

2. Bake, uncovered, 55-60 minutes until meat loaf is no longer pink and a thermometer reads 160°.

FREEZE OPTION *Cover and freeze one uncooked meat loaf for up to 3 months. To use, partially thaw in refrigerator overnight. Preheat oven to 350°. Unwrap meat loaf; place on a greased shallow baking pan. Bake, uncovered, until heated through and a thermometer inserted in center reads 165°.*

NOTES

_____
_____
_____
_____
_____
_____
_____
_____
_____

BUBBLY & GOLDEN MEXICAN BEEF COBBLER

Add whatever you like to this recipe to make it yours...black beans, sour cream, even guacamole!

—**MARY BROOKS** CLAY, MI

PREP: 20 MIN. • **BAKE:** 35 MIN.
MAKES: 6 SERVINGS

- 1 **pound ground beef**
- 1 **envelope taco seasoning**
- ¾ **cup water**
- 1 **jar (16 ounces) salsa**
- 1 **can (8¾ ounces) whole kernel corn, drained**
- 2 **cups (8 ounces) shredded sharp cheddar cheese**
- 3⅓ **cups biscuit/baking mix**
- 1⅓ **cups 2% milk**
- ⅛ **teaspoon salt**
- ⅛ **teaspoon pepper**

1. Preheat oven to 350°. In a large skillet, cook beef over medium heat 6-8 minutes or until no longer pink, breaking into crumbles; drain. Stir in taco seasoning and water. Bring to a boil; cook until liquid is evaporated.
2. Transfer to an 11x7-in. baking dish; layer with salsa, corn and cheese.
3. In a large bowl, mix biscuit mix and milk just until blended; drop by tablespoonfuls over cheese (dish will be full). Sprinkle with salt and pepper.
4. Bake, uncovered, 35-45 minutes or until bubbly and topping is golden brown.

Cook to Cook

My family of 6 loved this recipe. It was a little watery with the salsa added. I ended up draining some out after cooking. I added a can of black beans with the meat. I will probably add even more black beans next time. There was a lot of biscuit, but we really liked it. I won't change that next time.
—**POWELLCOU**

LEAVE IT TO THE OVEN

MEAT-AND-POTATO CASSEROLE

For variety, you can use another kind of cream soup (cream of mushroom, for instance). But try it this way first!

—**MARNA HEITZ** FARLEY, IA

PREP: 10 MIN. • **BAKE:** 50 MIN.
MAKES: 6 SERVINGS

- 4 **cups thinly sliced peeled potatoes**
- 2 **tablespoons butter, melted**
- ½ **teaspoon salt**
- 1 **pound ground beef**
- 1 **package (10 ounces) frozen corn**
- 1 **can (10¾ ounces) condensed cream of celery soup, undiluted**
- ⅓ **cup milk**
- ¼ **teaspoon garlic powder**
- ⅛ **teaspoon pepper**
- 1 **tablespoon chopped onion**
- 1 **cup (4 ounces) shredded cheddar cheese, divided**
  Minced fresh parsley, optional

1. Preheat oven 400°. Toss potatoes with butter and salt; arrange on the bottom and up the sides of a greased 13x9-in. baking dish. Bake, uncovered, 25-30 minutes or until potatoes are almost tender.

2. Meanwhile, in a large skillet, cook beef over medium heat until no longer pink; drain. Sprinkle beef and corn over potatoes. Combine the soup, milk, garlic powder, pepper, onion and ½ cup cheese; pour over beef mixture.

3. Bake, uncovered, 20 minutes or until vegetables are tender. Sprinkle with remaining cheese. Bake 2-3 minutes longer or until cheese is melted. Sprinkle with parsley if desired.

ITALIAN SHEPHERD'S PIES

Made in individual baking cups, these hearty little pies have biscuit-like tops and a saucy filling. You can also prepare the mixture in a 1½-quart baking dish.

—**SONYA LABBE** WEST HOLLYWOOD, CA

PREP: 20 MIN. • **BAKE:** 15 MIN.
MAKES: 4 SERVINGS

- 1 **pound ground beef**
- 1 **medium onion, finely chopped**
- 2 **cups marinara sauce**
- ⅛ **teaspoon salt**
- ⅛ **teaspoon pepper**

TOPPING

- 1 **cup all-purpose flour**
- ¼ **cup grated Parmesan cheese**
- 1½ **teaspoons baking powder**
- ½ **teaspoon salt**
- ¼ **teaspoon Italian seasoning**
- ½ **cup 2% milk**
- ¼ **cup butter, melted**

1. Preheat oven to 450°. In a skillet, cook beef and onion over medium heat until meat is no longer pink; drain. Add marinara sauce, salt and pepper; cook and stir 8-10 minutes or until thickened. Spoon into four 8-oz. ramekins or custard cups; set aside.
2. In a small bowl, combine the flour, cheese, baking powder, salt and Italian seasoning. Stir in milk and butter just until moistened. Spoon dough over meat mixture; place ramekins on a baking sheet.
3. Bake 12-15 minutes or until golden brown.

FREEZE OPTION *Cover and freeze unbaked pies. To use, remove from freezer 30 minutes before baking (do not thaw). Preheat oven to 400°. Place pie on a baking sheet; cover edge loosely with foil. Bake as directed, increasing time as necessary to heat through and for a thermometer inserted in center to read 165°.*

Cook to Cook

My family and I love this recipe. The only thing I do different is to use half ground beef and half sausage. Quick tip: I make the sauce ahead of time and place in the fridge—when I get home from work, I make the dough (topping) and I'm good to go. I have made it in a 2-quart dish and in ramekins. Personally, I prefer the recipe in the ramekins. With a salad, this makes a nice meal. —**TAMMY_GIRL**

LEAVE IT TO THE OVEN

SPIRAL STROMBOLI

Two types of deli meat and three kinds of cheese make this satisfying sandwich the perfect filler-upper! I frequently fix this on days when I need a fast meal.

—JEAN GRUENERT BURLINGTON, WI

PREP: 10 MIN. • **BAKE:** 25 MIN.
MAKES: 4 SERVINGS

- 1 **tube (11 ounces) refrigerated crusty French loaf**
- ¾ **cup shredded part-skim mozzarella cheese**
- ¾ **cup shredded cheddar cheese**
- ¼ **pound each thinly sliced deli salami and ham**
- ¼ **cup chopped roasted red peppers or 1 jar (2 ounces) pimientos, drained**
- 1 **tablespoon butter, melted**
- 2 **tablespoons shredded Parmesan cheese**

1. Preheat oven to 375°. Unroll dough and pat into a 14x12-in. rectangle. Sprinkle with mozzarella and cheddar cheese to within ½ in. of edges; top with meat and red peppers. Roll up jelly-roll style, starting with a short side; seal seam and tuck ends under.

2. Place seam side down on a greased baking sheet. Brush with butter; sprinkle with Parmesan cheese. Bake 25-30 minutes or until golden brown. Slice with a serrated knife.

Cook to Cook

My family LOVES this. I have made it with different types of meat, such as pepperoni, turkey, etc. It's always a favorite. **—KLUESNER5**

BEEF TACO LASAGNA

This recipe makes two big pans. Cook and serve one tonight and freeze one for later.

—**STACEY COMPTON** TOLEDO, OH

PREP: 30 MIN. • **BAKE:** 35 MIN. + STANDING
MAKES: 2 CASSEROLES (8 SERVINGS EACH)

- 24 **lasagna noodles**
- 2 **pounds lean ground beef (90% lean)**
- 2 **envelopes taco seasoning**
- 4 **egg whites**
- 2 **cartons (15 ounces each) ricotta cheese**
- 8 **cups (2 pounds) shredded cheddar cheese**
- 2 **jars (24 ounces each) chunky salsa**

1. Preheat oven to 350°. Cook noodles according to package directions.

2. Meanwhile, in a large skillet, cook beef over medium heat until no longer pink; drain. Stir in taco seasoning. In a small bowl, combine egg whites and ricotta cheese. Drain noodles.

3. In each of two 13x9-in. baking dishes, layer four noodles, ¾ cup ricotta mixture, half the beef mixture and 1⅓ cups cheddar cheese. Top each with four noodles, ¾ cup ricotta mixture, 1½ cups salsa and 1⅓ cups cheese. Repeat.

4. Bake, uncovered, 35-40 minutes or until heated through. Let stand 10 minutes before cutting.

FREEZE OPTION *Cover and freeze unbaked casserole. To use, partially thaw in refrigerator overnight. Remove from refrigerator 30 minutes before baking. Preheat oven to 350°. Bake as directed, increasing time as necessary to heat through and for a thermometer inserted in center to read 165°.*

NOTES

_____

_____

_____

_____

_____

_____

_____

LEAVE IT TO THE OVEN

FREEZE IT

CHEESE BEEF SPIRALS

My mom shared this easy-to-assemble casserole years ago. It's very good with garlic toast. Large shell macaroni or ziti noodles can be used instead of spiral pasta.
—**BRENDA MARSCHALL** POPLAR BLUFF, MO

PREP: 25 MIN. • **BAKE:** 30 MIN.
MAKES: 8-10 SERVINGS

- 2 **cups uncooked spiral pasta**
- 2 **pounds ground beef**
- 2 **small onions, chopped**
- 1 **garlic clove, minced**
- 1 **jar (26 ounces) spaghetti sauce**
- 1 **jar (4½ ounces) sliced mushrooms, drained**
- ½ **cup sour cream**
- ½ **pound process cheese (Velveeta), cubed**
- 2 **cups (8 ounces) shredded part-skim mozzarella cheese**

1. Preheat oven to 350°. Cook pasta according to package directions.
2. Meanwhile, in a large saucepan, cook the beef, onions and garlic over medium heat until meat is no longer pink; drain. Stir in spaghetti sauce and mushrooms; bring to a boil. Reduce heat; cover and simmer 20 minutes.
3. Place ½ cup of meat sauce in a greased shallow 2½-qt. baking dish. Drain pasta; place half over sauce. Top with half the remaining meat sauce; spread with sour cream. Top with the process cheese and remaining pasta and meat sauce. Sprinkle with the mozzarella cheese.
4. Cover and bake 25-30 minutes. Uncover; bake 5-10 minutes longer or until bubbly.

FREEZE OPTION *Freeze individual portions of cooled casserole in freezer containers. To use, partially thaw in refrigerator overnight. Heat through in a saucepan, stirring occasionally and adding a little spaghetti sauce if necessary.*

MOSTACCIOLI

A friend shared the recipe for this cheese-filled baked pasta years ago. It's great for entertaining.

—**MARGARET MCNEIL** GERMANTOWN, TN

PREP: 25 MIN. • **BAKE:** 25 MIN.
MAKES: 2 CASSEROLES (6 SERVINGS EACH)

- 1 **package (16 ounces) mostaccioli**
- 1½ **pounds ground beef**
- 1¼ **cups chopped green pepper**
- 1 **cup chopped onion**
- 1 **jar (26 ounces) spaghetti sauce**
- 1 **can (10¾ ounces) condensed cheddar cheese soup, undiluted**
- 1½ **teaspoons Italian seasoning**
- ¾ **teaspoon pepper**
- 2 **cups (8 ounces) shredded part-skim mozzarella cheese, divided**

1. Preheat oven to 350°. Cook mostaccioli according to package directions.
2. Meanwhile, in a large skillet, cook beef, green pepper and onion over medium heat until meat is no longer pink; drain. Stir in spaghetti sauce, soup, Italian seasoning and pepper.
3. Drain mostaccioli. Add mostaccioli and 1½ cups cheese to the beef mixture. Transfer to two greased 11x7-in. baking dishes. Sprinkle with the remaining cheese.

Cook to Cook

I made this tonight and we LOVED IT! I actually used 1 pound ground beef and 1 pound sausage. I used way more shredded cheese because we love lots of cheese. I used a little more spaghetti sauce, too. This will become a regular in our house now. The chedder cheese soup gives it a creamy good taste. I get so excited when I try a recipe and it's this good! Can't wait to try out on friends and other family members. —TBIOWA

4. Cover and bake 20 minutes. Uncover; bake 5-10 minutes longer or until bubbly and cheese is melted.

FREEZE OPTION *Cover and freeze unbaked casseroles up to 3 months. To use, thaw in refrigerator overnight. Remove from refrigerator 30 minutes before baking. Preheat oven to 350°. Cover and bake 50-60 minutes or until heated through, a thermometer reads 165° and the cheese is melted.*

LEAVE IT TO THE OVEN

SWEET POTATO ENCHILADA STACK

Mexican flavors abound in this awesome enchilada stack that's jam-packed with black beans and sweet potato.

—TASTE OF HOME TEST KITCHEN

PREP: 20 MIN. • **BAKE:** 20 MIN.
MAKES: 6 SERVINGS

- 1 large sweet potato, peeled and cut into ½-inch cubes
- 1 tablespoon water
- 1 pound ground beef
- 1 medium onion, chopped
- 1 can (15 ounces) black beans, rinsed and drained
- 1 can (10 ounces) enchilada sauce
- 2 teaspoons chili powder
- ½ teaspoon dried oregano
- ½ teaspoon ground cumin
- 3 flour tortillas (8 inches)
- 2 cups (8 ounces) shredded cheddar cheese

1. Preheat oven to 400°. In a large microwave-safe bowl, combine sweet potato and water. Cover; microwave on high 4-5 minutes or until potato is almost tender.

2. Meanwhile, in a skillet, cook beef and onion over medium heat until meat is no longer pink; drain. Stir in beans, enchilada sauce, chili powder, oregano, cumin and sweet potato; heat through.

3. Place a flour tortilla in a greased 9-in. deep-dish pie plate; layer with a third of the beef mixture and cheese. Repeat layers twice. Bake for 20-25 minutes or until bubbly.

NOTE *This recipe was tested in a 1,100-watt microwave.*

NOTES
_____
_____
_____
_____
_____
_____

ITALIAN POT ROAST

I get so many requests for this recipe that I made up cards to hand out every time I serve it at a get-together. My husband and son think it's world-class eating!

—CAROLYN WELLS NORTH SYRACUSE, NY

PREP: 20 MIN. • **BAKE:** 2 HOURS
MAKES: 8-10 SERVINGS (3 CUPS GRAVY)

- 1 **tablespoon all-purpose flour**
- 1 **large oven roasting bag**
- 1 **boneless beef chuck roast (3 pounds)**
- 1⅔ **cups water**
- 1 **can (10¾ ounces) condensed tomato soup, undiluted**
- 1 **envelope onion soup mix**
- 1½ **teaspoons Italian seasoning**
- 1 **garlic clove, minced**
- ¼ **cup cornstarch**
- ¼ **cup cold water**

1. Preheat oven to 325°. Sprinkle flour into oven bag; shake to coat. Place in a 13x9-in. baking pan; add roast. In a small bowl, combine the water, tomato soup, soup mix, Italian seasoning and garlic; pour into oven bag.

2. Cut six ½-in. slits in top of bag; close with tie provided. Bake 2 to 2½ hours or until meat is tender.

3. Remove roast to a serving platter and keep warm. Transfer cooking juices to a small saucepan; skim fat. Bring to a boil. Combine cornstarch and cold water until smooth; stir into cooking juices. Return to a boil; cook and stir 2 minutes or until thickened. Slice roast; serve with gravy.

Cook to Cook

I've made this roast as directed, but also added cut-up potatoes, celery, carrots and onion. The veggies cook along with the roast in the flavorful soup mixture. It's so tasty and cleanup is a breeze! Try it...I think you'll like it as much as we do.
—XPRINCESS

LEAVE IT TO THE OVEN

FREEZE IT

BAKED HAM SANDWICHES

Minced onion and prepared mustard put a flavorful spin on these ham and cheese sandwiches. I freeze a few and simply take the foil-wrapped sandwiches from the freezer and warm in the oven for an effortless meal.

—CHARLOTTE ROWE ALTO, NM

START TO FINISH: 20 MIN.
MAKES: 8 SERVINGS

- ⅓ cup butter, softened
- ½ cup dried minced onion
- ⅓ to ½ cup prepared mustard
- 2 tablespoons poppy seeds
- 8 hamburger buns, split
- 16 slices deli ham
- 8 slices Swiss cheese

1. Preheat oven to 350°. In a small bowl, combine the butter, onion, mustard and poppy seeds; spread about 2 tablespoons on each bun. Layer with ham and cheese; replace tops. Wrap each sandwich in foil.
2. Bake 6-10 minutes or until cheese is melted.

FREEZE OPTION *Freeze unbaked sandwiches up to 2 months. To use, preheat oven to 350°. Bake 30-35 minutes or until cheese is melted.*

MEATY CORN BREAD CASSEROLE

Here's a bake that is as indulgent as it is delicious. This is stick-to-your-ribs, down-home comfort food at its finest!

—**JUSTINA WILSON** WEST SALEM, WI

PREP: 20 MIN. • **BAKE:** 15 MIN.
MAKES: 6 SERVINGS

- ½ **pound ground beef**
- ½ **pound bulk pork sausage**
- 1¾ **cups frozen corn, thawed**
- 1 **cup water**
- 1 **envelope brown gravy mix**
- 1 **package (8½ ounces) corn bread/ muffin mix**
- 1 **tablespoon real bacon bits**
- 1½ **teaspoons pepper**
- ⅛ **teaspoon garlic powder**
- 1 **envelope country gravy mix**

1. Preheat oven to 400°. In a large skillet, cook beef and sausage over medium heat until no longer pink; drain. Stir in corn, water and brown gravy mix. Bring to a boil; cook and stir 1 minute or until thickened. Spoon into a greased 8-in.-square baking dish.

2. Prepare the corn bread batter according to package directions; stir in bacon bits, pepper and garlic powder. Spread over meat mixture.

3. Bake, uncovered, 15-20 minutes or until a toothpick inserted into corn bread layer comes out clean.

4. Meanwhile, prepare country gravy mix according to package directions; serve with casserole.

Cook to Cook

Really unique and delicious! I used all hamburger instead of half sausage and half hamburger. Instead of bacon bits, I added a can of green chiles to the corn bread. Very good! —HARTMR

SAUSAGE BROCCOLI CALZONE

You know how people sometimes drop in unexpectedly and often a little famished? To remain calm in your own kitchen, reach for packaged French bread dough, sausage, cheese and veggies—then roll out the red carpet and this tasty bite to eat.

—ANGIE COLOMBO OLDSMAR, FL

PREP: 20 MIN. • **BAKE:** 20 MIN.
MAKES: 6 SERVINGS

- 12 **ounces bulk pork sausage**
- 1½ **teaspoons minced fresh sage**
- 1 **tube (11 ounces) refrigerated crusty French loaf**
- 2 **cups frozen chopped broccoli, thawed and drained**
- 1 **cup (4 ounces) shredded part-skim mozzarella cheese**
- 1 **cup (4 ounces) shredded cheddar cheese**

1. Preheat oven to 350°. In a small skillet, cook sausage over medium heat until no longer pink; drain. Stir in sage.
2. On an ungreased baking sheet, unroll dough starting at the seam; pat into a 14x12-in. rectangle. Spoon sausage lengthwise across center of dough. Sprinkle with broccoli and cheeses. Bring long sides of dough to the center over filling; pinch seams to seal. Turn calzone seam side down.
3. Bake 20-25 minutes or until golden brown. Serve warm.

NOTES

_____
_____
_____
_____
_____
_____

FREEZE IT

SAUSAGE RICE CASSEROLE

I fiddled around with this dish, trying to adjust it to my family's tastes. When my pickiest child cleaned her plate, I knew I'd found the right flavor combination.
—**JENNIFER TROST** WEST LINN, OR

PREP: 30 MIN. • **BAKE:** 40 MIN.
MAKES: 2 CASSEROLES (8 SERVINGS EACH)

- 2 **packages (7.2 ounces each) rice pilaf**
- 2 **pounds bulk pork sausage**
- 6 **celery ribs, chopped**
- 4 **medium carrots, sliced**
- 1 **can (10¾ ounces) condensed cream of chicken soup, undiluted**
- 1 **can (10¾ ounces) condensed cream of mushroom soup, undiluted**
- 2 **teaspoons onion powder**
- ½ **teaspoon garlic powder**
- ¼ **teaspoon pepper**

1. Preheat oven to 350°. Prepare rice mixes according to package directions.
2. Meanwhile, in a large skillet, cook the sausage, celery and carrots over medium heat until meat is no longer pink; drain.
3. In a large bowl, combine sausage mixture, rice, soups, onion powder, garlic powder and pepper. Transfer to two greased 11x7-in. baking dishes.
4. Cover and bake 40-45 minutes or until vegetables are tender.

FREEZE OPTION *Cover and freeze unbaked casseroles up to 3 months. To use, partially thaw in refrigerator overnight. Remove from refrigerator 30 minutes before baking. Preheat oven to 350°. Bake as directed, increasing time as necessary to heat through and for a thermometer inserted in center to read 165°.*

LEAVE IT TO
THE OVEN

ROAST PORK WITH APPLES & ONIONS

The sweetness of the apples and onions really complements this roast. With its crisp skin and melt-in-your-mouth flavor, it's my one of my family's favorite dinners.

—**LILY JULOW** LAWRENCEVILLE, GA

PREP: 25 MIN. • **BAKE:** 45 MIN. + STANDING
MAKES: 8 SERVINGS

- 1 **boneless whole pork loin roast (2 pounds)**
- ¼ **teaspoon salt**
- ¼ **teaspoon pepper**
- 1 **tablespoon olive oil**
- 3 **large Golden Delicious apples, cut into wedges**
- 2 **large onions, cut into wedges**
- 5 **garlic cloves, peeled**
- 1 **tablespoon minced fresh rosemary or 1 teaspoon dried rosemary, crushed**

1. Preheat oven to 350°. Sprinkle the roast with salt and pepper. In a large nonstick skillet, brown roast in oil on all sides. Place in a shallow roasting pan coated with cooking spray. Arrange the apples, onions and garlic around roast; sprinkle with rosemary.

2. Bake, uncovered, 45-60 minutes or until meat reaches desired doneness (for medium-rare, a thermometer should read 145°; medium, 160°), turning apples, onions and garlic once. Let meat stand 10 minutes before slicing.

AU GRATIN HAM POTPIE

We first had Aunt Dolly's potpie at a family get-together. We loved it and were so happy she shared the recipe. Now, we make it almost every time we bake a ham.
—**MARY ZINSMEISTER** SLINGER, WI

PREP: 15 MIN. • **BAKE:** 40 MIN.
MAKES: 4-6 SERVINGS

- 1 package (4.9 ounces) au gratin potatoes
- 1½ cups boiling water
- 2 cups frozen peas and carrots
- 1½ cups cubed fully cooked ham
- 1 can (10¾ ounces) condensed cream of chicken soup, undiluted
- 1 can (4 ounces) mushroom stems and pieces, drained
- ½ cup milk
- ½ cup sour cream
- 1 jar (2 ounces) diced pimientos, drained
- 1 sheet refrigerated pie pastry

1. Preheat oven to 400°. In a large bowl, combine potatoes, contents of sauce mix and water. Stir in peas and carrots, ham, soup, mushrooms, milk, sour cream and pimientos. Transfer to an ungreased 2-qt. round baking dish.
2. Roll out pastry to fit top of dish; place over potato mixture. Flute edges; cut slits in pastry. Bake 40-45 minutes or until crust is golden brown. Let stand 5 minutes before serving.

Cook to Cook

Great taste and easy to make. Just be sure to let the potatoes sit in the hot water for a while to soften. I did not have a pie crust, so I used crushed corn flakes sprayed with Pam. Excellent. Highly recommend. —**SLMURRAY7**

LEAVE IT TO THE OVEN

NOTES

_____

_____

_____

_____

_____

_____

HAM & CHEESE POTATO CASSEROLE

My recipe makes two cheesy, delicious casseroles. Have one tonight and put the other on ice for a future busy weeknight. It's like having money in the bank when things get hectic!

—**KARI ADAMS** FORT COLLINS, CO

PREP: 15 MIN. • **BAKE:** 50 MIN. + STANDING
MAKES: 2 CASSEROLES (5 SERVINGS EACH)

- 2 cans (10¾ ounces each) condensed cream of celery soup, undiluted
- 2 cups (16 ounces) sour cream
- ½ cup water
- ½ teaspoon pepper
- 2 packages (28 ounces each) frozen O'Brien potatoes
- 1 package (16 ounces) process cheese (Velveeta), cubed
- 2½ cups cubed fully cooked ham

1. Preheat oven to 375°. In a large bowl, combine soup, sour cream, water and pepper. Stir in potatoes, cheese and ham.

2. Transfer to two greased 11x7-in. baking dishes. Cover and bake for 40 minutes. Uncover and bake 10-15 minutes longer or until bubbly. Let stand 10 minutes before serving.

FREEZE OPTION _Cover and freeze unbaked casseroles up to 3 months. To use, partially thaw in refrigerator overnight. Remove from refrigerator 30 minutes before baking. Preheat oven to 375°. Bake as directed, increasing time as necessary to heat through and for a thermometer inserted in center to read 165°._

ROSEMARY-APRICOT PORK TENDERLOIN

You'll be surprised at how quickly this dish comes together for an easy weeknight meal. With very little effort, you'll have tender and juicy meat that begs to be added to a salad or sandwich the next day.

—**MARIE RIZZIO** INTERLOCHEN, MI

PREP: 15 MIN. • **BAKE:** 25 MIN.
MAKES: 8 SERVINGS

- 3 **tablespoons minced fresh rosemary or 1 tablespoon dried rosemary, crushed**
- 3 **tablespoons olive oil, divided**
- 4 **garlic cloves, minced**
- 1 **teaspoon salt**
- ½ **teaspoon pepper**
- 2 **pork tenderloins (1 pound each)**

GLAZE
- 1 **cup apricot preserves**
- 3 **tablespoons lemon juice**
- 2 **garlic cloves, minced**

1. Preheat oven to 425°. In a small bowl, mix rosemary, 1 tablespoon oil, garlic, salt and pepper; brush over pork.
2. In a large ovenproof skillet, brown pork in remaining oil on all sides. Bake 15 minutes.

3. In a small bowl, combine the glaze ingredients; brush over pork. Bake 10-15 minutes longer or until meat reaches desired doneness (for medium-rare, a thermometer should read 145°; medium, 160°), basting occasionally with pan juices. Let stand 5 minutes before slicing.

Cook to Cook

I have prepared many recipes for pork tenderloin and this one was the best! I prepared it according to the recipe and didn't change a thing. The rosemary rub gave it a lot of flavor and the preserves provided the sweetness. Great flavors combined! Browning it sears in the juices and the flavor of the rosemary and garlic. —**MIDGED**

LEAVE IT TO THE OVEN

FRENCH MEAT AND VEGETABLE PIE

Some time ago, a co-worker brought a meat pie to lunch. The aroma was familiar—and after one taste, I was amazed to discover it was the same pie my grandmother used to serve when I was a youngster! My friend wrote down the recipe, and I've been enjoying it ever since.

—RITA WINTERBERGER HUSON, MT

PREP: 20 MIN. • **BAKE:** 30 MIN.
MAKES: 8 SERVINGS

- 2 **tablespoons canola oil**
- 1 **large onion, thinly sliced**
- 1 **pound ground beef**
- 1 **pound ground pork**
- 1 **cup mashed potatoes**
- 1 **can (8 ounces) mixed vegetables, drained**
- 2 **teaspoons ground allspice**
- 1 **teaspoon salt**
- ¼ **teaspoon pepper**
  Pastry for double-crust pie (9 inches)
- 1 **egg, lightly beaten, optional**

1. Preheat oven to 375°. In a skillet, heat oil over medium heat. Saute onion until tender. Remove and set aside.
2. Cook beef and pork over medium heat until no longer pink; drain. Combine onion, meat, potatoes, vegetables and seasonings.
3. Line pie plate with pastry; fill with meat mixture. Top with crust; seal and flute edges. Make slits in top crust. Brush with egg if desired.
4. Bake 30-35 minutes or until crust is golden brown.

Cook to Cook

This is a great tasting pie. It reminds me of a great-tasting turkey stuffing that our French grandmother used to make (minus the crust). It would be even better if you cubed the potatoes and cooked them with the onions and used frozen mixed vegetables or your own fresh vegetables from your garden or the farmers market. Grandmother did not have the canned vegetables.
—MPRK2B7W

THREE-CHEESE HAM LOAF

This golden loaf relies on the convenience of refrigerated dough that's stuffed with ham and cheese. I created the recipe by experimenting with a few simple ingredients my family loves. It makes a delicious hot sandwich in no time.

—**GLORIA LINDELL** WELCOME, MN

PREP: 15 MIN. • **BAKE:** 30 MIN.
MAKES: 6 SERVINGS

- 1 **tube (13.8 ounces) refrigerated pizza crust**
- 10 **slices deli ham**
- ¼ **cup sliced green onions**
- 1 **cup (4 ounces) shredded part-skim mozzarella cheese**
- 1 **cup (4 ounces) shredded cheddar cheese**
- 4 **slices provolone cheese**
- 1 **tablespoon butter, melted**

1. Preheat oven to 350°. Unroll dough onto a greased baking sheet; top with the ham, onions and cheeses. Roll up tightly jelly-roll style, starting with a long side; pinch seam to seal and tuck ends under. Brush with butter.
2. Bake 30-35 minutes or until golden brown. Let stand 5 minutes; cut into 1-in. slices.

FREEZE OPTION *Cool unsliced loaf on a wire rack. Spray a large piece of foil with cooking spray. Wrap loaf in prepared foil and freeze up to 3 months. To use, thaw at room temperature 2 hours. Preheat oven to 350°. Unwrap and place on a greased baking sheet. Bake 15-20 minutes or until heated through. Let stand 5 minutes; cut into 1-in. slices.*

NOTES

HAM WITH APPLE-RAISIN SAUCE

Since I ran across this recipe several years ago, I've used it often for special dinners. What I really like is the ease of preparation. You don't have a lot of cleanup because everything is done right there in the bag.

—SANDY OLBERDING SPENCER, IA

PREP: 10 MIN. • **BAKE:** 2 HOURS
MAKES: 16 SERVINGS

- 1 **tablespoon all-purpose flour**
- 1 **large oven roasting bag**
- 4 **medium tart apples, peeled and chopped**
- 2 **cups apple juice**
- 1 **cup raisins**
- ½ **cup packed brown sugar**
- 1 **teaspoon ground cinnamon**
- 1 **boneless fully cooked ham (about 6 pounds)**

1. Preheat oven to 350°. Shake flour in the oven roasting bag. Place in an ungreased 13x9-in. baking pan. Place apples, apple juice, raisins, brown sugar and cinnamon in the bag; mix well. Place ham in bag. Close bag. Cut six ½-in. slits in top of bag.

2. Bake 2 to 2¼ hours or until a thermometer reads 140°. Serve with the sauce.

Cook to Cook

I made this for our Easter dinner, and my husband loved it! He said I could make it anytime. I have to say, it was one of the best hams I have ever made...and that sauce...wow! I told my husband that I'm going to make just the sauce and it would probably be good over ice cream or angel food cake! Definitely two thumbs up! —CELTICSONG54

SAVORY CRESCENT TURKEY POTPIES

My comforting entree promises to warm you up on winter's chilliest nights.

—**JUDY WILSON** SUN CITY WEST, AZ

PREP: 30 MIN. • **BAKE:** 10 MIN.
MAKES: 8 SERVINGS

- **1** small onion, chopped
- **¼** cup all-purpose flour
- **3** cups chicken stock
- **3** cups cubed cooked turkey or chicken breast
- **1** package (16 ounces) frozen peas and carrots, thawed
- **2** medium red potatoes (about ⅔ pound), cubed and cooked
- **3** tablespoons minced fresh parsley
- **1** tablespoon minced fresh thyme or 1 teaspoon dried thyme
- **¼** teaspoon pepper
- **2** tubes (8 ounces each) refrigerated seamless crescent dough sheet
- **1** egg white
- **1** teaspoon water
- **½** teaspoon kosher salt

1. Preheat oven to 400°. Heat a Dutch oven coated with cooking spray over medium-high heat. Add onion; cook and stir 4-6 minutes or until tender. In a small bowl, mix flour and stock until smooth; stir into onion. Bring to a boil, stirring constantly; cook and stir 1-2 minutes or until thickened.

2. Gently stir in turkey, peas and carrots, potatoes, parsley, thyme and pepper. Divide among eight ungreased 10-oz. ramekins (about 4-in. diameter).

3. On a lightly floured surface, unroll crescent dough and roll each sheet into a 13x9-in. rectangle. Cut four 4½-in. squares from each sheet. (Squares must be large enough for corners to drape over ramekins; save remaining dough for another use.) Place squares over ramekins, gently pressing edges of dough over rims.

4. In a small bowl, whisk egg white with water; brush over tops. Sprinkle with salt. Place ramekins on baking sheets. Bake 10-14 minutes or until crust is golden brown and the filling is heated through.

LEAVE IT TO THE OVEN

LATTICE-TOP CHICKEN STEW

Convenient crescent roll dough turns into the pretty topping on this creamy bake filled with chicken and vegetables. While it's cooking, I prepare a simple salad and dessert. It's a nice meal for company, too.
—JANET ASELAGE SIDNEY, OH

PREP: 10 MIN. • **BAKE:** 35 MIN.
MAKES: 6-8 SERVINGS

- 1 package (16 ounces) frozen California-blend vegetables, thawed and drained
- 2 cups cubed cooked chicken
- 1 can (10¾ ounces) condensed cream of potato soup, undiluted
- 1 cup milk
- ½ cup shredded cheddar cheese
- ½ cup french-fried onions
- ½ teaspoon seasoned salt
- 1 tube (8 ounces) refrigerated crescent rolls

1. Preheat oven to 350°. In a large bowl, combine vegetables, chicken, soup, milk, cheese, onions and seasoned salt. Transfer to a greased 13x9-in. baking dish.
2. Bake, uncovered, 20 minutes.
3. Meanwhile, separate crescent dough into two rectangles. Seal perforations; cut each rectangle lengthwise into four strips. Working quickly, weave strips over warm filling, forming a lattice crust. Bake 15 minutes longer or until crust is golden brown.

NOTES

_____
_____
_____
_____
_____
_____

ROSEMARY TURKEY BREAST

I season turkey with a blend of rosemary, garlic and paprika. Because I rub that mixture directly on the meat under the skin, I can remove the skin before serving and not lose any of the flavor. The result is a lower-in-fat, yet delicious entree.

—DOROTHY PRITCHETT WILLS POINT, TX

PREP: 10 MIN.
BAKE: 1½ HOURS + STANDING
MAKES: 15 SERVINGS

- 2 **tablespoons olive oil**
- 8 **to 10 garlic cloves, peeled**
- 3 **tablespoons chopped fresh rosemary or 3 teaspoons dried rosemary, crushed**
- 1 **teaspoon salt**
- 1 **teaspoon paprika**
- ½ **teaspoon coarsely ground pepper**
- 1 **bone-in turkey breast (5 pounds)**

1. Preheat oven to 325°. In a food processor, place first six ingredients; cover and process until the garlic is coarsely chopped.

2. With your fingers, carefully loosen the skin from both sides of the turkey breast. Spread half the garlic mixture over the meat under the skin. Smooth skin over meat and secure to underside of breast with toothpicks. Spread the remaining garlic mixture over the skin.

3. Place turkey breast on a rack in a shallow roasting pan. Bake, uncovered, 1½ to 2 hours or until a thermometer reads 170°. Let stand 15 minutes before slicing. Discard toothpicks.

Cook to Cook

This was wonderful. Very moist and very garlicky. I would love to make it again! **—NATALIEPOOH**

LEAVE IT TO THE OVEN

211

CRUMB-COATED RANCH CHICKEN

How do you get so much flavor out of a five-ingredient-or-fewer recipe? Ranch dressing is the key! Enjoy this simple dish on busy weeknights or with company for special occasions.

—**LADONNA REED** PONCA CITY, OK

PREP: 10 MIN. • **BAKE:** 30 MIN.
MAKES: 4 SERVINGS

- ⅔ **cup ranch salad dressing**
- 2 **cups coarsely crushed cornflakes**
- 1 **tablespoon Italian seasoning**
- 1 **teaspoon garlic powder**
- 4 **boneless skinless chicken breast halves (8 ounces each)**

1. Preheat oven to 400°. Pour salad dressing into a shallow bowl. In another shallow bowl, mix cornflake crumbs, Italian seasoning and garlic powder. Dip chicken in dressing, then coat with crumb mixture.

2. Place in a greased shallow baking pan. Bake 30-35 minutes or until a meat thermometer reads 165°.

Cook to Cook

So easy and so good! I used spicy ranch dressing and mixed some Parmesan in with the cornflakes. —**SWANDLW**

BALSAMIC ROAST CHICKEN

Balsamic, wine and rosemary are classic flavors that work so well together. This recipe has all the makings for a special dinner with friends and family.

—TRACY TYLKOWSKI OMAHA, NE

PREP: 20 MIN. **BAKE:** 2¼ HOURS + STANDING
MAKES: 12 SERVINGS
(1½ CUPS ONION SAUCE)

- 1 **roasting chicken (6 to 7 pounds)**
- 2 **tablespoons minced fresh rosemary or 2 teaspoons dried rosemary, crushed**
- 3 **garlic cloves, minced**
- 1 **teaspoon salt**
- 1 **teaspoon pepper**
- 2 **medium red onions, chopped**
- ½ **cup dry red wine or reduced-sodium chicken broth**
- ½ **cup balsamic vinegar**

1. Preheat oven to 350°. Pat chicken dry. In a small bowl, combine the rosemary, garlic, salt and pepper; rub under skin of chicken. Place onions in a shallow roasting pan; top with chicken. Combine wine and balsamic vinegar; pour over chicken.

2. Bake, uncovered, 2¼ to 2¾ hours or until a thermometer inserted in the thigh reads 170°-175°, basting occasionally with pan juices. (Cover loosely with foil if the chicken browns too quickly.)

3. Let stand 15 minutes before carving. Remove and discard skin before serving. Pour onion sauce into a small bowl; skim fat. Serve with the chicken.

NOTES

_____
_____
_____
_____
_____
_____

LEAVE IT TO THE OVEN

CHICKEN AND RICE DINNER

The chicken in this recipe bakes up to a beautiful golden brown, while the moist rice is packed with flavor. The taste is simply unbeatable!

—DENISE BAUMERT DALHART, TX

PREP: 15 MIN. • **BAKE:** 55 MIN.
MAKES: 6 SERVINGS

- 1 broiler/fryer chicken (3½ to 4 pounds), cut up
- ¼ to ⅓ cup all-purpose flour
- 2 tablespoons canola oil
- 2⅓ cups water
- 1½ cups uncooked long grain rice
- 1 cup milk
- 1 teaspoon salt
- 1 teaspoon poultry seasoning
- ½ teaspoon pepper
  Minced fresh parsley

1. Preheat oven to 350°. Dredge chicken in flour. In a large skillet, brown chicken in oil on all sides over medium heat.

2. In a large bowl, combine the water, rice, milk, salt, poultry seasoning and pepper. Pour into a greased 13x9-in. baking dish. Top with chicken.

3. Cover and bake 55 minutes or until chicken juices run clear. Garnish with the parsley.

TURKEY AND BLACK BEAN ENCHILADAS

Hearty and satisfying, these slimmed-down enchiladas with whole wheat tortillas have a moist and delicious filling that you and your family will appreciate.

—**SARAH BURLESON** SPRUCE PINE, NC

PREP: 30 MIN. • **BAKE:** 15 MIN.
MAKES: 8 SERVINGS

- 2 **cans (15 ounces each) black beans, rinsed and drained, divided**
- 1 **pound lean ground turkey**
- 1 **medium green pepper, chopped**
- 1 **small onion, chopped**
- 1 **can (15 ounces) enchilada sauce, divided**
- 1 **cup (4 ounces) shredded reduced-fat Mexican cheese blend, divided**
- 8 **whole wheat tortillas (8 inches), warmed**

1. Preheat oven to 425°. In a small bowl, mash 1 can black beans; set aside. In a large nonstick skillet, cook the turkey, pepper and onion over medium heat until meat is no longer pink; drain. Add the mashed beans, remaining beans, half the enchilada sauce and ½ cup cheese; heat through.
2. Place ⅔ cupful of bean mixture down the center of each tortilla. Roll up and place seam side down in two 11x7-in. baking dishes coated with cooking spray.
3. Pour remaining enchilada sauce over the top; sprinkle with remaining cheese. Bake, uncovered, 15-20 minutes or until heated through.

FREEZE OPTION *Cover and freeze unbaked casseroles up to 3 months. To use, partially thaw in refrigerator overnight. Remove from refrigerator*

Cook to Cook

This is a fantastic recipe! I've made it many times with variations on the vegetables I put in (add diced tomatoes for a fresh taste or jalapenos for a spicier taste, etc). It's also very easy to make into a vegetarian dish by substituting TVP (textured vegetable protein) or brown rice for the ground turkey! I've never served it to someone who didn't like it! —**NELLOYELLO11**

30 minutes before baking. Preheat oven to 425°. Bake as directed, increasing time as necessary to heat through and for a thermometer inserted in center to read 165°.

NOTES

LEAVE IT TO
THE OVEN

CREAMY CHICKEN CASSEROLE

I created this when my husband was craving a dish his aunt used to make. It tastes and smells great and is now a staple in our house.

—**MARI WARNKE** FREMONT, WI

PREP: 20 MIN. • **BAKE:** 40 MIN.
MAKES: 2 CASSEROLES (5 SERVINGS EACH)

- 4 cups uncooked egg noodles
- 4 cups cubed cooked chicken
- 1 package (16 ounces) frozen peas and carrots
- 2 cups milk
- 2 cans (10¾ ounces each) condensed cream of celery soup, undiluted
- 2 cans (10¾ ounces each) condensed cream of chicken soup, undiluted
- 1 cup chopped onion
- 2 tablespoons butter, melted
- ½ teaspoon salt
- ½ teaspoon pepper

1. Preheat oven to 350°. Cook noodles according to package directions.
2. Meanwhile, in a large bowl, combine remaining ingredients. Drain noodles; add to chicken mixture.
3. Transfer to two greased 8-in.-square baking dishes. Cover and bake 30 minutes. Uncover and bake for 10-15 minutes longer or until heated through.

FREEZE OPTION *Cover and freeze unbaked casseroles up to 3 months. To use, partially thaw in refrigerator overnight. Remove from refrigerator 30 minutes before baking. Cover and microwave on high 10-12 minutes or until heated through and a thermometer inserted in the center reads 165°, stirring twice.*

Cook to Cook

I made one casserole for my family and one for a friend. Everyone liked it! My husband doesn't like peas, so I used California blend veggies and added mushrooms to my family's dish. Great for using up leftover chicken, also.
—**AB0628**

ROASTED CHICKEN WITH VEGGIES

A golden brown chicken surrounded by bright vegetables creates an appealing meal-in-one dish.

—**MARY BETH HANSEN** COLUMBIA, TN

PREP: 20 MIN. • **BAKE:** 1½ HOURS
MAKES: 6 SERVINGS

- 1 broiler/fryer chicken (3 to 3½ pounds)
- 1 tablespoon canola oil
- ⅛ teaspoon salt
- ⅛ teaspoon pepper
- 6 medium carrots, cut into 1-inch pieces
- 4 celery ribs, cut into 1-inch pieces
- 3 medium baking potatoes, cut into 1½-inch pieces
- 2 medium onions, cut into wedges
- 2 tablespoons butter, melted
- 4 teaspoons minced fresh thyme or 1 teaspoon dried thyme

1. Preheat oven to 375°. Place the chicken, breast side up, in a shallow roasting pan. Rub with oil; sprinkle with salt and pepper. Bake, uncovered, 45 minutes.

2. Arrange the vegetables around chicken. Combine butter and thyme; drizzle over chicken and vegetables.

3. Cover and bake 45-60 minutes longer or until a thermometer inserted in a thigh reads 170°-175° and the vegetables are tender.

LEAVE IT TO
THE OVEN

EASY CHICKEN PICCATA

My chicken dish is ready to serve in a half hour. It takes just a few minutes in the oven to bake to tender perfection. I like to serve this over noodles.

—HANNAH WILLIAMS MALIBU, CA

START TO FINISH: 30 MIN.
MAKES: 4 SERVINGS

- 4 **boneless skinless chicken breast halves (6 ounces each)**
- ½ **teaspoon salt**
- ¼ **teaspoon pepper**
- ½ **cup all-purpose flour**
- 3 **tablespoons olive oil**
- 1 **cup chicken stock**
- 3 **to 4 tablespoons capers, drained**
- 2 **to 3 tablespoons lemon juice**
- 3 **tablespoons butter**

1. Preheat oven to 350°. Cut chicken breasts in half crosswise. Pound with a meat mallet to ½-in. thickness; season with salt and pepper. Place flour in a shallow bowl. Dip chicken in flour to coat both sides; shake off excess.
2. In a large skillet, heat 1 tablespoon oil over medium-high heat. Brown chicken in batches, adding additional oil as needed. Transfer chicken to an ungreased 13x9-in. baking dish.
3. Add stock, capers and lemon juice to pan, stirring to loosen browned bits from pan. Whisk in butter, 1 tablespoon at a time, until creamy. Pour sauce over chicken. Bake 5-10 minutes or until no longer pink.

SKILLET-ROASTED LEMON CHICKEN WITH POTATOES

This is a meal I have my students make in our nutrition unit. It has a delicious lemon-herb flavor and is simple to make.

—MINDY ROTTMUND LANCASTER, PA

PREP: 20 MIN. • **BAKE:** 25 MIN.
MAKES: 4 SERVINGS

- 1 **tablespoon olive oil, divided**
- 1 **medium lemon, thinly sliced**
- 4 **garlic cloves, minced and divided**
- ¼ **teaspoon grated lemon peel**
- ½ **teaspoon salt, divided**
- ¼ **teaspoon pepper, divided**
- 8 **boneless skinless chicken thighs (4 ounces each)**
- ¼ **teaspoon dried rosemary, crushed**
- 1 **pound fingerling potatoes, halved lengthwise**
- 8 **cherry tomatoes**

1. Preheat oven to 450°. Grease a 10-in. cast-iron skillet with 1 teaspoon oil. Arrange lemon slices in a single layer in skillet.

2. Combine 1 teaspoon oil, 2 minced garlic cloves, lemon peel, ¼ teaspoon salt and ⅛ teaspoon pepper; rub over chicken. Place over lemon.

3. In a large bowl, combine rosemary and the remaining oil, garlic, salt and pepper. Add potatoes and tomatoes; toss to coat. Arrange over chicken.

4. Bake, uncovered, 25-30 minutes or until chicken is no longer pink and potatoes are tender.

Cook to Cook

Very good! I liked the pronounced lemon flavor with the rosemary. I used halved small red potatoes instead of fingerlings, and a very coarsely chopped fresh tomato instead of cherry tomatoes. Use what you have!
—BIGMAMACOOKS

LEAVE IT TO THE OVEN

ITALIAN CHICKEN ROLL-UPS

Because I have a busy schedule, I like to keep a batch of these tender chicken rolls in the freezer. Coated with golden crumbs, they are fancy enough for company.

—**BARBARA WOBSER** SANDUSKY, OH

PREP: 20 MIN. • **BAKE:** 25 MIN.
MAKES: 8 SERVINGS

- 8 **boneless skinless chicken breast halves (4 ounces each)**
- 8 **thin slices (4 ounces) deli ham**
- 4 **slices provolone cheese, halved**
- ⅔ **cup seasoned bread crumbs**
- ½ **cup grated Romano or Parmesan cheese**
- ¼ **cup minced fresh parsley**
- ½ **cup milk**
  Cooking spray

1. Preheat oven to 425°. Flatten chicken to ¼-in. thickness. Place a slice of ham and half slice of provolone cheese on each piece of chicken. Roll up from a short side and tuck in ends; secure with a toothpick.

2. In a shallow bowl, combine bread crumbs, Romano cheese and parsley. Pour milk into another bowl. Dip chicken rolls in milk, then roll in crumb mixture.

3. Place roll-ups, seam side down, on a greased baking sheet. Spritz chicken with cooking spray. Bake, uncovered, 25 minutes or until meat is no longer pink. Remove toothpicks.

FREEZE OPTION *Wrap unbaked chicken roll-ups individually in plastic wrap; place in a large resealable freezer bag. Freeze up to 2 months. To use, completely thaw in the refrigerator. Preheat oven to 425°. Unwrap roll-ups and place on a greased baking sheet. Spritz with nonstick cooking spray. Bake, uncovered, 30 minutes or until juices run clear.*

Cook to Cook

This was an extremely easy recipe! And I was able to freeze half, so I have plenty for another dinner. I did substitute Swiss cheese for the provolone, so it was a little more like a Cordon Bleu, which was fun. This is great for beginning cooks who want to impress their guests! —**SDAWSONH**

HUNGARIAN CHICKEN PAPRIKASH

My mom learned to make this tender chicken dish when she volunteered to help prepare the dinners served at her church. It's my favorite main dish, and the gravy, seasoned with paprika, sour cream and onions, is the best!

—**PAMELA EATON** MONCLOVA, OH

PREP: 20 MIN. • **BAKE:** 1½ HOURS
MAKES: 6 SERVINGS

- 1 **large onion, chopped**
- ¼ **cup butter, cubed**
- 4 **to 5 pounds broiler/fryer chicken pieces**
- 2 **tablespoons paprika**
- 1 **teaspoon salt**
- ½ **teaspoon pepper**
- 1½ **cups water**
- 2 **tablespoons cornstarch**
- 2 **tablespoons cold water**
- 1 **cup (8 ounces) sour cream**

1. Preheat oven to 350°. In a skillet, saute onion in butter until tender.

2. Sprinkle chicken with paprika, salt and pepper; place in an ungreased roasting pan. Spoon onion mixture over chicken. Add the water.

3. Cover and bake 1½ hours or until chicken juices run clear. Remove chicken and keep warm.

4. Pour drippings and loosened browned bits from the roasting pan into a saucepan. Skim fat. In a small bowl, combine the cornstarch and cold water until smooth. Stir into pan juices with onion. Bring to a boil; cook and stir 2 minutes or until thickened. Remove from heat. Stir in sour cream. Serve with chicken.

LEAVE IT TO THE OVEN

221

TUNA PUFF SANDWICHES

My husband and I can't get enough of this great supper sandwich. The cheese-covered tomato slices are wonderful over the mild tuna salad.

—**STELLA DOBMEIER** KAMLOOPS, BC

START TO FINISH: 30 MIN.
MAKES: 6 SERVINGS

- ¾ cup mayonnaise, divided
- 2 tablespoons chopped green pepper
- 1½ teaspoons grated onion
- 1½ teaspoons prepared mustard
- ¼ teaspoon Worcestershire sauce
- 1 pouch (6.4 ounces) tuna
- 3 hamburger buns, split
- 6 slices tomato
- ¾ cup shredded cheddar cheese

1. Preheat oven to 400°. In a small bowl, combine ¼ cup mayonnaise, green pepper, onion, mustard and Worcestershire sauce; stir in tuna. Spread over each bun half; top each with a tomato slice. Arrange the sandwiches on a baking sheet.

2. In another bowl, combine the cheese and remaining mayonnaise; spoon cheese mixture over tomato.

3. Bake 11-13 minutes or until topping is puffy and golden brown.

Cook to Cook

This was pretty good. Beats your everyday tuna fish sandwich. The cheese really dresses it up. Flavor was terrific. I did slap a bun on top; it looked pretty, but we wanted to eat it like a sandwich! —**LINSVIN**

SHRIMP & MACARONI CASSEROLE

Mac and cheese goes upscale in this delicious variation. The shrimp gives a unique twist to the popular standard.

—**MICHAEL COHEN** LOS ANGELES, CA

PREP: 20 MIN. • **BAKE:** 20 MIN.
MAKES: 3 SERVINGS

- 1 **cup uncooked elbow macaroni**
- 1 **egg, beaten**
- ¼ **cup half-and-half cream**
- 2 **tablespoons butter, melted**
- ½ **cup grated Parmesan cheese**
- ¾ **cup shredded part-skim mozzarella cheese, divided**
- 1 **garlic clove, minced**
- ¼ **teaspoon salt**
- ⅛ **teaspoon pepper**
- ¼ **pound uncooked shrimp, peeled, deveined and chopped**
- ¾ **cup chopped fresh spinach**

1. Preheat oven to 350°. Cook the macaroni according to the package directions.

2. Meanwhile, in a small bowl, combine egg, cream and butter; set aside. Drain macaroni; transfer to another bowl. Add Parmesan cheese, ½ cup mozzarella cheese, garlic, salt, pepper and reserved egg mixture to macaroni; toss to coat. Stir in shrimp and spinach.

3. Transfer to a 1-qt. baking dish coated with cooking spray. Sprinkle with remaining mozzarella cheese.

4. Bake, uncovered, 20-25 minutes or until shrimp turn pink and the cheese is melted.

LEAVE IT TO THE OVEN

OVEN-FRIED FISH NUGGETS

My husband and I love fresh fried fish, but we're both trying to cut back on fats. I made up this recipe and it was a huge hit. He tells me that he likes it as much as deep-fried fish, and that's saying a lot!

—**LADONNA REED** PONCA CITY, OK

START TO FINISH: 25 MIN.
MAKES: 4 SERVINGS

- ⅓ cup seasoned bread crumbs
- ⅓ cup crushed cornflakes
- 3 tablespoons grated Parmesan cheese
- ½ teaspoon salt
- ¼ teaspoon pepper
- 1½ pounds cod fillets, cut into 1-inch cubes
- Butter-flavored cooking spray

1. Preheat oven to 375°. In a shallow bowl, mix bread crumbs, cornflakes, Parmesan cheese, salt and pepper. Coat fish with butter-flavored spray, then roll in crumb mixture.

2. Place on a baking sheet coated with cooking spray. Bake 15-20 minutes or until fish flakes easily with a fork.

PARSLEY-CRUSTED COD

Struggling to get more fish in your family's diet? You'll appreciate this easy cod with ingredients you likely have on hand. The flavors are mild and delicious, so even picky eaters won't complain.

—JUDY GREBETZ RACINE, WI

START TO FINISH: 30 MIN.
MAKES: 4 SERVINGS

- ¾ **cup dry bread crumbs**
- 1 **tablespoon minced fresh parsley**
- 2 **teaspoons grated lemon peel**
- 1 **garlic clove, minced**
- ¼ **teaspoon kosher salt**
- ¼ **teaspoon pepper**
- 2 **tablespoons olive oil**
- 4 **cod fillets (6 ounces each)**

1. Preheat oven to 400°. In a shallow bowl, combine the first six ingredients. Brush oil over one side of fillets; gently press into crumb mixture.

2. Place crumb side up in a 13x9-in. baking dish coated with cooking spray. Bake 15-20 minutes or until fish flakes easily with a fork.

Cook to Cook

I usually do not care for fish but had some tilapia in the freezer for my hubby and decided to try this recipe to use it up. This was really good! We both enjoyed it and are looking forward to trying it with the cod next time.
—HIGHJINX1

NOTES

LEAVE IT TO THE OVEN

BUSY-DAY BAKED FISH

An onion soup-and-sour cream mixture really adds zip to this beautiful baked fish. Your family will never guess how quickly and easily it comes together.

—**BEVERLY KRUEGER** YAMHILL, OR

START TO FINISH: 30 MIN.
MAKES: 6-8 SERVINGS

- 1 cup (8 ounces) sour cream
- 2 tablespoons onion soup mix
- 1½ cups seasoned bread crumbs
- 2½ pounds fish fillets
- ¼ cup butter, melted
- ⅓ cup shredded Parmesan cheese

1. Preheat oven to 425°. In a shallow bowl, combine sour cream and soup mix. Place bread crumbs in another shallow bowl. Cut fish into serving-size pieces; coat with sour cream mixture, then roll in crumbs.

2. Place in two greased 13x9-in. baking dishes. Drizzle with the butter. Bake, uncovered, 12 minutes. Sprinkle with cheese; bake 2-6 minutes longer or until fish flakes easily with a fork.

Cook to Cook

I want to say this is the easiest and tastiest fish dish we've tried. Excellent! One time, I was out of fish so I tried it with pork chops. Also excellent! Would also be good with chicken breasts. Of course, you'll adjust the cooking time— but keep the other ingredients the same. A winner in our family through and through! —**ANONYMOUS**

FREEZE IT

SIX-CHEESE LASAGNA

This hearty lasagna couldn't be much easier to make. No-boil noodles and prepared spaghetti sauce save time and also cut down on the cleanup.

—**JODI ANDERSON** OVERBROOK, KS

PREP: 25 MIN. • **BAKE:** 1 HOUR + STANDING
MAKES: 12 SERVINGS

- 1 **pound ground beef**
- 1 **pound bulk Italian sausage**
- 1 **jar (24 ounces) meatless spaghetti sauce**
- 2 **eggs, beaten**
- 1 **carton (15 ounces) ricotta cheese**
- 1½ **cups (12 ounces) 4% cottage cheese**
- ¼ **cup grated Parmesan cheese**
- ¼ **cup grated Romano or Asiago cheese**
- 8 **no-cook lasagna noodles**
- 4 **cups (16 ounces) shredded part-skim mozzarella cheese**
- 6 **slices provolone cheese, quartered**

1. Preheat oven to 350°. In a large skillet, cook beef and sausage over medium heat until no longer pink; drain. Stir in spaghetti sauce.

2. In a large bowl, combine the eggs, ricotta, cottage, Parmesan and Romano cheeses.

3. Spread 1½ cups sauce mixture in a greased 13x9-in. baking dish. Top with four noodles. Spread 1½ cups sauce to edges of the noodles. Sprinkle with 2 cups mozzarella cheese. Top with ricotta mixture, provolone cheese and the remaining noodles, sauce and mozzarella cheese.

4. Cover and bake 50 minutes or until a thermometer reads 160°. Uncover; bake 10 minutes or until cheese is lightly browned. Let stand 15 minutes before cutting.

FREEZE OPTION *Cover and freeze unbaked lasagna up to 3 months. To use, thaw in refrigerator overnight. Remove from refrigerator 30 minutes before baking. Preheat oven to 350°. Bake as directed.*

LEAVE IT TO THE OVEN

FOUR-CHEESE BAKED ZITI

This pasta dish, made with Alfredo sauce, is delightfully different from typical tomato-based recipes. It is rich with cheese and goes together quickly. I find it to be very popular at potlucks.

—LISA VARNER EL PASO, TX

PREP: 20 MIN. • **BAKE:** 30 MIN.
MAKES: 8 SERVINGS

- 1 package (16 ounces) ziti or small tube pasta
- 2 cartons (10 ounces each) refrigerated Alfredo sauce
- 1 cup (8 ounces) sour cream
- 2 eggs, lightly beaten
- 1 carton (15 ounces) ricotta cheese
- ½ cup grated Parmesan cheese, divided
- ¼ cup grated Romano cheese
- ¼ cup minced fresh parsley
- 1¾ cups shredded part-skim mozzarella cheese

1. Preheat oven to 350°. Cook ziti according to package directions; drain and return to the pan. Stir in Alfredo sauce and sour cream. Spoon half into a lightly greased 3-qt. baking dish.
2. In a small bowl, combine the eggs, ricotta cheese, ¼ cup Parmesan cheese, Romano cheese and parsley; spread over pasta. Top with remaining pasta mixture; sprinkle with the mozzarella and remaining Parmesan.
3. Cover and bake 25 minutes or until a thermometer reads 160°. Uncover; bake 5-10 minutes or until bubbly.

CHICKEN MANICOTTI

When a girlfriend came home from the hospital with her newborn, I sent over this freezer casserole. She and her family raved over how good it was. Try substituting olives for the mushrooms or using veal instead of chicken.

—**JAMIE VALOCCHI** MESA, AZ

PREP: 25 MIN. • **BAKE:** 65 MIN.
MAKES: 2 CASSEROLES (4 SERVINGS EACH)

- 1 **tablespoon garlic powder**
- 1½ **pounds boneless skinless chicken breasts**
- 16 **uncooked manicotti shells**
- 2 **jars (26 ounces each) spaghetti sauce, divided**
- 1 **pound bulk Italian sausage, cooked and drained**
- ½ **pound fresh mushrooms, sliced**
- 4 **cups (16 ounces) shredded part-skim mozzarella cheese**
- ⅔ **cup water**

1. Preheat oven to 375°. Rub garlic powder over chicken; cut into 1-in. strips. Stuff chicken into manicotti shells. Spread 1 cup spaghetti sauce in each of two greased 13x9-in. baking dishes.
2. Place eight stuffed manicotti shells in each dish. Sprinkle with sausage and mushrooms. Pour remaining spaghetti sauce over top. Sprinkle with cheese.
3. Drizzle water around the edge of each dish. Cover and bake 65-70 minutes or until chicken is no longer pink and pasta is tender.

FREEZE OPTION *Cover and freeze unbaked casseroles for up to 1 month. To use, partially thaw in refrigerator overnight. Remove from refrigerator 30 minutes before baking. Preheat oven to 375°. Bake casseroles as directed, increasing time as necessary to heat through and for a thermometer inserted in center to read 165°.*

NOTES

Cook to Cook

My family loves this! I love that it makes two casseroles. I usually make one with the sausage and mushrooms and the second without the mushrooms. I have never frozen it because whatever is left over always gets eaten for lunch the next day, and there is usually a battle over who will get it! It is a great dish to serve for company, too.
—**CAROLASTAFF**

LEAVE IT TO
THE OVEN

CREAMY SPINACH SAUSAGE PASTA

So rich and creamy, this pasta dish is wonderfully cheesy and delicious! And for time-saving convenience, I like to assemble it the night before, then bake it the next day.

—**SUSIE SIZEMORE** COLLINSVILLE, VA

PREP: 15 MIN. • **BAKE:** 45 MIN.
MAKES: 5 SERVINGS

- 3 **cups uncooked rigatoni or large tube pasta**
- 1 **pound bulk Italian sausage**
- 1 **cup finely chopped onion**
- 1 **can (14½ ounces) Italian diced tomatoes, undrained**
- 1 **package (10 ounces) frozen creamed spinach, thawed**
- 1 **package (8 ounces) cream cheese, softened**
- 2 **cups (8 ounces) shredded part-skim mozzarella cheese, divided**

1. Preheat oven to 350°. Cook pasta according to package directions.
2. Meanwhile, in a Dutch oven, cook sausage and onion over medium heat until meat is no longer pink; drain.
3. Stir in the tomatoes, spinach, cream cheese and 1 cup mozzarella cheese. Drain the pasta; add to the sausage mixture. Transfer to a greased 11x7-in. baking dish.
4. Cover and bake 35 minutes. Uncover; sprinkle with the remaining cheese. Bake 10 minutes longer or until cheese is melted.

Cook to Cook

This was absolutely heavenly. My husband asked if I could make it every day! I used Italian Seasoned Jenni-o ground turkey (tastes just like Italian sausage), low-fat cream cheese and part-skim mozzarella... and it was one of the best things I have ever eaten. Can I give it 6 stars? —**MRSWRAY**

CHEESY RIGATONI BAKE

This is a family favorite. One of our four children likes it so much, he always asks for it as a birthday dinner.

—NANCY URBINE LANCASTER, OH

PREP: 20 MIN. • **BAKE:** 30 MIN.
MAKES: 2 CASSEROLES (6 SERVINGS EACH)

- 1 package (16 ounces) rigatoni or large tube pasta
- 2 tablespoons butter
- ¼ cup all-purpose flour
- ½ teaspoon salt
- 2 cups milk
- ¼ cup water
- 4 eggs, lightly beaten
- 2 cans (8 ounces each) tomato sauce
- 2 cups (8 ounces) shredded part-skim mozzarella cheese, divided
- ¼ cup grated Parmesan cheese, divided

1. Preheat oven to 375°. Cook pasta according to package directions.
2. Meanwhile, in a small saucepan, melt butter. Stir in flour and salt until smooth; gradually add milk and water. Bring to a boil; cook and stir 2 minutes or until thickened.
3. Drain pasta; place in a large bowl. Add eggs. Spoon into two greased 8-in.-square baking dishes. Layer each with one can tomato sauce, half the mozzarella cheese and half the white sauce. Sprinkle each with half the Parmesan cheese.
4. Bake, uncovered, 30-35 minutes or until a thermometer reads 160°.

FREEZE OPTION *Cover and freeze unbaked casseroles up to 3 months. To use, partially thaw in refrigerator overnight. Remove from refrigerator 30 minutes before baking. Preheat oven to 375°. Cover and bake 40 minutes. Uncover; bake 7-10 minutes or until a thermometer reads 165°.*

LEAVE IT TO THE OVEN

SPAGHETTI CASSEROLE

Here's an easy dish to prepare ahead of time and bake just before dinnertime. Sour cream and canned mushroom soup make this casserole luscious.

—**KIM ROCKER** LAGRANGE, GA

PREP: 20 MIN. • **BAKE:** 55 MIN.
MAKES: 2 CASSEROLES (6 SERVINGS EACH)

- 1 **package (16 ounces) spaghetti**
- 1½ **pounds ground beef**
- 1 **jar (26 ounces) spaghetti sauce**
- 2 **cans (8 ounces each) tomato sauce**
- 1 **can (10¾ ounces) condensed cream of mushroom soup, undiluted**
- 1 **cup (8 ounces) sour cream**
- 2 **cups (8 ounces) shredded Colby-Monterey Jack cheese**

1. Preheat oven to 350°. Cook pasta according to package directions.
2. Meanwhile, in a large skillet, cook beef over medium heat until no longer pink; drain. Stir in spaghetti sauce and tomato sauce. Remove from heat.
3. Drain pasta. Combine soup and sour cream. In two 8-in.-square baking dishes, layer half of the meat sauce, pasta, soup mixture and cheese. Repeat the layers.
4. Cover and bake 55-65 minutes or until cheese is melted.

FREEZE OPTION *Cover and freeze unbaked casseroles up to 3 months. To use, partially thaw in refrigerator overnight. Remove from refrigerator 30 minutes before baking. Preheat oven to 350°. Bake, increasing time as necessary to heat through and for a thermometer inserted in center to read 165°.*

6

NO-FUSS SLOW COOKER

Just toss in the food, set the slow cooker and go about your day.

NO-FUSS SLOW COOKER INDEX

Cook to Cook

Look for
THESE boxes
for helpful tidbits!

MELT-IN-YOUR-MOUTH POT ROAST

Slow-simmered and seasoned with rosemary, mustard and thyme, this tender and tasty pot roast is so easy to make and always a hit. Substitute burgundy or brandy plus a half cup of water for the broth...the aroma is wonderful!

—JEANNIE KLUGH LANCASTER, PA

PREP: 10 MIN. • **COOK:** 6 HOURS
MAKES: 6-8 SERVINGS

- 1 pound medium red potatoes, quartered
- 1 cup fresh baby carrots
- 1 boneless beef chuck roast (3 to 4 pounds)
- ¼ cup Dijon mustard
- 2 teaspoons dried rosemary, crushed
- 1 teaspoon garlic salt
- ½ teaspoon dried thyme
- ½ teaspoon pepper
- ⅓ cup chopped onion
- 1½ cups beef broth

1. Place potatoes and carrots in a 5-qt. slow cooker. Cut the roast in half. In a small bowl, mix mustard, rosemary, garlic salt, thyme and pepper; rub over the roast. Place in slow cooker; top with onion and broth.

2. Cover and cook on low 6-8 hours or until meat and vegetables are tender.

CHIPOTLE-BLACK BEAN CHILI

This thick chili is special to me because it "cooks itself" while I'm at work. My family and friends love it. It's really nice served with corn bread.

—**PATRICIA NIEH** PORTOLA VALLEY, CA

PREP: 15 MIN. • **COOK:** 7 HOURS
MAKES: 8 SERVINGS

- 2 **cans (15 ounces each) black beans, rinsed and drained**
- 2 **cans (14½ ounces each) fire-roasted diced tomatoes, undrained**
- 1 **large onion, finely chopped**
- 1 **medium green pepper, finely chopped**
- 2 **chipotle peppers in adobo sauce, finely chopped**
- 2 **tablespoons adobo sauce**
- 2 **garlic cloves, minced**
- 1 **boneless beef chuck roast (2 pounds), cut into 1-inch cubes**
- 1 **tablespoon ground cumin**
- 1 **tablespoon dried oregano**
- ½ **teaspoon salt**
- ½ **teaspoon pepper**
  Optional toppings: shredded Monterey Jack cheese, reduced-fat sour cream, minced fresh cilantro and lime wedges

1. In a large bowl, combine beans, tomatoes, onion, green pepper, chipotle peppers, adobo sauce and garlic. In another bowl, combine beef, cumin, oregano, salt and pepper.

2. Pour half the tomato mixture into a 4- or 5-qt. slow cooker; add the beef. Top with remaining tomato mixture.

3. Cover and cook on low 7-9 hours or until meat is tender. Serve with the toppings of your choice.

SMOTHERED ROUND STEAK

Try affordable round steak and gravy served over egg noodles for a hearty meal. Satisfying and chock-full of veggies, this slow cooker creation will take the worry out of what's-for-supper any weeknight.

—KATHY GARRETT CAMDEN, WV

PREP: 20 MIN. • **COOK:** 7 HOURS
MAKES: 4 SERVINGS

- ⅓ cup all-purpose flour
- 1 teaspoon salt
- ¼ teaspoon pepper
- 1½ pounds beef top round steak, cut into 1½-inch strips
- 1 large onion, sliced
- 1 large green pepper, sliced
- 1 can (14½ ounces) diced tomatoes, undrained
- 1 jar (4 ounces) sliced mushrooms, drained
- 3 tablespoons soy sauce
- 2 tablespoons molasses
  Hot cooked egg noodles, optional

1. In a large resealable plastic bag, combine the flour, salt and pepper. Add the beef and shake to coat. Transfer to a 3-qt. slow cooker. Add onion, green pepper, tomatoes, mushrooms, soy sauce and molasses.

2. Cover and cook on low 7-8 hours or until the meat is tender. Serve with noodles if desired.

Cook to Cook

I made this shortly after my issue (of *Taste of Home*) arrived, and it was wonderful; it was even better the next day! I used the molasses, although it sounded odd, but it was really delicious. Thank goodness for recipe search, though, since I can't find the issue with this recipe in it. **—MELINDAB**

NOTES

TRADITIONAL BEEF STEW

The aroma of this classic beef stew is irresistible, making it impossible not to dig in the moment you walk in the door!

—ROSANA PAPE HAMILTON, IN

PREP: 15 MIN. • **COOK:** 8 HOURS
MAKES: 4 SERVINGS

- 1 **pound beef stew meat, cut into 1-inch cubes**
- 1 **pound fresh baby carrots**
- 2 **medium potatoes, cut into chunks**
- 2 **medium onions, cut into wedges**
- 1 **cup drained diced tomatoes**
- 1 **cup beef broth**
- 1 **celery rib, cut into ½-inch pieces**
- 2 **tablespoons quick-cooking tapioca**
- 1 **teaspoon Worcestershire sauce**
- ¼ **teaspoon salt**
- ¼ **teaspoon pepper**

1. In a 3-qt. slow cooker, combine all the ingredients.

2. Cover and cook on low 8-10 hours or until meat and vegetables are tender.

FREEZE IT

TENDER SALSA BEEF

This is my Mexican-style twist on comfort food. To keep it kid-friendly, use mild salsa.
—**STACIE STAMPER** NORTH WILKESBORO, NC

PREP: 15 MIN. • **COOK:** 8 HOURS
MAKES: 8 SERVINGS

- 1½ **pounds beef stew meat, cut into ¾-inch cubes**
- 2 **cups salsa**
- 1 **tablespoon brown sugar**
- 1 **tablespoon reduced-sodium soy sauce**
- 1 **garlic clove, minced**
- 4 **cups hot cooked brown rice**

1. In a 3-qt. slow cooker, combine beef, salsa, brown sugar, soy sauce and garlic.
2. Cover and cook on low 8-10 hours or until meat is tender. Using a slotted spoon, serve beef with rice.

FREEZE OPTION *Freeze individual portions of cooled stew in freezer containers. To use, partially thaw in refrigerator overnight. Heat through in a saucepan, stirring occasionally and adding a water if necessary.*

CORNED BEEF DINNER

This flavorful meal is a must for St. Patrick's Day, but it's great any time of the year. Don't forget the fresh rye bread!

—**MICHELLE RHODES** FORT BLISS, TX

PREP: 25 MIN. • **COOK:** 8 HOURS
MAKES: 8 SERVINGS

- **4 to 5 medium red potatoes,** quartered
- **2 cups fresh baby carrots, halved** lengthwise
- **3 cups chopped cabbage**
- **1 corned beef brisket with spice** packet (3½ pounds)
- **3 cups water**
- **1 tablespoon caraway seeds**

1. Place potatoes, carrots and cabbage in a 5-qt. slow cooker. Cut brisket in half; place over vegetables. Add the water, caraway seeds and contents of spice packet.

2. Cover and cook on low 8-10 hours or until meat and vegetables are tender.

NOTES

BEEF BURGUNDY

I trim the meat, cut up the vegetables and store them in separate containers in the refrigerator the night before. The next day, I toss all the ingredients into the slow cooker. Shortly before dinnertime, I cook the noodles and bake some cheesy garlic toast to complete the meal.

—MARY JO MILLER MANSFIELD, OH

PREP: 10 MIN. • **COOK:** 5 HOURS
MAKES: 6 SERVINGS

- 1½ **pounds beef stew meat, cut into 1-inch cubes**
- ½ **pound whole fresh mushrooms, halved**
- 4 **medium carrots, chopped**
- 1 **can (10¾ ounces) condensed golden mushroom soup, undiluted**
- 1 **large onion, cut into thin wedges**
- ½ **cup Burgundy wine or beef broth**
- ¼ **cup quick-cooking tapioca**
- ½ **teaspoon salt**
- ¼ **teaspoon dried thyme**
- ¼ **teaspoon pepper**
  Hot cooked egg noodles

1. In a 5-qt. slow cooker, combine the first 10 ingredients.
2. Cover and cook on low 5-6 hours or until the meat is tender. Serve with the noodles.

Cook to Cook

I added a little more Burgundy wine and some sour cream at the end. Cooked noodles separately. Thought it could use a little more flavor. Minute tapioca helped to thicken gravy and did dissolve completely. Gravy was wonderful! Will definitely make again. **—R. FUGIT**

FREEZE IT

ROAST BEEF AND GRAVY

This is by far the simplest way to make roast beef and gravy. On busy days, I can put this main dish in the slow cooker and forget about it. My family likes it with mashed potatoes and fruit salad.

—**ABBY METZGER** LARCHWOOD, IA

PREP: 15 MIN. • **COOK:** 8 HOURS
MAKES: 8-10 SERVINGS

- 1 **boneless beef chuck roast (3 pounds)**
- 2 **cans (10¾ ounces each) condensed cream of mushroom soup, undiluted**
- ⅓ **cup sherry or beef broth**
- 1 **envelope onion soup mix**

1. Cut roast in half; place in a 3-qt. slow cooker. In a large bowl, combine the remaining ingredients; pour over roast.
2. Cover and cook on low 8-10 hours or until meat is tender.

FREEZE OPTION *Place sliced pot roast in freezer containers; top with cooking juices. Cool and freeze. To use, partially thaw in refrigerator overnight. Heat through in a covered saucepan, gently stirring and adding a little water if necessary.*

MACHACA BEEF DIP SANDWICHES

The winning combination of beef, cumin, chili powder and the spicy heat of chipotle peppers makes these sandwiches game-day food at its finest!

—KAROL CHANDLER-EZELL

NACOGDOCHES, TX

PREP: 20 MIN. • **COOK:** 8 HOURS
MAKES: 6 SERVINGS

- 1 **boneless beef chuck roast (2 to 3 pounds)**
- 1 **large sweet onion, thinly sliced**
- 1 **can (14½ ounces) reduced-sodium beef broth**
- ½ **cup water**
- 3 **chipotle peppers in adobo sauce, chopped**
- 1 **tablespoon adobo sauce**
- 1 **envelope au jus gravy mix**
- 1 **tablespoon Creole seasoning**
- 1 **tablespoon chili powder**
- 2 **teaspoons ground cumin**
- 6 **French rolls, split**
  Guacamole and salsa, optional

1. Place roast in a 3- to 4-qt. slow cooker; top with onion. Mix broth, water, chipotle peppers, adobo sauce, gravy mix, Creole seasoning, chili powder and cumin; pour over meat.
2. Cover and cook on low 8-10 hours or until meat is tender.
3. Remove roast; cool slightly. Skim fat from cooking juices. Shred beef with two forks and return to slow cooker; heat through. Using a slotted spoon, place meat on rolls. Serve with cooking juices and guacamole or salsa if desired.

FREEZE OPTION *Freeze individual portions of cooled meat mixture and juices in freezer containers. To use, partially thaw in the refrigerator overnight. Heat through in a saucepan, stirring occasionally and adding a little water if necessary. Serve on rolls with guacamole and salsa if desired.*

NOTE *Wear disposable gloves when cutting hot peppers; the oils can burn skin. Avoid touching your face. The following spices may be substituted for 1 tablespoon Creole seasoning: ¾ teaspoon each salt, garlic powder and paprika; and a pinch each of dried thyme, ground cumin and cayenne pepper.*

Cook to Cook

My husband said that this was the best beef dip sandwich he has ever had. It has a great flavor and was easy to prepare. I will be making this one again. GREAT recipe! **—BMLINK627**

NOTES

_____
_____
_____
_____
_____
_____

Cook to Cook

This was a delicious change of pace from the usual "pot roast." I did add a can of diced tomatoes (Italian style) and this enhanced the gravy. I also added more carrots because we really like them. Wonderful recipe and definitely a keeper! —DEDEH

[FREEZE IT]

STEAK SAN MARINO

I'm a busy pastor's wife and mother of three, and this delicious, inexpensive dish helps my day run smoother. The steak is so tender and flavorful, my kids gobble it up and my husband asks for seconds!

—**LAEL GRIESS** HULL, IA

PREP: 15 MIN. • **COOK:** 7 HOURS
MAKES: 6 SERVINGS

¼ cup all-purpose flour
½ teaspoon salt
½ teaspoon pepper
1 beef top round steak (1½ pounds), cut into six pieces
2 large carrots, sliced
1 celery rib, sliced
1 can (8 ounces) tomato sauce
2 garlic cloves, minced
1 bay leaf
1 teaspoon Italian seasoning
½ teaspoon Worcestershire sauce
3 cups hot cooked brown rice

1. In a large resealable plastic bag, combine the flour, salt and pepper. Add beef, a few pieces at a time, and shake to coat. Transfer to a 4-qt. slow cooker.
2. In a small bowl, combine carrots, celery, tomato sauce, garlic, bay leaf, Italian seasoning and Worcestershire sauce. Pour over beef.
3. Cover and cook on low 7-9 hours or until beef is tender. Discard bay leaf. Serve with rice.

FREEZE OPTION *Place steak and vegetables in freezer containers; top with cooking sauce. Cool and freeze. To use, partially thaw in refrigerator overnight. Heat through in a covered saucepan, gently stirring and adding a little water if necessary.*

MUSHROOM STEAK

Usually, I'd make this dish in the oven. But when I knew I wouldn't have time for it to bake one night, I let it simmer all day in the slow cooker and had great results. The leftovers are wonderful!

—SANDY PETTINGER LINCOLN, NE

PREP: 20 MIN. • **COOK:** 7 HOURS
MAKES: 6 SERVINGS

- ⅓ **cup all-purpose flour**
- ½ **teaspoon salt**
- ½ **teaspoon pepper, divided**
- 1 **beef top round steak (2 pounds), cut into 1½-inch strips**
- 2 **cups sliced fresh mushrooms**
- 1 **small onion, cut into thin wedges**
- 1 **can (10¾ ounces) condensed golden mushroom soup, undiluted**
- ¼ **cup sherry or beef broth**
- ½ **teaspoon dried oregano**
- ¼ **teaspoon dried thyme**
  Hot cooked egg noodles

1. In a large resealable plastic bag, combine the flour, salt and ¼ teaspoon pepper. Add beef, a few pieces at a time, and shake to coat.

2. In a 3-qt. slow cooker combine the mushrooms, onion and beef. Combine the soup, sherry, oregano, thyme and remaining pepper; pour over top.

3. Cover and cook on low 7-9 hours or until beef is tender. Serve with noodles.

FREEZE IT

ITALIAN SHREDDED BEEF SANDWICHES

Everyone goes for these easy sandwiches! For extra pizzazz, top them with provolone cheese and banana pepper rings.
—MARGIE WILLIAMS MT. JULIET, TN

PREP: 15 MIN. • **COOK:** 9 HOURS
MAKES: 12 SERVINGS

- **1 beef rump roast or bottom round roast (3 pounds)**
- **2 cups water**
- **1 envelope zesty Italian salad dressing mix**
- **1 envelope au jus gravy mix**
- **1 medium onion, thinly sliced**
- **1 can (4 ounces) chopped green chilies**
- **12 Italian rolls, split**

1. Cut roast in half. Place in a 4-qt. slow cooker. Combine the water and salad dressing and au jus mixes; pour over meat. Top with onion and chilies.
2. Cover and cook on low 9-11 hours or until meat is tender. Remove meat. When cool enough to handle, shred meat. Skim fat from cooking juices. Return meat to slow cooker; heat through. Serve on rolls.

FREEZE OPTION *Freeze individual portions of cooled meat mixture and juices in freezer containers. To use, partially thaw in the refrigerator overnight. Heat through in a saucepan, stirring occasionally and adding a little water if necessary. Serve on rolls.*

HUNGARIAN GOULASH

You will love how easily this version of a beloved ethnic dish comes together. My son shared the recipe with me many years ago, and it is on my meal rotation list.

—JACKIE KOHN DULUTH, MN

PREP: 15 MIN. • **COOK:** 8 HOURS
MAKES: 6-8 SERVINGS

- 2 **pounds beef top round steak, cut into 1-inch cubes**
- 1 **cup chopped onion**
- 2 **tablespoons all-purpose flour**
- 1½ **teaspoons paprika**
- 1 **teaspoon garlic salt**
- ½ **teaspoon pepper**
- 1 **can (14½ ounces) diced tomatoes, undrained**
- 1 **bay leaf**
- 1 **cup (8 ounces) sour cream**
  Hot cooked egg noodles

1. Place beef and onion in a 3-qt. slow cooker. Combine the flour, paprika, garlic salt and pepper; sprinkle over beef and stir to coat. Stir in tomatoes; add bay leaf.

2. Cover and cook on low 8-10 hours or until meat is tender.

3. Discard the bay leaf. Just before serving, stir in the sour cream; heat through. Serve with noodles.

FREEZE OPTION *Before adding sour cream, cool stew. Freeze stew in freezer containers. To use, partially thaw in refrigerator overnight. Heat through in a saucepan, stirring occasionally and adding a little broth if necessary. Remove from heat; stir in sour cream.*

CIDER MUSHROOM BRISKET

Apple juice and gingersnaps give an autumn feel to this tender brisket. It's quick to prep, and the pleasing aroma will linger for hours.

—**COLLEEN WESTON** DENVER, CO

PREP: 10 MIN. • **COOK:** 6 HOURS
MAKES: 12 SERVINGS

- 1 **fresh beef brisket (6 pounds)**
- 2 **jars (12 ounces each) mushroom gravy**
- 1 **cup apple cider or juice**
- 1 **envelope onion mushroom soup mix**
- ⅓ **cup crushed gingersnap cookies**

1. Cut brisket into thirds; place in a 5- or 6-qt. slow cooker. In a large bowl, combine the gravy, cider, soup mix and cookie crumbs; pour over beef.
2. Cover and cook on low 6-8 hours or until the meat is tender.
3. Thinly slice meat across the grain. Skim fat from cooking juices; thicken if desired.

NOTE *This is a fresh beef brisket, not corned beef.*

Cook to Cook

The meat was flavorful and tender. Couldn't believe adding ginger snaps would make such a flavorful gravy. Family LOVED it! Definitely a keeper!
—**DYLYNNE30**

FREEZE IT

SMOKY BEAN STEW

I start this satisfying sausage-and-bean stew in the slow cooker, then spend the afternoon curled up with a good book. It's an effortless meal that tastes great.
—**GLENDA HOLMES** RILEY, KS

PREP: 10 MIN. • **COOK:** 4 HOURS
MAKES: 6-8 SERVINGS

- 1 package (16 ounces) miniature smoked sausage links
- 1 can (16 ounces) baked beans
- 2 cups frozen cut green beans
- 2 cups frozen lima beans
- ½ cup packed brown sugar
- ½ cup thinly sliced fresh carrots
- ½ cup chopped onion
- ½ cup ketchup
- 1 tablespoon cider vinegar
- 1 teaspoon prepared mustard

In a 3-qt. slow cooker, combine all the ingredients. Cover and cook on high 4-5 hours or until the vegetables are tender.

FREEZE OPTION *Freeze cooled stew in freezer containers. To use, partially thaw in the refrigerator overnight. Heat through in a saucepan, stirring occasionally and adding a little water if necessary.*

NOTES

Cook to Cook

Excellent! I was in a rush and mixed all ingredients together, then poured them over the ribs instead of putting the rub on first. They were still delicious. We'll make these again. —NICELI

SWEET AND SPICY JERK RIBS

Here's a no-fuss ribs recipe that the whole family will love. The spicy rub and sweet sauce make it an instant favorite.
—GERI LESCH NEW PORT RICHEY, FL

PREP: 10 MIN. • **COOK:** 6 HOURS
MAKES: 5 SERVINGS

- 4½ **pounds pork baby back ribs**
- 3 **tablespoons olive oil**
- ⅓ **cup Caribbean jerk seasoning**
- 3 **cups honey barbecue sauce**
- 3 **tablespoons apricot preserves**
- 2 **tablespoons honey**

1. Cut ribs into serving-size pieces; brush with the oil and rub with jerk seasoning. Place in a 5- or 6-qt. slow cooker. Mix the remaining ingredients; pour over ribs.

2. Cover and cook on low 6-8 hours or until meat is tender. Skim fat from the sauce before serving.

FREEZE IT

PORK BURRITOS

As a working mother, I depend on my slow cooker to help feed my family. We all love the zesty but slightly sweet flavor of these tender burritos.

—KELLY GENGLER THERESA, WI

PREP: 25 MIN. • **COOK:** 8 HOURS
MAKES: 10 BURRITOS

- 1 **boneless pork shoulder butt roast (3 to 4 pounds)**
- 1 **can (14½ ounces) diced tomatoes with mild green chilies, undrained**
- ¼ **cup chili powder**
- 3 **tablespoons minced garlic**
- 2 **tablespoons lime juice**
- 2 **tablespoons honey**
- 1 **tablespoon chopped seeded jalapeno pepper**
- 1 **teaspoon salt**
- 10 **flour tortillas (8 inches), warmed Sliced avocado and sour cream, optional**

1. Cut roast in half; place in a 5-qt. slow cooker. In a blender, combine the tomatoes, chili powder, garlic, lime juice, honey, jalapeno and salt; cover and process until smooth. Pour over the pork.

2. Cover and cook on low 8-10 hours or until meat is tender.

3. Remove roast; cool slightly. Shred pork with two forks and return to slow cooker. Using a slotted spoon, place about ½ cup pork mixture down the center of each tortilla; top with avocado and sour cream if desired. Fold sides and ends over filling and roll up.

FREEZE OPTION *Omit avocado and sour cream. Individually wrap cooled burritos in paper towels and foil; freeze in a resealable plastic freezer bag. To use, remove foil; place paper towel-wrapped burrito on a microwave-safe plate. Microwave on high 3-4 minutes or until heated through, turning once. Let stand 20 seconds. Serve with sliced avocado and sour cream if desired.*

NOTE *Wear disposable gloves when cutting hot peppers; the oils can burn skin. Avoid touching your face.*

HAM TETRAZZINI

I modified a recipe that came with my slow cooker to reduce the fat without sacrificing the flavor. I've served this at parties, family dinners and potlucks. Everyone is pleasantly surprised to find out that it's lighter than traditional fare.

—**SUSAN BLAIR** STERLING, MI

PREP: 15 MIN. • **COOK:** 4 HOURS
MAKES: 5 SERVINGS

- 1 can (10¾ ounces) reduced-sodium condensed cream of mushroom soup, undiluted
- 1 cup sliced fresh mushrooms
- 1 cup cubed fully cooked ham
- ½ cup fat-free evaporated milk
- 2 tablespoons white wine or water
- 1 teaspoon prepared horseradish
- 1 package (7 ounces) spaghetti
- ½ cup shredded Parmesan cheese

1. In a 3-qt. slow cooker, mix soup, mushrooms, ham, milk, wine and horseradish.

2. Cover and cook on low 4 hours.

3. Cook the spaghetti according to package directions; drain. Add the spaghetti and cheese to slow cooker; toss to coat.

GARLIC-APPLE PORK ROAST

Here's the meal I have become famous for, and it is so simple to prepare. The garlic and apple flavors really complement the pork. This roast is great with steamed fresh asparagus and roasted red potatoes.

—JENNIFER LOOS WASHINGTON BORO, PA

PREP: 10 MIN. • **COOK:** 8 HOURS + STANDING
MAKES: 12 SERVINGS

- 1 **boneless pork loin roast (3½ to 4 pounds)**
- 1 **jar (12 ounces) apple jelly**
- ½ **cup water**
- 2½ **teaspoons minced garlic**
- 1 **tablespoon dried parsley flakes**
- 1 **to 1½ teaspoons seasoned salt**
- 1 **to 1½ teaspoons pepper**

1. Cut the roast in half; place in a 5-qt. slow cooker. In a small bowl, combine jelly, water and garlic; pour over roast. Sprinkle with parsley, salt and pepper.
2. Cover and cook on low 8-10 hours or until the meat is tender. Let stand 15 minutes before slicing. Serve with cooking juices if desired.

Cook to Cook

This was so moist and very flavorful. I added some potatoes to the slow cooker to make a whole meal. It was delicious and so easy to make! **—DREAMYCOW**

PULLED PORK SANDWICHES

Foolproof and wonderfully delicious describes my barbecue pork recipe. Just four ingredients make a fabulous dish—with hardly any effort from you.

—SARAH JOHNSON CHICAGO, IL

PREP: 15 MIN. • **COOK:** 7 HOURS
MAKES: 6 SERVINGS

- 1 **Hormel lemon-garlic pork loin filet (1⅓ pounds)**
- 1 **can (12 ounces) Dr Pepper**
- 1 **bottle (18 ounces) barbecue sauce**
- 6 **hamburger buns, split**

1. Place pork in a 3-qt. slow cooker. Pour Dr Pepper over top. Cover and cook on low 7-9 hours or until the meat is tender.

2. Remove meat; cool slightly. Discard cooking juices. Shred meat with two forks and return to slow cooker. Stir in barbecue sauce; heat through. Serve on the buns.

FREEZE OPTION *Place individual portions of cooled meat mixture and juice in freezer containers. To use, partially thaw in the refrigerator overnight. Microwave, covered, on high in a microwave-safe dish until heated through, gently stirring and adding a little water if necessary.*

NOTES

PORK CHOP DINNER

Canned soup creates a comforting gravy for tender pork and potatoes in this simple supper idea. Feel free to vary the amount of onion soup mix in the recipe to suit your family's tastes.

—**MIKE AVERY** BATTLE CREEK, MI

PREP: 10 MIN. • **COOK:** 6 HOURS
MAKES: 4 SERVINGS

- 6 **to 8 medium carrots (1 pound), coarsely chopped**
- 3 **to 4 medium potatoes, cubed**
- 4 **boneless pork loin chops (¾ inch thick)**
- 1 **large onion, sliced**
- 1 **envelope onion soup mix**
- 2 **cans (10¾ ounces each) condensed cream of mushroom soup, undiluted**

1. Place carrots and potatoes in a 3-qt. slow cooker. Top with pork chops, onion, soup mix and soup.
2. Cover and cook on low 6-8 hours or until meat and vegetables are tender.

> **Cook to Cook**
>
> I browned chops first, changed the onion soup mix to leek soup mix, used salt-free mushroom soup, and added some sliced fresh mushrooms. I left out the potatoes and used mashed ones for a side with the gravy. It was wonderful. I will be making this again. —MARG1940

CREAMY MUSHROOM HAM & POTATOES

Everyone loves these potatoes and always comes back for seconds. I like this recipe because it uses only seven ingredients and takes just a few minutes of prep.

—TRACI MEADOWS MONETT, MO

PREP: 25 MIN. • **COOK:** 4 HOURS
MAKES: 4 SERVINGS

- 1 can (10¾ ounces) condensed cream of mushroom soup, undiluted
- ½ cup 2% milk
- 1 tablespoon dried parsley flakes
- 6 medium potatoes, peeled and thinly sliced
- 1 small onion, chopped
- 1½ cups cubed fully cooked ham
- 6 slices process American cheese

1. In a small bowl, combine the soup, milk and parsley. In a greased 3-qt. slow cooker, layer half the potatoes, onion, ham, cheese and soup mixture. Repeat layers.

2. Cover and cook on low 4-5 hours or until potatoes are tender.

ITALIAN SHREDDED PORK STEW

Need a warm meal for a blustery night? Put together this nutritious stew with fresh sweet potatoes, kale and Italian seasoning. The shredded pork is so tender, you're going to want to make this often.

—ROBIN JUNGERS CAMPBELLSPORT, WI

PREP: 20 MIN. • **COOK:** 8 HOURS
MAKES: 9 SERVINGS (3½ QUARTS)

- 2 medium sweet potatoes, peeled and cubed
- 2 cups chopped fresh kale
- 1 large onion, chopped
- 3 garlic cloves, minced
- 1 boneless pork shoulder butt roast (2½ to 3½ pounds)
- 1 can (14 ounces) white kidney or cannellini beans, rinsed and drained
- 1½ teaspoons Italian seasoning
- ½ teaspoon salt
- ½ teaspoon pepper
- 3 cans (14½ ounces each) chicken broth
  Sour cream, optional

1. Place sweet potatoes, kale, onion and garlic in a 5-qt. slow cooker. Place roast on vegetables. Add the beans and seasonings. Pour broth over top.

2. Cover and cook on low 8-10 hours or until meat is tender.

3. Remove meat; cool slightly. Skim fat from cooking juices. Shred pork with two forks and return to slow cooker; heat through. Garnish servings with sour cream if desired.

FREEZE IT

SLOW COOKER SPLIT PEA SOUP

When I have leftover ham in the fridge, I always like to make this soup. Just throw the ingredients in the slow cooker, turn it on—and dinner is done!

—PAMELA CHAMBERS WEST COLUMBIA, SC

PREP: 15 MIN. • **COOK:** 8 HOURS
MAKES: 8 SERVINGS

- 1 package (16 ounces) dried green split peas, rinsed
- 2 cups cubed fully cooked ham
- 1 large onion, chopped
- 1 cup julienned or chopped carrots
- 3 garlic cloves, minced
- ½ teaspoon dried rosemary, crushed
- ½ teaspoon dried thyme
- 1 carton (32 ounces) reduced-sodium chicken broth
- 2 cups water

In a 4- or 5-qt. slow cooker, combine all ingredients. Cover and cook on low for 8-10 hours or until peas are tender.

FREEZE OPTION *Freeze cooled soup in freezer containers. To use, thaw in the refrigerator overnight. Heat through in a saucepan over medium heat, stirring occasionally.*

Cook to Cook

This is excellent! I added a couple diced potatoes, a dash of Penzey's Shallot Pepper and pinch of sea salt. I also used 3 cups of water. In place of the cooked ham, I used 3 small boneless smoked pork chops. Give this one a try; you won't be sorry! —JERSEYGAL262

BARBECUED PORK CHOP SUPPER

I can start these barbecued pork chops in the morning and enjoy a tasty supper at night without any last-minute work.

—JACQUELINE JONES ROUND LAKE BEACH, IL

PREP: 10 MIN. • **COOK:** 8 HOURS
MAKES: 8 SERVINGS

- 6 **small red potatoes, cut into quarters**
- 6 **medium carrots, cut into 1-inch pieces**
- 8 **bone-in pork loin or rib chops (½ inch thick and 8 ounces each)**
- 1 **teaspoon salt**
- ¼ **teaspoon pepper**
- 1 **bottle (28 ounces) barbecue sauce**
- 1 **cup ketchup**
- 1 **cup cola**
- 2 **tablespoons Worcestershire sauce**

1. Place potatoes and carrots in a 5-qt. slow cooker. Top with the pork chops. Sprinkle with salt and pepper. In a small bowl, combine barbecue sauce, ketchup, cola and Worcestershire sauce; pour over chops.

2. Cover and cook on low 8-9 hours or until meat and vegetables are tender.

NOTES

SECRET'S IN THE SAUCE BBQ RIBS

Slow cooking makes these ribs so tender that the meat literally falls off the bones. And the sweet, rich sauce is simply wonderful. Yum!

—TANYA REID WINSTON SALEM, NC

PREP: 10 MIN. • **COOK:** 6 HOURS
MAKES: 5 SERVINGS

- 4½ **pounds pork baby back ribs**
- 1½ **teaspoons pepper**
- 2½ **cups barbecue sauce**
- ¾ **cup cherry preserves**
- 1 **tablespoon Dijon mustard**
- 1 **garlic clove, minced**

1. Cut ribs into serving-size pieces; sprinkle with pepper. Place in a 5- or 6-qt. slow cooker. Combine all the remaining ingredients; pour over ribs.
2. Cover and cook on low 6-8 hours or until meat is tender. Serve with sauce.

SWEET 'N' SOUR PORK CHOPS

These tangy, tender pork chops are moist and simply delicious. They couldn't be much simpler to make, since the recipe uses only five ingredients!

—**LAURIE STAFFORD** WATERVILLE, NY

PREP: 5 MIN. • **COOK:** 4 HOURS
MAKES: 4 SERVINGS

- 1 can (8 ounces) crushed pineapple, undrained
- 1 cup honey barbecue sauce
- ⅓ cup finely chopped onion
- 2 tablespoons chili sauce
- 4 bone-in pork loin chops (8 ounces each)

1. In a small bowl, combine pineapple, barbecue sauce, onion and chili sauce. Pour half into a greased 3-qt. slow cooker. Top with pork chops and remaining sauce.

2. Cover and cook on low 4-5 hours or until meat is tender.

Cook to Cook

These are delicious! I added minced garlic and a little Worcestershire and soy sauce. I used Sweet Baby Ray's original BBQ sauce, so I added 1 tablespoon honey. I brown my chops first and have used both the bone-in and the boneless. Both are terrific—great recipe! We love these with mashed potatoes.

—**BADKITTY**

NOTES

PORK CHOPS & POTATOES IN MUSHROOM SAUCE

This recipe is really a keeper! Everyone loves the potatoes with the chops, and they always go back for seconds.

—LINDA FOREMAN LOCUST GROVE, OK

PREP: 25 MIN. • **COOK:** 3½ HOURS
MAKES: 6 SERVINGS

- 1 can (10¾ ounces) condensed cream of mushroom soup, undiluted
- ¼ cup chicken broth
- ¼ cup country-style Dijon mustard
- 1 garlic clove, minced
- ½ teaspoon dried thyme
- ¼ teaspoon salt
- ¼ teaspoon pepper
- 6 medium red potatoes, sliced
- 1 medium onion, halved and thinly sliced
- 6 boneless pork loin chops (5 ounces each)

1. In a 5-qt. slow cooker, combine the first seven ingredients. Stir in potatoes and onion. Top with pork chops.

2. Cover and cook on low 4-6 hours or until potatoes are tender.

ZESTY CHICKEN MARINARA

A friend served this delicious Italian-style chicken before a church social, and I fell in love with it. My husband says it tastes like something you'd get at a restaurant.

—LINDA BAUMANN RICHFIELD, WI

PREP: 15 MIN. • **COOK:** 4 HOURS
MAKES: 4 SERVINGS

- 4 **bone-in chicken breast halves (12 to 14 ounces each), skin removed**
- 2 **cups marinara sauce**
- 1 **medium tomato, chopped**
- ½ **cup Italian salad dressing**
- 1½ **teaspoons Italian seasoning**
- 1 **garlic clove, minced**
- ½ **pound uncooked angel hair pasta**
- ½ **cup shredded part-skim mozzarella cheese**

1. Place chicken in a 4-qt. slow cooker. In a small bowl, combine the marinara sauce, tomato, salad dressing, Italian seasoning and garlic; pour over the chicken.

2. Cover and cook on low 4-5 hours or until chicken is tender.

3. Cook pasta according to package directions; drain. Serve chicken and sauce with pasta; sprinkle with cheese.

Cook to Cook

My whole family loved this—I added fresh mushrooms a little more than halfway through and used ½ can Italian tomatoes in place of a fresh one. Would definitely make again.
—SIMPSON5TOGO

FREEZE IT

ITALIAN TURKEY SANDWICHES

I hope you enjoy these delicious turkey sandwiches as much as our family does. The recipe makes plenty, so it's great for potlucks. Leftovers are just as good reheated the next day.

—**CAROL RILEY** OSSIAN, IN

PREP: 10 MIN. • **COOK:** 5 HOURS
MAKES: 12 SERVINGS

- 1 **bone-in turkey breast (6 pounds), skin removed**
- 1 **medium onion, chopped**
- 1 **small green pepper, chopped**
- ¼ **cup chili sauce**
- 3 **tablespoons white vinegar**
- 2 **tablespoons dried oregano or Italian seasoning**
- 4 **teaspoons beef bouillon granules**
- 12 **kaiser or hard rolls, split**

1. Place turkey breast in a greased 5-qt. slow cooker. Add the onion and green pepper. Combine the chili sauce, vinegar, oregano and bouillon; pour over turkey and vegetables.
2. Cover and cook on low 5-6 hours or until turkey is tender.
3. Shred turkey with two forks and return to the slow cooker; heat through. Spoon ½ cup onto each roll.

FREEZE OPTION *Place cooled meat and juice mixture in freezer containers. To use, partially thaw in refrigerator overnight. Microwave, covered, on high in a microwave-safe dish until heated through, gently stirring and adding a little water if necessary.*

SPICY CHICKEN CHILI

The prep work for this chili is easy, thanks to several pantry staples. It's loaded with shredded chicken and beans. The spicy heat can be tamed a bit by cool sour cream.

—FRED LOCKWOOD PLANO, TX

PREP: 25 MIN. • **COOK:** 5 HOURS
MAKES: 10 SERVINGS (3½ QUARTS)

- 4 bone-in chicken breast halves (14 ounces each)
- 2 medium onions, chopped
- 2 medium green peppers, chopped
- 1 cup pickled jalapeno slices
- 1 can (4 ounces) chopped green chilies
- 2 jars (16 ounces each) salsa verde
- 2 cans (15½ ounces each) navy beans, rinsed and drained
- 1 cup (8 ounces) sour cream
- ½ cup minced fresh cilantro
  Optional toppings: shredded Colby-Monterey Jack cheese, sour cream and crushed tortilla chips

1. Place the chicken, onions, peppers, jalapeno and chilies in a 5- or 6-qt. slow cooker. Pour salsa over top.

2. Cover and cook on low 5-6 hours or until chicken is tender.

3. Remove chicken; cool slightly. Shred the chicken with two forks, discarding skin and bones; return meat to slow cooker. Stir in the beans, sour cream and cilantro; heat through. Serve with toppings of your choice.

FREEZE OPTION *Before adding sour cream, cilantro and toppings, cool chili. Freeze chili in freezer containers. To use, partially thaw in the refrigerator overnight. Heat through in a saucepan, stirring occasionally and adding a little water if needed. Stir in sour cream and cilantro. Serve with desired toppings.*

NOTE *Wear disposable gloves when cutting hot peppers; the oils can burn skin. Avoid touching your face.*

Cook to Cook

I love the combination of the slow-cooked vegetables and the sour cream! I lightened up the recipe with fat-free sour cream, and made more of a "Christmas" (i.e., red and green) version since I had red peppers and regular salsa on hand. But it was still great! Really hearty, and a nice combination of flavors. **—DFAUSNACHT**

NOTES

SQUASH 'N' CHICKEN STEW

We created a satisfying stew that's nutritious, full-flavored and family-friendly. Chicken thighs are simmered with stewed tomatoes and butternut squash for one-dish meal convenience.

—TASTE OF HOME TEST KITCHEN

PREP: 15 MIN. • **COOK:** 6 HOURS
MAKES: 5 SERVINGS

- 2 **pounds boneless skinless chicken thighs, cut into ½-inch pieces**
- 1 **can (28 ounces) stewed tomatoes, cut up**
- 3 **cups cubed peeled butternut squash**
- 2 **medium green peppers, cut into ½-inch pieces**
- 1 **small onion, sliced and separated into rings**
- 1 **cup water**
- 1 **teaspoon salt**
- 1 **teaspoon ground cumin**
- ½ **teaspoon ground coriander**
- ½ **teaspoon pepper**
- 2 **tablespoons minced fresh parsley**
  Hot cooked couscous, optional

1. In a 5-qt. slow cooker, combine the first 10 ingredients.
2. Cover and cook on low for 6-7 hours or until chicken is no longer pink. Sprinkle with parsley. Serve with couscous if desired.

ROSEMARY MUSHROOM CHICKEN

A delicate hint of rosemary lightly seasons the rich, creamy mushroom gravy in this savory dish. Cooking the chicken and gravy together cuts so much time during the dinner rush. Add noodles or rice for a complete supper.

—GENNY MONCHAMP REDDING, CA

PREP: 30 MIN. • **COOK:** 7 HOURS
MAKES: 6 SERVINGS

- 6 **chicken leg quarters, skin removed**
- 2 **cups sliced fresh mushrooms**
- 2 **cans (10¾ ounces each) condensed cream of mushroom soup, undiluted**
- ½ **cup white wine or chicken broth**
- 1 **teaspoon garlic salt**
- 1 **teaspoon dried rosemary, crushed**
- ½ **teaspoon paprika**
- ⅛ **teaspoon pepper**
  Hot cooked egg noodles

1. Place chicken in a 5- or 6-qt. slow cooker coated with cooking spray; top with mushrooms. Combine the soup, wine, garlic salt, rosemary, paprika and pepper; pour over top.

2. Cover and cook on low 7-9 hours or until the chicken is tender. Serve with the noodles.

Cook to Cook

So easy and delicious! Seven hours was definitely long enough in my slow cooker. I added an additional 1 teaspoon rosemary near the end, and then added 2-3 cups cooked spinach just before serving. (The recipe didn't need improving, but I wanted to use up the spinach!) Served it with baked potatoes. Thanks for a great addition to my slow cooker recipe options!

—MARLAD98

MAPLE MUSTARD CHICKEN

This recipe is one of my husband's favorites. It calls for only four ingredients, and we try to always have them on hand for a delicious and cozy dinner anytime!

—JENNIFER SEIDEL MIDLAND, MI

PREP: 5 MIN. • **COOK:** 3 HOURS
MAKES: 6 SERVINGS

- 6 **boneless skinless chicken breast halves (6 ounces each)**
- ½ **cup maple syrup**
- ⅓ **cup stone-ground mustard**
- 2 **tablespoons quick-cooking tapioca**
  Hot cooked brown rice

1. Place the chicken in a 3-qt. slow cooker. In a small bowl, combine the syrup, mustard and tapioca; pour over the chicken.

2. Cover and cook on low 3-4 hours or until tender. Serve with rice.

NACHO CHICKEN & RICE

You can simmer up a low-fat, delicious meal with just a few basic ingredients. Your family is sure to be delighted with this colorful medley with tender chicken and a zippy cheese sauce.

—LINDA FOREMAN LOCUST GROVE, OK

PREP: 20 MIN. • **COOK:** 5 HOURS
MAKES: 6 SERVINGS

- 2½ **pounds boneless skinless chicken breast halves, cubed**
- 1 **each small green, sweet red and orange peppers, cut into thin strips**
- 1 **can (10¾ ounces) condensed nacho cheese soup, undiluted**
- ½ **cup chunky salsa**
- ⅛ **teaspoon chili powder**
- 4½ **cups hot cooked rice**

1. In a 3-qt. slow cooker, combine the chicken, peppers, soup, salsa and chili powder.
2. Cover and cook on low 5-6 hours or until the chicken is tender. Serve with the rice.

Cook to Cook

This recipe is amazing! It made my apartment smell heavenly while it was cooking—and tasted just as great. Only suggestion would be to add a little bit of salt. Otherwise great recipe! I added some onions too. **—HRWHEELER**

NOTES

SLOW-ROASTED CHICKEN WITH VEGETABLES

The aroma of rosemary and garlic is mouthwatering, and this recipe could not be easier. Just a few minutes of prep and you'll come home to a delicious dinner. Even a beginner cook could make this and have it turn out perfectly.

—ANITA BELL HERMITAGE, TN

PREP: 15 MIN. • **COOK:** 6 HOURS + STANDING
MAKES: 6 SERVINGS

- 2 medium carrots, halved lengthwise and cut into 3-inch pieces
- 2 celery ribs, halved lengthwise and cut into 3-inch pieces
- 8 small red potatoes, quartered
- ¾ teaspoon salt, divided
- ⅛ teaspoon pepper
- 1 medium lemon, halved
- 2 garlic cloves, crushed
- 1 broiler/fryer chicken (3 to 4 pounds)
- 1 tablespoon dried rosemary, crushed
- 1 tablespoon lemon juice
- 1 tablespoon olive oil
- 2 teaspoons paprika

1. Place the carrots, celery and potatoes in a 6-qt. slow cooker; toss with ¼ teaspoon salt and pepper. Place lemon halves and garlic in chicken cavity. Tuck wings under chicken; tie drumsticks together. Place chicken over vegetables in slow cooker, breast side up. Mix rosemary, lemon juice, oil, paprika and remaining salt; rub over the chicken.

2. Cover and cook on low 6-8 hours or until a thermometer inserted in a thigh reads 170°-175° and the vegetables are tender.

3. Remove chicken to a serving platter; tent with foil. Let stand 15 minutes before carving. Serve with vegetables.

SPICY BEANS WITH TURKEY SAUSAGE

Here's a jambalaya-type dish that comes together in the slow cooker. It works well for casual get-togethers or family dinners. For extra pizzazz, top each bowlful with sour cream or shredded cheese.

—**DOROTHY JORDAN** COLLEGE STATION, TX

PREP: 25 MIN. • **COOK:** 5 HOURS
MAKES: 6 SERVINGS

- 1 **pound smoked turkey sausage, halved and sliced**
- 1 **can (16 ounces) kidney beans, rinsed and drained**
- 1 **can (15½ ounces) great northern beans, rinsed and drained**
- 1 **can (15 ounces) black beans, rinsed and drained**
- 1½ **cups frozen corn**
- 1½ **cups salsa**
- 1 **large green pepper, chopped**
- 1 **large onion, chopped**
- ½ **to 1 cup water**
- 3 **garlic cloves, minced**
- 1 **teaspoon ground cumin**

In a 5-qt. slow cooker, combine all the ingredients. Cover and cook on low 5-6 hours or until heated through. Stir before serving.

FREEZE OPTION *Freeze cooled stew in freezer containers. To use, partially thaw in the refrigerator overnight. Heat through in a saucepan, stirring occasionally and adding a little water if necessary.*

Cook to Cook

Great comfort food—and bonus points for also being a slow cooker recipe. Perfect for a weeknight family dinner. I made a minor substitution, using pinto beans instead of northern, because that's what I had. I opted for mild salsa since I'm not into "spicy" food. However, for those who like more heat, you can adjust accordingly. Leftovers the next day were just as tasty as the first time. Easy, tasty and filling! Definitely adding it to my menu rotation. —**DELORES14**

CRANBERRY CHICKEN

I've been married for more than 40 years. I love to collect cookbooks and try new dishes. This is delicious, easy and nice served with rice and a vegetable.

—**EDITH HOLLIDAY** FLUSHING, MI

PREP: 10 MIN. • **COOK:** 5 HOURS
MAKES: 6 SERVINGS

- 1 broiler/fryer chicken (3 to 4 pounds), cut up
- 1 can (14 ounces) whole-berry cranberry sauce
- 1 cup barbecue sauce
- 1 small onion, finely chopped
- 1 celery rib, finely chopped
- ½ teaspoon salt
- ¼ teaspoon pepper
  Hot cooked rice

1. Place chicken in a 3-qt. slow cooker. In a small bowl, combine the cranberry sauce, barbecue sauce, onion, celery, salt and pepper; pour over chicken.

2. Cover and cook on low 5-6 hours or until chicken is tender. Serve with rice.

FREEZE IT

SIMPLE CHICKEN TAGINE

I like to sprinkle my stew with toasted almonds or cashews and serve it with hot couscous. Flavored with cinnamon and a touch of sweetness from the apricots, this tastes like you spent all day in the kitchen!
—ANGELA BUCHANAN LONGMONT, CO

PREP: 15 MIN. • **COOK:** 6 HOURS
MAKES: 6 SERVINGS

- **2¼ pounds bone-in chicken thighs, skin removed**
- **1 large onion, chopped**
- **2 medium carrots, sliced**
- **¾ cup unsweetened apple juice**
- **1 garlic clove, minced**
- **1 teaspoon salt**
- **½ teaspoon ground cinnamon**
- **½ teaspoon pepper**
- **1 cup chopped dried apricots**
  Hot cooked couscous

1. Place chicken, onion and carrots in a 3- or 4-qt. slow cooker coated with cooking spray. In a small bowl, mix the apple juice, garlic, salt, cinnamon and pepper; pour over vegetables.

2. Cover and cook on low 6-8 hours or until chicken is tender.

3. Remove the chicken from slow cooker; shred the meat with two forks. Skim fat from cooking juices; stir in the apricots. Return the shredded chicken to slow cooker; heat though. Serve with the couscous.

FREEZE OPTION *Freeze cooled stew in freezer containers. To use, partially thaw in refrigerator overnight. Heat through in a saucepan, stirring occasionally and adding a little water if necessary. Serve with couscous.*

GARDEN CHICKEN CACCIATORE

Here's the perfect Italian meal to serve company. It frees you up to visit with your guests and always receives compliments. I like to serve it with hot cooked pasta, green salad and a dry red wine. Mangia!

—MARTHA SCHIRMACHER
STERLING HEIGHTS, MI

PREP: 15 MIN. • **COOK:** 8½ HOURS
MAKES: 12 SERVINGS

- 12 **boneless skinless chicken thighs (about 3 pounds)**
- 2 **medium green peppers, chopped**
- 1 **can (14½ ounces) diced tomatoes with basil, oregano and garlic, undrained**
- 1 **can (6 ounces) tomato paste**
- 1 **medium onion, sliced**
- ½ **cup reduced-sodium chicken broth**
- ¼ **cup dry red wine or additional reduced-sodium chicken broth**
- 3 **garlic cloves, minced**
- ¾ **teaspoon salt**
- ⅛ **teaspoon pepper**
- 2 **tablespoons cornstarch**
- 2 **tablespoons cold water**

1. Place chicken in a 4- or 5-qt. slow cooker. In a small bowl, combine green peppers, tomatoes, tomato paste, onion, broth, wine, garlic, salt and pepper; pour over chicken.

2. Cover and cook on low 8-10 hours or until chicken is tender.

3. In a small bowl, mix cornstarch and water until smooth; gradually stir into slow cooker. Cover and cook on high 30 minutes or until sauce is thickened.

Cook to Cook

This was pretty good. I like dark meat and my husband likes white meat, so we had a combination of the two. I loved both. I'd suggest adding a little crushed red pepper, though. We sprinkled some on our chicken when we went back for seconds. :)
—RWIPPEL

SLOW-COOKED SOUTHWEST CHICKEN

With just 15-minutes of prep, you'll be out of the kitchen in no time. This deliciously low-fat dish gets even better when served with reduced-fat sour cream and freshly-chopped cilantro.

—BRANDI CASTILLO SANTA MARIA, CA

PREP: 15 MIN. • **COOK:** 6 HOURS
MAKES: 6 SERVINGS

- 2 **cans (15 ounces each) black beans, rinsed and drained**
- 1 **can (14½ ounces) reduced-sodium chicken broth**
- 1 **can (14½ ounces) diced tomatoes with mild green chilies, undrained**
- ½ **pound boneless skinless chicken breast**
- 1 **jar (8 ounces) chunky salsa**
- 1 **cup frozen corn**
- 1 **tablespoon dried parsley flakes**
- 1 **teaspoon ground cumin**
- ¼ **teaspoon pepper**
- 3 **cups hot cooked rice**

1. In a 2- or 3-qt. slow cooker, combine the beans, broth, tomatoes, chicken, salsa, corn and seasonings.

2. Cover and cook on low 6-8 hours or until a thermometer reads 165°.

3. Shred chicken with two forks and return to the slow cooker; heat through. Serve with rice.

FREEZE OPTION *Freeze cooled stew in freezer containers. To use, partially thaw in the refrigerator overnight. Heat through in a saucepan, stirring occasionally and adding a little water if necessary.*

NOTES

SLOW COOKER TURKEY BREAST

Here's an easy recipe to try whenever you're craving turkey. It uses kitchen staples, which makes it handy.

—**MARIA JUCO** MILWAUKEE, WI

PREP: 10 MIN. • **COOK:** 5 HOURS
MAKES: 14 SERVINGS

- 1 **bone-in turkey breast (6 to 7 pounds), skin removed**
- 1 **tablespoon olive oil**
- 1 **teaspoon dried minced garlic**
- 1 **teaspoon seasoned salt**
- 1 **teaspoon paprika**
- 1 **teaspoon Italian seasoning**
- 1 **teaspoon pepper**
- ½ **cup water**

1. Brush turkey with oil. Combine the garlic, seasoned salt, paprika, Italian seasoning and pepper; rub over the turkey. Transfer to a 6-qt. slow cooker; add water.

2. Cover and cook on low 5-6 hours or until tender.

CHICKEN & VEGETABLES WITH MUSTARD-HERB SAUCE

My comforting and hearty chicken dinner is so easy, it is almost effortless!

—**MARIE RIZZIO** INTERLOCHEN, MI

PREP: 20 MIN. • **COOK:** 6 HOURS
MAKES: 4 SERVINGS

- 4 medium red potatoes, quartered
- 3 medium parsnips, cut into 1-inch pieces
- 2 medium leeks (white portion only), thinly sliced
- ¾ cup fresh baby carrots
- 4 chicken leg quarters, skin removed
- 1 can (10¾ ounces) condensed cream of chicken soup with herbs, undiluted
- 2 tablespoons minced fresh parsley
- 1 tablespoon snipped fresh dill or 1 teaspoon dill weed
- 1 tablespoon Dijon mustard

1. In a 5- or 6-qt. slow cooker, place the potatoes, parsnips, leeks, carrots and chicken; pour soup over top.
2. Cover and cook on low 6-8 hours or until chicken is tender.
3. Remove chicken and vegetables; cover and keep warm. Stir the parsley, dill and mustard into cooking juices; serve with the chicken and vegetables.

VEGETARIAN STUFFED PEPPERS

What a simple way to fix stuffed peppers without parboiling! Light and packed with Southwest flavor, these also come with 8 grams of fiber per serving. How can you go wrong?

—**MICHELLE GURNSEY** LINCOLN, NE

PREP: 15 MIN. • **COOK:** 3 HOURS
MAKES: 4 SERVINGS

- 4 **medium sweet red peppers**
- 1 **can (15 ounces) black beans, rinsed and drained**
- 1 **cup (4 ounces) shredded pepper jack cheese**
- ¾ **cup salsa**
- 1 **small onion, chopped**
- ½ **cup frozen corn**
- ⅓ **cup uncooked converted long grain rice**
- 1¼ **teaspoons chili powder**
- ½ **teaspoon ground cumin**
   Reduced-fat sour cream, optional

1. Cut and discard tops from peppers; remove seeds. In a large bowl, mix beans, cheese, salsa, onion, corn, rice, chili powder and cumin; spoon into peppers. Place in a 5-qt. slow cooker coated with cooking spray.

2. Cover and cook on low 3-4 hours or until peppers are tender and filling is heated through. If desired, serve with sour cream.

7

BREAKFAST FOR DINNER

No time for eggs and pancakes in the a.m.? Serve these yummy dishes for dinner!

BREAKFAST FOR DINNER INDEX

Cook to Cook

Look for
THESE boxes
for helpful tidbits!

CREAM CHEESE & CHIVE OMELET

The first bite of creamy filling lets you know this isn't any old omelet. Make it once, and I suspect you'll be fixing it often.

—**ANNE TROISE** MANALAPAN, NJ

START TO FINISH: 15 MIN.
MAKES: 2 SERVINGS

1	tablespoon olive oil
4	eggs
2	tablespoons minced chives
2	tablespoons water
⅛	teaspoon salt
⅛	teaspoon pepper
2	ounces cream cheese, cubed
	Salsa

1. In a large nonstick skillet, heat oil over medium-high heat. Whisk the eggs, chives, water, salt and pepper. Add egg mixture to skillet (mixture should set immediately at edges).

2. As eggs set, push cooked edges toward the center, letting uncooked portion flow underneath. When the eggs are set, sprinkle cream cheese on one side; fold other side over filling. Slide omelet onto a plate; cut in half. Serve with salsa.

SUNDAY BRUNCH CASSEROLE

"Isn't it about time for you to make your 'egg pie?'," my husband and sons inquire, using the nickname they've given this hearty casserole. It's nice enough for a special brunch and versatile enough for a satisfying family supper.

—PATRICIA THROLSON WILLMAR, MN

PREP: 20 MIN. **BAKE:** 35 MIN.
MAKES: 8 SERVINGS

- ½ **pound sliced bacon, chopped**
- ½ **cup chopped onion**
- ½ **cup chopped green pepper**
- 12 **eggs, lightly beaten**
- 1 **cup 2% milk**
- 1 **teaspoon salt**
- ½ **teaspoon pepper**
- ¼ **teaspoon dill weed**
- 1 **package (16 ounces) frozen shredded hash brown potatoes, thawed**
- 1 **cup (4 ounces) shredded cheddar cheese**

1. Preheat oven to 350°. In a large skillet, cook the bacon over medium heat until crisp. Remove with a slotted spoon; drain on paper towels. Discard drippings, reserving 2 tablespoons.
2. In the same skillet, saute the onion and green pepper in drippings until tender; remove with a slotted spoon.
3. In a large bowl, whisk eggs, milk and seasonings. Stir in the hash browns, cheese, onion mixture and bacon.
4. Transfer to a greased 13x9-in. baking dish. Bake, uncovered, 35-45 minutes or until a knife inserted near center comes out clean.

Cook to Cook

Very easy to make, turned out very tasty, and was very filling. As we had this for dinner, I did add some chopped kale and chard to increase the amount of nutrients. I don't think they influenced the taste in any way. For future dinners, I'd probably also add whatever green vegetable was in my fridge and needed to be used up. If I made for a brunch, I think I'd make as shown in the recipe.
—INTLANNE

HAM 'N' CHEESE QUICHE

When I was expecting our daughter, I made and froze these cheesy quiches as well as several other dishes. After her birth, it was nice to have dinner in the freezer when my husband and I were too tired to cook.

—**CHRISTENA PALMER** GREEN RIVER, WY

PREP: 20 MIN. • **BAKE:** 35 MIN.
MAKES: 2 QUICHES (6 SERVINGS EACH)

- 1 package (14.1 ounces) refrigerated pie pastry
- 2 cups diced fully cooked ham
- 2 cups (8 ounces) shredded sharp cheddar cheese
- 2 teaspoons dried minced onion
- 4 eggs
- 2 cups half-and-half cream
- ½ teaspoon salt
- ¼ teaspoon pepper

1. Preheat oven to 400°. Unroll pastry sheets into two 9-in. pie plates; flute edges. Line unpricked pastry shells with a double thickness of heavy-duty foil. Fill with pie weights, dried beans or uncooked rice. Bake 10-12 minutes or until light golden brown. Remove foil and weights; bake 3-5 minutes longer or until bottom is golden brown. Cool on wire racks.

2. Divide ham, cheese and onion between shells. In a large bowl, whisk eggs, cream, salt and pepper until blended. Pour into shells. Cover edges loosely with foil. Bake 35-40 minutes or until a knife inserted near the center comes out clean. Let stand 5-10 minutes before cutting.

FREEZE OPTION *Cover and freeze unbaked quiche. To use, remove from freezer 30 minutes before baking (do not thaw). Preheat oven to 350°. Place quiche on a baking sheet; cover edge loosely with foil. Bake as directed, increasing time as necessary for a knife inserted near the center to come out clean.*

NOTE *Let pie weights cool before storing. Beans and rice may be reused for pie weights, but not for cooking.*

POTATO & RED ONION FRITTATA

Here is a winning trio for a bistro-type brunch or casual night in. It's fancy but inexpensive...what better combination?

—**MARIA REGAKIS** SAUGUS, MA

PREP: 30 MIN. • **BAKE:** 15 MIN.
MAKES: 4 SERVINGS

- 1 large red onion, chopped
- ½ teaspoon minced fresh rosemary or ⅛ teaspoon dried rosemary, crushed
- 4 tablespoons butter, divided
- 1 garlic clove, minced
- ½ pound red potatoes (about 5 small), thinly sliced
- 6 eggs, lightly beaten
- ⅓ cup 2% milk
- ½ teaspoon salt
- ¼ teaspoon pepper
- ½ cup shredded Gruyere or Swiss cheese

1. Preheat oven to 350°. In a 10-in. ovenproof skillet, saute onion and rosemary in 1 tablespoon butter until tender. Add garlic; cook 1 minute longer. Remove from pan and set aside. In the same skillet, cook potatoes in 2 tablespoons butter until tender and golden brown. Remove and keep warm.

2. In a large bowl, whisk the eggs, milk, salt and pepper. Stir in the cheese and onion mixture. Melt remaining butter in the skillet; tilt pan to evenly coat. Add egg mixture.

3. Bake 8-10 minutes or until eggs are nearly set.

4. Top with potatoes; bake 3-5 minutes or until eggs are completely set. Let stand 5 minutes. Cut into wedges.

BREAKFAST PIZZA

I used to make this for my morning drivers when I worked at a pizza delivery place. And they just loved it! It's a quick and easy eye-opener that appeals to all ages.

—CATHY SHORTALL EASTON, MD

START TO FINISH: 25 MIN.
MAKES: 8 SLICES

- 1 **tube (13.8 ounces) refrigerated pizza crust**
- 2 **tablespoons olive oil, divided**
- 6 **eggs**
- 2 **tablespoons water**
- 1 **package (3 ounces) real bacon bits**
- 1 **cup (4 ounces) shredded Monterey Jack cheese**
- 1 **cup (4 ounces) shredded cheddar cheese**

1. Preheat oven to 400°. Unroll crust into a greased 15x10x1-in. baking pan; flatten dough and build up edges slightly. Brush with 1 tablespoon oil. Prick dough thoroughly with a fork. Bake the crust 7-8 minutes or until lightly browned.

2. Meanwhile, in a small bowl, whisk eggs and water. In a small skillet, heat remaining oil until hot. Add eggs; cook and stir over medium heat until eggs are completely set.

3. Spoon eggs over crust. Sprinkle with bacon and cheeses. Bake 5-7 minutes longer or until cheese is melted.

Cook to Cook

My boys love this kind of pizza. They like it when I spread a little white gravy over the crust before adding the other ingredients. Also, for a fun twist, you can press the dough into muffin tins, fill up with the ingredients, and bake as usual. Very yummy! **—CANMARRIN64**

SAUSAGE EGG BAKE

This satisfying egg dish is wonderful for any meal of the day. I fix it frequently for special occasions, too, because it's easy to prepare and really versatile. For a change, use spicier sausage or substitute a flavored cheese blend.

—**MOLLY SWALLOW** POCATELLO, ID

PREP: 10 MIN. • **BAKE:** 40 MIN.
MAKES: 12 SERVINGS

- 1 **pound bulk Italian sausage**
- 2 **cans (10¾ ounces each) condensed cream of potato soup, undiluted**
- 9 **eggs, lightly beaten**
- ¾ **cup 2% milk**
- ¼ **teaspoon pepper**
- 1 **cup (4 ounces) shredded cheddar cheese**

1. Preheat oven to 375°. In a large skillet, cook sausage over medium heat until no longer pink; drain. Stir in soup.
2. In a large bowl, whisk eggs, milk and pepper; stir in sausage mixture. Transfer to a lightly greased 2-qt. baking dish. Sprinkle with cheese.
3. Bake, uncovered, 40-45 minutes or until a knife inserted near the center comes out clean.

Cook to Cook

I made this for a potluck yesterday. It was gone in no time! I added some onions and mushrooms to it and used Mexican cheese blend and Monterey Jack. —**PSPMAGS**

BREAKFAST BISCUIT CUPS

The first time I made these biscuit cups, my husband and his assistant basketball coach came in as I was pulling them out of the oven. They loved them!

—**DEBRA CARLSON** COLUMBUS JUNCTION, IA

PREP: 30 MIN. • **BAKE:** 20 MIN.
MAKES: 8 SERVINGS

- ⅓ **pound bulk pork sausage**
- 1 **tablespoon all-purpose flour**
- ⅛ **teaspoon salt**
- ½ **teaspoon pepper, divided**
- ¾ **cup plus 1 tablespoon 2% milk, divided**
- ½ **cup frozen cubed hash brown potatoes, thawed**
- 1 **tablespoon butter**
- 2 **eggs**
- ⅛ **teaspoon garlic salt**
- 1 **can (16.3 ounces) large refrigerated flaky biscuits**
- ½ **cup shredded Colby-Monterey Jack cheese**

1. Preheat oven to 375°. In a large skillet, cook sausage over medium heat until no longer pink; drain. Stir in the flour, salt and ¼ teaspoon pepper until blended; gradually add ¾ cup milk. Bring to a boil; cook and stir 2 minutes or until thickened. Remove from heat and set aside.

2. In another large skillet over medium heat, cook potatoes in butter until tender. Whisk the eggs, garlic salt and remaining milk and pepper; add to skillet. Cook and stir until almost set.

3. Press each biscuit onto the bottom and up the sides of eight ungreased muffin cups. Spoon the egg mixture, half the cheese and sausage into cups; sprinkle with remaining cheese.

4. Bake 18-22 minutes or until golden brown. Cool 5 minutes; remove from pan. Serve warm.

FREEZE OPTION *Cool biscuit cups. Place on a waxed paper-lined baking sheet until firm. Transfer to a resealable plastic freezer bag and freeze up to 3 months. To use, microwave one frozen biscuit cup on high 50-60 seconds or until heated through.*

NOTES

BREAKFAST
FOR DINNER

FREEZE IT
BACON QUICHE

Light and fluffy, this scrumptious quiche is ideal for breakfast or brunch, but can also be served at dinnertime. Serve with a cluster of chilled grapes or other fresh fruit on the side.

—**COLLEEN BELBEY** WARWICK, RI

PREP: 15 MIN. • **BAKE:** 40 MIN. + STANDING
MAKES: 6 SERVINGS

- 1 **sheet refrigerated pie pastry**
- ¼ **cup sliced green onions**
- 1 **tablespoon butter**
- 6 **eggs**
- 1½ **cups heavy whipping cream**
- ¼ **cup unsweetened apple juice**
- 1 **pound sliced bacon, cooked and crumbled**
- ⅛ **teaspoon salt**
- ⅛ **teaspoon pepper**
- 2 **cups (8 ounces) shredded Swiss cheese**

1. Preheat oven to 350°. Line a 9-in. pie plate with pastry; trim and flute edges. Set aside. In a small skillet, saute green onions in butter until tender.
2. In a large bowl, whisk eggs, cream and juice. Stir in bacon, salt, pepper and green onions. Pour into pastry; sprinkle with cheese.

3. Bake 40-45 minutes or until a knife inserted near center comes out clean. Let stand 10 minutes before cutting.

FREEZE OPTION *Securely wrap individual portions of cooled quiche in plastic wrap and foil; freeze. To use, partially thaw in refrigerator overnight. Remove from refrigerator 30 minutes before baking. Preheat oven to 350°. Unwrap quiche; reheat in oven until heated through and a thermometer inserted in center reads 165°.*

HASH BROWN SAUSAGE BAKE

This is one of my son's favorites. Buttery hash browns form a mouthwatering crust for the yummy filling of sausage and cheese. It's sure to please at breakfast, brunch or even lunch.

—**VICKY DEMPSEY** LOUISVILLE, MS

PREP: 30 MIN. • **BAKE:** 40 MIN.
MAKES: 6-8 SERVINGS

- 1 **package (20 ounces) refrigerated shredded hash brown potatoes**
- ⅓ **cup butter, melted**
- 1 **teaspoon beef bouillon granules**
- 1 **pound bulk pork sausage**
- ⅓ **cup chopped onion**
- 1 **cup (8 ounces) 4% cottage cheese**
- 3 **eggs, lightly beaten**
- 4 **slices process American cheese, chopped**

1. Preheat oven to 350°. In a large bowl, combine the hash browns, butter and bouillon. Press onto the bottom and up the sides of a greased 10-in. pie plate. Bake 25-30 minutes or until edges are lightly browned.

2. Meanwhile, in a large skillet, cook sausage and onion over medium heat until meat is no longer pink; drain. In a large bowl, combine the sausage mixture, cottage cheese, eggs and American cheese.

3. Pour into crust. Bake at 350° for 40-45 minutes or until a knife inserted near the center comes out clean. Let stand 5 minutes before cutting.

Cook to Cook

I made this for Christmas, and it has become our favorite casserole! This is great anytime of day, not just breakfast. The only change I made is to swap out the American cheese for mild cheddar.
—ELISHAL

BREAKFAST
FOR DINNER

EGGS IN MUFFIN CUPS

My mother used to make these all the time for our family, and now I carry on the tradition with my own. The eggs are quick to put together, and I get ready for the day while they're in the oven. My children loved them even when they were toddlers.

—LISA WALDER URBANA, IL

START TO FINISH: 30 MIN.
MAKES: 6 SERVINGS (2 EACH)

- 12 **thin slices deli roast beef**
- 6 **slices process American cheese, quartered**
- 12 **eggs**

1. Preheat oven to 350°. Press one slice of beef onto the bottom and up the sides of each greased muffin cup, forming a shell. Arrange two cheese pieces in each shell. Break one egg into each cup.
2. Bake, uncovered, 20-25 minutes or until eggs are completely set.

NOTES

BREAKFAST WRAPS

We like quick and simple morning meals during the week, and these wraps are great when prepared ahead of time. It takes just a minute in the microwave to reheat them.

—BETTY KLEBERGER FLORISSANT, MO

START TO FINISH: 15 MIN.
MAKES: 4 SERVINGS

- 6 **eggs**
- 2 **tablespoons milk**
- ¼ **teaspoon pepper**
- 1 **tablespoon canola oil**
- 1 **cup (4 ounces) shredded cheddar cheese**
- ¾ **cup diced fully cooked ham**
- 4 **flour tortillas (8 inches), warmed**

1. In a small bowl, whisk the eggs, milk and pepper. In a large skillet, heat oil. Add egg mixture; cook and stir over medium heat until eggs are completely set. Stir in cheese and ham.

2. Spoon egg mixture down the center of each tortilla; roll up.

FREEZE OPTION *Wrap cooled egg wrap in plastic wrap and freeze in a resealable plastic bag for up to 1 month. To use, thaw in refrigerator overnight. Remove plastic wrap; wrap tortilla in a moist paper towel. Microwave on high for 30-60 seconds or until heated through. Serve immediately.*

Cook to Cook

These were an easy Saturday lunch that did not take a lot of time. I will keep this recipe in mind the next time I need to use up some eggs. **—KAYLEES**

TRUE BELGIAN WAFFLES

It was on a visit to my husband's relatives in Belgium that I was given this recipe. Back in the U.S., I served the waffles to his Belgian-born grandmother. She said they tasted just like home.

—**ROSE DELEMEESTER** ST. CHARLES, MI

START TO FINISH: 20 MIN.
MAKES: 10 WAFFLES (ABOUT 4½ INCHES)

- 2 **cups all-purpose flour**
- ¾ **cup sugar**
- 3½ **teaspoons baking powder**
- 2 **eggs, separated**
- 1½ **cups milk**
- 1 **cup butter, melted**
- 1 **teaspoon vanilla extract**
   Sliced fresh strawberries or syrup

1. In a bowl, combine flour, sugar and baking powder. In another bowl, lightly beat egg yolks. Add milk, butter and vanilla; mix well. Stir into the dry ingredients just until combined. Beat egg whites until stiff peaks form; fold into batter.

2. Bake in a preheated waffle iron according to manufacturer's directions until golden brown. Serve the waffles with strawberries or syrup.

Cook to Cook

This is the most ridiculously good waffle recipe I've tried to date. I halved the recipe but kept the full teaspoon of vanilla and they are marvelous! The texture is amazing, they came out nice and crispy and airy. Yes they're a little sweet, but I like that. I had them topped with more butter, syrup and strawberries, and they were fantastic. If you don't like them as sweet, simply reduce the sugar. This is my new permanent waffle recipe, I don't think I'll ever have the nerve to test another!

—**LROCKER5515**

BREAKFAST SCRAMBLE

One weekend morning, my husband and I were hungry for a breakfast without the traditional sausage or bacon. I reached for some ground beef and tossed in other ingredients as I went. This was the mouthwatering result.

—**MARY LILL** ROCK CAVE, WV

PREP: 10 MIN. • **COOK:** 45 MIN.
MAKES: 4-6 SERVINGS

- 1 **pound ground beef**
- 1 **medium onion, chopped**
- 3 **cups diced peeled potatoes**
- ½ **cup water**
  Salt and pepper to taste
- 1 **can (14½ ounces) diced tomatoes, undrained**
- 4 **eggs, lightly beaten**
- 4 **ounces process cheese (Velveeta), sliced**

1. In a large skillet, cook beef and onion over medium heat until meat is no longer pink; drain. Add potatoes, water, salt and pepper. Cover and simmer 20 minutes or until potatoes are tender.

2. Add tomatoes; cook 5 minutes. Pour eggs over mixture. Cook and stir until eggs are completely set. Top with the cheese. Cover and cook 1 minute or until the cheese is melted.

BANANA BLUEBERRY PANCAKES

This recipe is a favorite in our home. My kids don't even realize how healthy it is!

—**KELLY REINICKE** WISCONSIN RAPIDS, WI

PREP: 15 MIN. • **COOK:** 5 MIN./BATCH
MAKES: 14 PANCAKES

- 1 cup whole wheat flour
- ½ cup all-purpose flour
- 2 tablespoons sugar
- 2 teaspoons baking powder
- ½ teaspoon salt
- 1 egg, lightly beaten
- 1¼ cups fat-free milk
- 3 medium ripe bananas, mashed
- 1 teaspoon vanilla extract
- 1½ cups fresh or frozen blueberries
  Maple syrup, optional

1. In a large bowl, combine the flours, sugar, baking powder and salt. Mix the egg, milk, bananas and vanilla; stir into dry ingredients just until moistened.

2. Pour batter by ¼ cupfuls onto a hot griddle coated with cooking spray; sprinkle with blueberries. Turn when bubbles form on top; cook until second side is golden brown. Serve with syrup if desired.

NOTE *If using frozen blueberries, do not thaw.*

MUSHROOM QUICHE LORRAINE

Family and friends will delight in this savory quiche. Mushrooms and green onions bring fresh flavor, while cheese and bacon lend a touch of decadence.

—**MICHELLE FINCHER** LYMAN, SC

PREP: 15 MIN. • **BAKE:** 30 MIN.
MAKES: 6 SERVINGS

- 1 **unbaked pastry shell (9 inches)**
- 1 **cup sliced fresh mushrooms**
- ½ **cup chopped green onions**
- 2 **tablespoons butter**
- 4 **eggs**
- 1¼ **cups half-and-half cream**
- ⅛ **teaspoon pepper**
- 1 **cup (4 ounces) shredded Swiss cheese**
- 4 **bacon strips, cooked and crumbled**

1. Preheat oven to 450°. Line unpricked pastry shell with a double thickness of heavy-duty foil. Bake 8 minutes. Remove foil; bake 5 minutes longer. Remove from the oven; reduce heat to 375°.

2. Meanwhile, in a small skillet, saute mushrooms and onions in butter until tender. In a large bowl, beat the eggs, cream and pepper. Using a slotted spoon, transfer mushrooms and onions to egg mixture. Stir in cheese and bacon.

3. Pour into the crust. Cover edges loosely with foil. Bake 30-35 minutes or until a knife inserted near the center comes out clean. Let stand 5 minutes before cutting.

FREEZE OPTION *Securely wrap individual portions of cooled quiche in plastic wrap and foil; freeze. To use, partially thaw in refrigerator overnight. Remove from refrigerator 30 minutes before baking. Preheat oven to 375°. Unwrap quiche; reheat in oven until heated through and a thermometer inserted in center reads 165°.*

Cook to Cook

I used this recipe to make quiche for the first time for Mother's Day. I modified the recipe by adding zucchini, using cheddar instead of Swiss, and ham instead of bacon. I had to cook it longer than the recipe states, but it was worth it and turned out great! —**MRSHANNA**

BREAKFAST FOR DINNER

GREEN CHILI EGG PUFF

Green chilies add a touch of Southwest flavor to this fluffy egg dish. The cottage cheese offers nice texture, and people always adore the gooey Monterey Jack cheese melted throughout.

—**LAUREL LESLIE** SONORA, CA

PREP: 15 MIN. • **BAKE:** 35 MIN.
MAKES: 12 SERVINGS

- 10 **eggs**
- ½ **cup all-purpose flour**
- 1 **teaspoon baking powder**
- ½ **teaspoon salt**
- 4 **cups (16 ounces) shredded Monterey Jack cheese**
- 2 **cups (16 ounces) 4% cottage cheese**
- 1 **can (4 ounces) chopped green chilies**

1. Preheat oven to 350°. In a large bowl, beat eggs on medium-high speed 3 minutes or until light and lemon-colored. Combine flour, baking powder and salt; gradually add to eggs and mix well. Stir in the cheeses and chilies.
2. Pour into a greased 13x9-in. baking dish. Bake, uncovered, 35-40 minutes or until a knife inserted near the center comes out clean. Let stand 5 minutes before serving.

Cook to Cook

I have to admit, this was pretty amazing. However, I would make the following two changes: 1) The fat content is extremely high on this puff and there are easy ways to tone it down. Buy lower-milk fat cottage cheese and lower-milk fat Monterey cheese. This also significantly lowers the calorie count, while not affecting the protein count (which is one of the reasons I love this recipe.) 2) I didn't taste the green chilies at all and I am NOT a fan of spicy food. I used a 4- oz. can and next time will use closer to 6 oz. Note: This puff tastes amazing with salsa on top! :) —**AFAMOUSSTATUE**

NOTES

UPSIDE-DOWN BACON PANCAKE

Make a big impression when you present one family-size bacon pancake. The brown sugar adds sweetness that complements the salty bacon. If you can fit more bacon in the skillet and want to add more, go for it!

—**MINDIE HILTON** SUSANVILLE, CA

START TO FINISH: 30 MIN.
MAKES: 6 SERVINGS

- 6 **bacon strips, coarsely chopped**
- ¼ **cup packed brown sugar**
- 2 **cups complete buttermilk pancake mix**
- 1½ **cups water**
  Maple syrup and butter, optional

1. Preheat oven to 350°. In a large ovenproof skillet, cook bacon over medium heat until crisp. Using a slotted spoon, remove bacon to paper towels. Remove drippings, reserving 2 tablespoons. Return bacon to pan with reserved drippings; sprinkle with brown sugar.

2. In a small bowl, combine pancake mix and water just until moistened. Pour into pan.

3. Bake 18-20 minutes or until a toothpick inserted near the center comes out clean. Cool 10 minutes before inverting onto a serving plate. Serve warm with maple syrup and butter if desired.

BREAKFAST CREPES WITH BERRIES

After a long day of blackberry picking, I whipped up a sauce to dress up some crepes I had on hand. This speedy dish really hit the spot and tied everything together beautifully! The crepes make an elegant addition to any brunch, and the sauce is delectable over warm waffles, too.
—**JENNIFER WEISBRODT** OCONOMOWOC, WI

START TO FINISH: 20 MIN.
MAKES: 8 SERVINGS

- 1½ **cups fresh raspberries**
- 1½ **cups fresh blackberries**
- 1 **cup (8 ounces) sour cream**
- ½ **cup confectioners' sugar**
- 1 **carton (6 ounces) orange creme yogurt**
- 1 **tablespoon lime juice**
- 1½ **teaspoons grated lime peel**
- ½ **teaspoon vanilla extract**
- ⅛ **teaspoon salt**
- 8 **prepared crepes (9 inches)**

1. In a large bowl, combine raspberries and blackberries; set aside. In a small bowl, combine the sour cream and confectioners' sugar until smooth. Stir in yogurt, lime juice, lime peel, vanilla and salt.

2. Spread 2 tablespoons sour cream mixture over each crepe; top with about ⅓ cup berries. Roll up; drizzle with remaining sour cream mixture. Serve immediately.

SPECIAL BRUNCH BAKE

This eye-opener features buttermilk biscuits. If you don't have Canadian bacon, try it with turkey bacon or ham.

—NICKI WOODS SPRINGFIELD, MO

PREP: 10 MIN. • **BAKE:** 30 MIN.
MAKES: 12 SERVINGS

- 2 tubes (4 ounces each) refrigerated buttermilk biscuits
- 3 cartons (8 ounces each) egg substitute
- 7 ounces Canadian bacon, chopped
- 1 cup (4 ounces) shredded reduced-fat cheddar cheese
- 1 cup (4 ounces) shredded part-skim mozzarella cheese
- ½ cup chopped fresh mushrooms
- ½ cup finely chopped onion
- ¼ teaspoon pepper

1. Preheat oven to 350°. Arrange biscuits in a 13x9-in. baking dish coated with cooking spray. In a large bowl, combine remaining ingredients; pour over biscuits.

2. Bake, uncovered, 30-35 minutes or until a knife inserted near the center comes out clean.

Cook to Cook

Really tasty! My husband and I both agreed it would be great with some diced red bell pepper added in...will try that next time! **—SHELTON463**

NOTES

HAM 'N' EGG SANDWICH

Whenever the whole family gets together for a holiday or long weekend, they request this big breakfast sandwich. I can feed everyone by stacking our favorite breakfast fixings inside a loaf of French bread. Then I simply pop it in the oven to warm it up.

—**DEEDEE NEWTON** TORONTO, ON

PREP: 30 MIN. • **BAKE:** 15 MIN.
MAKES: 6-8 SERVINGS

- 1 **unsliced loaf (1 pound) French bread**
- 4 **tablespoons butter, softened, divided**
- 2 **tablespoons mayonnaise**
- 8 **thin slices deli ham**
- 1 **large tomato, sliced**
- 1 **small onion, thinly sliced**
- 8 **eggs, lightly beaten**
- 8 **slices cheddar cheese**

1. Preheat oven to 375°. Cut bread in half lengthwise; carefully hollow out top and bottom, leaving ½-in. shells (discard removed bread or save for another use). Spread 3 tablespoons butter and all of the mayonnaise inside bread shells. Line bottom bread shell with ham; top with tomato and onion.
2. In a large skillet, melt remaining butter; add eggs. Cook over medium heat, stirring occasionally until edges are almost set.
3. Spoon into bottom bread shell; top with cheese. Cover with bread top. Wrap in greased foil. Bake 15-20 minutes or until heated through. Cut into serving-size pieces.

NOTES

_____
_____
_____
_____
_____
_____

HAM AND SWISS OMELET

This easy omelet will be a snap to fix for breakfast or dinner.

—**AGNES WARD** STRATFORD, ON

START TO FINISH: 20 MIN.
MAKES: 1 SERVING

- 1 tablespoon butter
- 3 eggs
- 3 tablespoons water
- ⅛ teaspoon salt
- ⅛ teaspoon pepper
- ½ cup cubed fully cooked ham
- ¼ cup shredded Swiss cheese

1. In a small nonstick skillet, melt butter over medium-high heat. Whisk the eggs, water, salt and pepper. Add egg mixture to skillet (mixture should set immediately at edges).

2. As eggs set, push cooked edges toward the center, letting uncooked portion flow underneath. When the eggs are set, place ham on one side and sprinkle with cheese; fold other side over filling. Slide omelet onto a plate.

Cook to Cook

I'm a beginner cook and have never made an omelet before, so this helped out quite a bit on technique. Lots of different possible takes on the omelet.
—**N_COLE**

APPLE DUTCH BABY

This dish is a longtime family favorite for Christmas morning. It's light and airy, filled with eggs and juicy apples and delicious with bacon on the side.

—**TEENY MCCLOY** RED DEER, AB

PREP: 10 MIN. • **BAKE:** 35 MIN.
MAKES: 8 SERVINGS

- ¼ **cup butter, cubed**
- 3 **to 4 medium tart apples, peeled and sliced**
- ¼ **cup packed brown sugar**
- 1 **teaspoon ground cinnamon**
- 6 **eggs, separated**
- ⅔ **cup all-purpose flour**
- ⅓ **cup milk**
- 1 **teaspoon baking powder**
- ½ **teaspoon salt**
- ¼ **cup sugar**
  Confectioners' sugar, optional

1. Preheat oven to 400°. Place butter in a 13x9-in. baking dish. Heat 5-8 minutes or until melted. Stir in apples, brown sugar and cinnamon. Bake 15-18 minutes longer or until apples are tender.

2. Meanwhile, in a small bowl, whisk egg yolks, flour, milk, baking powder and salt until smooth. In a large bowl, beat egg whites on medium speed until soft peaks form. Gradually add sugar, 1 tablespoon at a time, beating on high until stiff peaks form.

3. Fold egg whites into egg yolk mixture. Spread over apples. Bake at 400° 12-15 minutes or until set and golden. If desired, sprinkle with confectioner's sugar.

8

DESSERTS IN A FLASH

Add a sweet note to any meal with these effortless treats.

DESSERTS IN A FLASH INDEX

Cook to Cook

Look for
THESE boxes
for helpful tidbits!

SALTINE TOFFEE BARK

Get ready for a new family favorite—like brittle, but even better. This sweet-and-salty treasure is great for munching, but also makes a thoughtful gift.

—**LAURA COX** BREWSTER, MA

START TO FINISH: 25 MIN.
MAKES: 2 LBS.

- 40 saltines
- 1 cup butter, cubed
- ¾ cup sugar
- ¾ cup creamy peanut butter
- 2 cups (12 ounces) semisweet chocolate chips
- 1 package (8 ounces) milk chocolate English toffee bits

1. Preheat oven to 350°. Line a 15x10x1-in. baking pan with heavy-duty foil. Arrange saltines in a single layer on foil; set aside.

2. In a large heavy saucepan over medium heat, melt butter. Stir in sugar. Bring to a boil; cook and stir 1-2 minutes or until sugar is dissolved. Pour evenly over crackers.

3. Bake 8-10 minutes or until bubbly. Immediately sprinkle with chocolate chips. Allow chips to soften for a few minutes, then spread over top. Sprinkle with toffee bits. Cool.

4. Cover and refrigerate 1 hour or until set. Break candy into pieces. Store in an airtight container.

MINI BROWNIE TREATS

I like to take these quick-and-easy treats to potlucks and family gatherings. They disappear so quickly!

—PAM KOKES NORTH LOUP, NE

PREP: 15 MIN. • **BAKE:** 20 MIN. + COOLING
MAKES: 4 DOZEN

- 1 **package fudge brownie mix (13-inch x 9-inch pan size)**
- 48 **striped or milk chocolate kisses**

1. Preheat oven to 350°. Prepare brownie mix according to package directions for fudgelike brownies. Fill paper-lined miniature muffin cups two-thirds full.

2. Bake 18-21 minutes or until a toothpick inserted near the center comes out clean.

3. Immediately top each with a chocolate kiss. Cool 10 minutes before removing from pans to wire racks to cool completely.

CHOCOLATE & PEANUT BUTTER PUDDING PIE WITH BANANAS

This pie was created in tribute to Elvis, who was my favorite entertainer, and to the town of Hershey, Pennsylvania, where I was born.

—PENNY HAWKINS MEBANE, NC

PREP: 30 MIN. + CHILLING
MAKES: 8 SERVINGS

- 1 **cup chocolate wafer crumbs (about 20 wafers)**
- ¼ **cup butter, melted**
- 2 **medium firm bananas**
- ¾ **cup creamy peanut butter**
- 2 **ounces semisweet chocolate, chopped**
- 2 **cups cold 2% milk**
- 2 **packages (3.4 ounces each) instant vanilla pudding mix**
- 2 **cups whipped topping, divided**
- 2 **tablespoons chopped salted peanuts**
  Peanut butter cups, optional

1. Preheat oven to 350°. In a small bowl, combine wafer crumbs and butter; press onto the bottom and up the sides of an ungreased 9-in. pie plate. Bake 8-10 minutes or until set. Cool completely on a wire rack.

2. Slice bananas; arrange on bottom of crust. In a microwave-safe bowl, combine peanut butter and chocolate; microwave on high 1 to 1½ minutes or until blended and smooth, stirring every 30 seconds. Spoon over bananas.

3. In a large bowl, whisk milk and pudding mix 2 minutes. Let stand 2 minutes or until soft-set. Fold in 1 cup whipped topping; spread over chocolate mixture. Pipe remaining whipped topping over edge.

Refrigerate, covered, at least 3 hours.
4. Sprinkle with peanuts just before serving. If desired, serve with cut-up peanut butter cups.

NOTE *Make this pie the night before you plan to serve it.*

Cook to Cook

I made this for our Sunday dinner with the neighbors. Everyone RAVED about it and there were NO leftovers. Incredible blend of chocolate, peanut butter and bananas! **—BILLLMUCK**

NOTES

TOFFEE PEANUT CLUSTERS

These are a favorite among all my family and friends. I can whip them together quickly, and the toffee adds a unique twist.

—JOY DULANEY HIGHLAND VILLAGE, TX

START TO FINISH: 30 MIN.
MAKES: 5 DOZEN

- 1½ **pounds milk chocolate candy coating, coarsely chopped**
- 1 **jar (16 ounces) dry roasted peanuts**
- 1 **package (8 ounces) milk chocolate English toffee bits**

1. In a microwave, melt candy coating; stir until smooth. Stir in peanuts and toffee bits.

2. Drop by rounded tablespoonfuls onto waxed paper-lined baking sheets. Let stand until set. Store in an airtight container.

Cook to Cook

This is so easy to make and so very delicious! I love the combination of toffee, salty peanuts and chocolate. Next time I'll add some dried fruit or something...there's a thousand different ways to make this simple but tasty recipe! **—SPARKLES033103**

PISTACHIO PUDDING PARFAITS

I made these parfaits for my children to take to school on St. Patrick's Day. Everyone loved them. The recipe can be made right before you eat it or a few hours beforehand.

—**ROSANNA FOWLER** BEDFORD, IN

START TO FINISH: 20 MIN.
MAKES: 8 SERVINGS

- 1 **package (8 ounces) cream cheese, softened**
- 1 **cup confectioners' sugar**
- 1½ **cups whipped topping**
- 1 **package (3.4 ounces) instant pistachio pudding mix**
- 10 **pecan shortbread cookies, coarsely crushed**

1. In a small bowl, beat cream cheese and confectioners' sugar. Fold in whipped topping; set aside. Prepare pudding according to package directions; set aside.

2. Spoon 1 tablespoon cookie crumbs into each of eight parfait glasses. Top with half the pudding and whipped topping mixture. Repeat layers. Top with remaining cookie crumbs. Chill until serving.

NOTES

_____

_____

_____

_____

_____

_____

CINNAMON-TOAST BLUEBERRY BAKES

What a treat! These little toast cups are brimming with juicy blueberries and so yummy served warm from the oven.

—**CLAIRE L. WATSON** CAPE GIRARDEU, MO

START TO FINISH: 30 MIN.
MAKES: 4 SERVINGS

- 6 **tablespoons butter, melted**
- 3 **tablespoons sugar**
- ½ **teaspoon ground cinnamon**
- 4 **slices whole wheat bread, cut into ½-inch cubes**
- 1 **cup fresh or frozen blueberries**
- ¼ **cup packed brown sugar**
- 2 **teaspoons lemon juice**

1. Preheat oven to 350°. In a large bowl, combine the butter, sugar and cinnamon. Add bread cubes; toss to coat. In a small bowl, combine the remaining ingredients; toss to coat.
2. Place half of bread mixture in four 8-oz. ramekins. Layer with blueberry mixture and remaining bread mixture.
3. Bake, uncovered, 15-20 minutes or until crisp and heated through.

Cook to Cook

I used 6 slices of honey wheat bread, decreased the butter to 4 tablespoons and increased the cinnamon to 1 teaspoon. I didn't have blueberries on hand, but had extra strawberries and blackberries so I used those. Top with whipped cream or a little powdered sugar and this is incredible!
—**COOKAHOLICWIFE**

FROSTY TOFFEE BITS PIE

To tame the heat of a steamy summer day or to finish off a wonderful meal any time, this cool and creamy dessert can't be beat.
—**LADONNA REED** PONCA CITY, OK

PREP: 10 MIN. + FREEZING
MAKES: 6-8 SERVINGS

- 1 **package (3 ounces) cream cheese, softened**
- 2 **tablespoons sugar**
- ½ **cup half-and-half cream**
- 1 **carton (8 ounces) frozen whipped topping, thawed**
- 1 **package (8 ounces) milk chocolate English toffee bits, divided**
- 1 **graham cracker crust (9 inches)**

1. In a large bowl, beat cream cheese and sugar until smooth. Beat in cream until blended. Fold in whipped topping and 1 cup toffee bits.

2. Spoon into crust; sprinkle with remaining toffee bits. Cover and freeze overnight. Remove from the freezer 10 minutes before serving.

NOTE *Make this pie the night before you plan to serve it.*

DESSERTS IN A FLASH

LEMON DELIGHT TRIFLE

I like to serve this lovely lemony treat in a trifle bowl. If you don't have one, a glass 13x9-in. dish will also work well.

—**KIM WALLACE** DENNISON, OH

PREP: 30 MIN. + CHILLING
MAKES: 12 SERVINGS (1 CUP EACH)

- 3½ **cups cold 2% milk**
- 2 **packages (3.4 ounces each) instant lemon pudding mix**
- 1 **package (8 ounces) cream cheese, softened**
- ½ **cup butter, softened**
- ½ **cup confectioners' sugar**
- 1 **carton (12 ounces) frozen whipped topping, thawed, divided**
- 1 **package (12 to 14 ounces) lemon cream-filled sandwich cookies, crushed**

1. In a large bowl, whisk milk and pudding mixes 2 minutes. Let stand 2 minutes or until soft-set.
2. In another bowl, beat the cream cheese, butter and confectioners' sugar until smooth. Gradually stir in pudding until blended.
3. Set aside ¼ cup each of whipped topping and crushed cookies for garnish. Fold remaining whipped topping into pudding mixture.
4. Place half the remaining cookies in a 3-qt. glass bowl; top with half the pudding mixture. Repeat the layers. Garnish with the reserved whipped topping and crushed cookies. Chill until serving.

NOTES

CHOCOLATE RASPBERRY SQUARES

Here's an elegant bar cookie that's loaded with wonderful flavors and very easy to assemble. A nice extra touch is to sprinkle the bars with confectioners' sugar.

—**MARILYN SWISHER** BERRIEN CENTER, MI

PREP: 15 MIN. • **BAKE:** 30 MIN. + COOLING
MAKES: 16 SERVINGS

- 1½ cups all-purpose flour
- 1½ cups quick-cooking or old-fashioned oats
- ½ cup sugar
- ½ cup packed brown sugar
- ¼ teaspoon salt
- 1 cup cold butter, cubed
- ¾ cup seedless raspberry jam
- 1 package (11½ ounces) semisweet chocolate chunks
- ¼ cup chopped walnuts

1. Preheat oven to 375°. In a large bowl, combine the flour, oats, sugars and salt. Cut in butter until mixture resembles coarse crumbs. Set aside 1 cup for topping. Press remaining crumb mixture into a greased 9-in.-square baking pan. Spread with jam; sprinkle with chocolate chunks

2. Combine walnuts and reserved crumb mixture; sprinkle over the top.

3. Bake 30-35 minutes or until lightly browned and bubbly. Cool on a wire rack. Cut into squares.

Cook to Cook

Really lovely recipe! I used hazelnuts for the walnuts, and it worked just as well! Top Tip? The jam/chocolate filling stays really runny for a long time after taking out of the oven. Once it's cooled a bit, put in fridge for an hour, then take out and cut with ease! Also, line your tin with baking parchment long enough to be able to lift the bars out once they've cooled a bit. This never lasts long in our house! —**WELSHIES GIRL**

CHOCOLATE MINT WAFERS

I created these melt-in-your-mouth thin mints for a cookie exchange, and everyone raved about them. To switch up the flavor, try using different extracts instead of peppermint.

—**MICHELLE KESTER** CLEVELAND, OH

PREP: 20 MIN. + STANDING
MAKES: ABOUT 1½ DOZEN

- **4 ounces dark chocolate candy coating**
- **⅛ to ¼ teaspoon peppermint extract**
- **18 to 24 vanilla wafers**

1. Place candy coating and extract in a microwave-safe bowl. Microwave, uncovered, on high 30-60 seconds or until smooth, stirring every 15 seconds.
2. Dip vanilla wafers in coating; allow excess to drip off. Place on waxed paper; let stand until set. Store in an airtight container.

NOTE *This recipe was tested in a 1,100-watt microwave.*

Cook to Cook

We have used this recipe in our family for a number of years. Instead of vanilla wafers, we use Ritz crackers. They taste like the famous mint cookies sold by the Girl Scouts and look like them too.
—**JUDYMARIE67**

MACADAMIA KEY LIME PIE

I make Key lime pie at least four times a month during summer, it's that refreshing! This shortbread crust adds a wonderful touch of richness.

—BRYNN LEMAIRE GUEYDAN, LA

PREP: 20 MIN. + CHILLING
MAKES: 8 SERVINGS

- 1 cup crushed shortbread cookies
- ½ cup finely chopped macadamia nuts
- ¼ cup sugar
- ⅓ cup butter, melted

FILLING

- 1 package (8 ounces) cream cheese, softened
- 1 can (14 ounces) sweetened condensed milk
- ½ cup Key lime juice or lime juice
- 1 cup heavy whipping cream
- ¼ cup coarsely chopped macadamia nuts

1. In a small bowl, mix cookie crumbs, macadamia nuts and sugar; stir in butter. Press onto bottom and up sides of a greased 9-in. pie plate. Refrigerate 30 minutes.

2. In a large bowl, beat cream cheese until smooth. Beat in milk and lime juice until blended. Transfer to crust. Refrigerate, covered, at least 4 hours.

3. In a small bowl, beat cream until soft peaks form; spoon or pipe onto pie. Top with macadamia nuts.

NO-COOK COCONUT PIE

A quick meal doesn't have to go without dessert. Just try my creamy No-Cook Coconut Pie and see what you can do!

—JEANETTE FUEHRING CONCORDIA, MO

START TO FINISH: 15 MIN.
MAKES: 6-8 SERVINGS

- 2 **packages (3.4 ounces each) instant vanilla pudding mix**
- 2¾ **cups cold 2% milk**
- 1 **teaspoon coconut extract**
- 1 **carton (8 ounces) frozen whipped topping, thawed**
- ½ **cup flaked coconut**
- 1 **graham cracker crust (9 inches) Toasted coconut**

1. In a large bowl, whisk the pudding mixes, milk and extract 2 minutes. Fold in whipped topping and coconut.

2. Pour into the crust. Sprinkle with toasted coconut. Chill until serving.

CHOCOLATE PEANUT BUTTER CRISP BARS

Invite the kids to roll up their sleeves and help make these crunchy, chocolaty bars. They're so easy and will surely satisfy anyone's sweet tooth.

—**KATHY MITCHELL** BROOKFIELD, WI

PREP: 25 MIN. **COOK:** 10 MIN. + STANDING
MAKES: 15 SERVINGS

- 1½ cups graham cracker crumbs
- 1 cup sugar
- ¾ cup packed brown sugar
- ¾ cup butter, cubed
- ⅓ cup 2% milk
- 2 sleeves butter-flavored crackers (about 80 crackers)
- 1 cup butterscotch chips
- 1 cup (6 ounces) semisweet chocolate chips
- ¾ cup creamy peanut butter

1. In a saucepan, combine the cracker crumbs, sugars, butter and milk. Bring to a boil, stirring constantly; cook and stir 5 minutes longer.

2. Place a single layer of crackers in a greased 13x9-in. dish; top with half of crumb mixture. Repeat layers. Top with remaining crackers.

3. In a small saucepan, combine the butterscotch chips, chocolate chips and peanut butter. Cook and stir until smooth. Pour over crackers. Let stand until set.

NOTE *This recipe was tested with Keebler Town House crackers.*

Cook to Cook

Loved, loved loved! I will definitely make these again. Love the sweet/salty/crunchy result, and they aren't sickeningly sweet. I used round crackers, but will probably use club crackers next time. I decreased the butterscotch chips to ¾ cup and increased the chocolate chips to 1¼ cups, because I don't like too strong a butterscotch flavor. And I used crunchy peanut butter, since that's what I had on hand. —**CONSHANTY**

NOTES

QUICK CHERRY TURNOVERS

Refrigerated crescent rolls let you make these fruit-filled pastries in a hurry. My family loves these turnovers for breakfast, but they're so delicious that they'd be welcome any time of day at all. Feel free to experiment with other pie fillings, too.

—ELLEEN OBERRUETER DANBURY, IA

START TO FINISH: 20 MIN.
MAKES: 4 SERVINGS

- 1 tube (8 ounces) refrigerated crescent rolls
- 1 cup cherry pie filling
- ½ cup confectioners' sugar
- 1 to 2 tablespoons milk

1. Preheat oven to 375°. Unroll crescent dough and separate into four rectangles; place on an ungreased baking sheet. Press perforations to seal. Place ¼ cup pie filling on one half of each rectangle. Fold dough over filling; pinch edges to seal.
2. Bake 10-12 minutes or until golden.
3. Place confectioners' sugar in a small bowl; stir in enough milk to achieve a drizzling consistency. Drizzle over turnovers. Serve warm.

PEANUT BUTTER S'MORES

I turn to this recipe when I need something fun and easy for dessert. It's a decadent take on classic campfire s'mores.

—**LILY JULOW** LAWRENCEVILLE, GA

START TO FINISH: 10 MIN.
MAKES: 4 SERVINGS

- **8 large chocolate chip cookies**
- **4 teaspoons hot fudge ice cream topping**
- **4 large marshmallows**
- **4 peanut butter cups**

1. Spread the bottoms of four cookies with fudge topping.

2. Using a long-handled fork, grill marshmallows 6 in. from medium-hot heat until golden brown, turning occasionally. Carefully place a marshmallow and a peanut butter cup on each fudge-topped cookie; top with remaining cookies. Serve immediately.

DESSERTS IN A FLASH

SWEET-TART RHUBARB CREPES

This recipe's name speaks to the well-balanced flavors of tart rhubarb and sweet orange. It's an elegant, fabulous, unique kind of dessert!

—**BETSY KING** DULUTH, MN

START TO FINISH: 30 MIN.
MAKES: 8 SERVINGS

- 5 **cups finely chopped fresh or frozen rhubarb, thawed**
- ¾ **cup sugar**
- 2 **tablespoons all-purpose flour**
- 2 **tablespoons orange juice**
- 1 **tablespoon butter**
- 1 **teaspoon grated orange peel**
- 16 **prepared crepes (9 inches)**
  Confectioners' sugar and additional grated orange peel, optional

1. In a large saucepan, combine the first five ingredients. Cook, stirring occasionally, over medium heat 15-18 minutes or until tender. Remove from heat; stir in orange peel.
2. Spread 2 tablespoons of filling down the center of each crepe; roll up.

Sprinkle with confectioners' sugar and additional orange peel if desired.

NOTE *If using frozen rhubarb, measure rhubarb while still frozen, then thaw completely. Drain in a colander, but do not press liquid out.*

Cook to Cook

Instead of granulated sugar I used ½ cup brown sugar; these still turned out very well. —**JOYFULCOOKING**

PEANUT BUTTER PIE

This is one dessert that's a real family favorite, so I make it every chance I get. When my youngest son wanted pies around his wedding cake, this was one of the few he requested—and it's so simple!

—LEE DENEAU LANSING, MI

START TO FINISH: 10 MIN.
MAKES: 8 SERVINGS

- ¾ cup peanut butter
- 4 ounces cream cheese, softened
- 1 cup confectioners' sugar
- 1 carton (8 ounces) frozen whipped topping, thawed
- 1 graham cracker crust (9 inches)
  Salted chopped peanuts

In a large bowl, beat the peanut butter, cream cheese and confectioners' sugar until smooth. Fold in the whipped topping; pour into prepared crust. Sprinkle with nuts. Chill until serving.

NOTES

_____
_____
_____
_____
_____
_____
_____
_____
_____

APPLE NACHOS

It doesn't get much easier than whipping together this colorful, crisp treat. These nacho look-alikes will delight young guests!

—**RAEANN GNATKOWSKI** CARROLLTON, MI

START TO FINISH: 20 MIN.
MAKES: 24 SERVINGS

- 36 **caramels**
- 1 **tablespoon water**
- 30 **large marshmallows**
- ⅓ **cup butter, cubed**
- 4 **medium tart apples, peeled and cut into ¼-inch slices**
- ⅓ **cup chopped dry roasted peanuts**
- ⅓ **cup miniature semisweet chocolate chips**
- 3 **tablespoons Halloween sprinkles or sprinkles of your choice**

1. In a microwave, melt caramels with water; stir until smooth.

2. Meanwhile, in a large saucepan, melt the marshmallows and butter. Arrange apple slices on a large platter. Drizzle with the caramel; top with the marshmallow mixture. Sprinkle with peanuts, chocolate chips and sprinkles. Serve immediately.

BANANAS FOSTER SUNDAES

I have wonderful memories of eating Bananas Foster in New Orleans, and since I am a dietitian, I wanted to find a healthier version. I combined the best of two recipes and added my own tweaks to create this Southern treat.

—**LISA VARNER** EL PASO, TX

START TO FINISH: 15 MIN.
MAKES: 6 SERVINGS

- 1 **tablespoon butter**
- 3 **tablespoons brown sugar**
- 1 **tablespoon orange juice**
- ¼ **teaspoon ground cinnamon**
- ¼ **teaspoon ground nutmeg**
- 3 **large firm bananas, sliced**
- 2 **tablespoons chopped pecans, toasted**
- ½ **teaspoon rum extract**
- 3 **cups reduced-fat vanilla ice cream**

1. In a large nonstick skillet, melt butter over medium-low heat. Stir in brown sugar, orange juice, cinnamon and nutmeg until blended.

2. Add the bananas and pecans; cook, stirring gently, 2-3 minutes or until bananas are glazed and slightly softened. Remove from heat; stir in the extract. Serve with ice cream.

Cook to Cook

I substituted 1 teaspoon of rum for the rum extract because I didn't have it in the house. We also used light ice cream, so I hope that compensated for the extra calories! —**PBROW68**

GOLDEN APPLE SNACK CAKE

This moist, old-fashioned cake is hard to beat, especially warmed up and finished off with a dollop of whipped topping.

—**CARRIE GRAVOT** BELLEVILLE, IL

PREP: 15 MIN. • **BAKE:** 35 MIN. + COOLING
MAKES: 9 SERVINGS

- ½ cup butter, softened
- 1 cup sugar
- 1 egg
- 1 cup all-purpose flour
- ½ teaspoon baking soda
- ½ teaspoon ground cinnamon
- 2½ cups chopped peeled tart apples
- ½ cup chopped pecans

1. Preheat oven to 350°. In a large bowl, cream butter and sugar until light and fluffy. Add egg. Combine the flour, baking soda and cinnamon; gradually beat into the creamed mixture. Fold in apples and pecans.

2. Transfer to a greased 9-in.-square baking pan. Bake 32-38 minutes or until a toothpick inserted near center comes out clean. Cool on a wire rack.

NOTES

CHOCOLATE CHEESECAKE PIE

Guests are always delighted with this rich pie. I sometimes top it with raspberry or cherry pie filling.

—SANDY SCHWARTZ BROOKLYN, NY

START TO FINISH: 30 MIN.
MAKES: 8 SERVINGS

- 1 package (8 ounces) cream cheese, softened
- ¼ cup butter, softened
- ⅓ cup sugar
- 1½ teaspoons vanilla extract
- 1½ cups milk chocolate chips, melted and cooled
- 1 carton (8 ounces) frozen whipped topping, thawed
- 1 graham cracker crust (9 inches)
  Chocolate curls, optional

In a large bowl, beat cream cheese, butter, sugar and vanilla until smooth. Beat in cooled chocolate. Fold in whipped topping. Spoon into crust. Refrigerate until serving. Decorate with chocolate curls as desired.

Cook to Cook

This pie is so delicious and easy to make. I made whipped cream to add to it and put on top. Everyone loved it. Will make again. —DARLENAM

Cook to Cook

My husband made this and it was WONDERFUL! The kids loved it, too. If you were to add chocolate, it would be like eating a banana split. We will definitely be having this again!
—JROLECHOW

STRAWBERRY-BANANA ANGEL TORTE

This pretty cake is the perfect ending to a light summer meal.

—**MILLIE VICKERY** LENA, IL

START TO FINISH: 20 MIN.
MAKES: 8-10 SERVINGS

- 1 prepared angel food cake (8 to 10 ounces)
- ½ cup sour cream
- ¼ cup sugar
- ¼ cup pureed fresh strawberries
- ¾ cup sliced ripe bananas
- ½ cup sliced fresh strawberries
- 1 cup heavy whipping cream, whipped
  Halved fresh strawberries

1. Split cake horizontally into three layers; place bottom layer on a serving plate. In a large bowl, combine the sour cream, sugar and pureed strawberries; fold in bananas and sliced strawberries. Fold in whipped cream.

2. Spread a third of the filling between each layer; spread the remaining filling over the top. Cover and refrigerate until serving. Garnish with the halved strawberries.

MICROWAVE CHERRY CRISP

Here's a crisp that uses a time-saving method to produce a treat with real old-fashioned flavor. It tastes just like the old-time crisps —with half the fuss!

—**DEBRA MORELLO** EDWARDS, CA

START TO FINISH: 20 MIN.
MAKES: 4 SERVINGS

- 1 **can (21 ounces) cherry pie filling**
- ¾ **cup packed brown sugar**
- ⅔ **cup quick-cooking oats**
- ⅓ **cup all-purpose flour**
- ¼ **cup butter, cubed**
  Vanilla ice cream, optional

1. Spoon pie filling into a greased 9-in. pie plate. In a small bowl, mix brown sugar, oats and flour; cut in butter until crumbly. Sprinkle over filling.
2. Microwave, uncovered, on high 7-9 minutes or until hot. If desired, serve warm with ice cream.

NOTE *This recipe was tested in a 1,100-watt microwave.*

DESSERTS
IN A FLASH

327

BERRY CHEESECAKE PARFAITS

I can whip up this dessert in no time. Impressive and delicious, it seems to offer just the right touch after a full meal. We also enjoy it as a great midnight snack.
—**JOYCE MART** WICHITA, KS

START TO FINISH: 10 MIN.
MAKES: 4 SERVINGS

- 1 **package (8 ounces) cream cheese, softened**
- 2 **to 4 tablespoons sugar**
- ½ **cup vanilla yogurt**
- 2 **cups fresh raspberries or berries of your choice**
- ½ **cup graham cracker crumbs (8 squares)**

1. In a large bowl, beat cream cheese and sugar until smooth. Stir in yogurt.
2. In four dessert glasses or bowls, alternate layers of berries, cream cheese mixture and cracker crumbs. Serve immediately or refrigerate up to 8 hours.

Cook to Cook

I made this using crumbled vanilla wafers, instead of the graham crackers, and blackberries. And it was delicious and easy! My family requests this on a regular basis! —SULYNN051467

PEACH CRISP DELIGHT

Crisps are a dessert that I really enjoy. Rice Chex make this one unique, while peaches and brown sugar provide loads of classic appeal. Best of all, it takes less than 30 minutes from start to finish!

—**TRACY GOLDER** BLOOMSBURG, PA

START TO FINISH: 25 MIN.
MAKES: 6 SERVINGS

- **2 cans (15 ounces each) sliced peaches, drained**
- **2 cups Rice Chex, crushed**
- **⅓ cup packed brown sugar**
- **¼ cup all-purpose flour**
- **3 tablespoons cold butter**
  Whipped topping or ice cream, optional

1. Preheat oven to 375°. Place peaches in a greased 8-in.-square baking dish. In a small bowl, combine the cereal, brown sugar and flour; cut in butter until mixture resembles coarse crumbs. Sprinkle over peaches.

2. Bake, uncovered, 15-20 minutes or until the topping is golden brown. Serve warm.

NOTES

NO-BAKE COOKIE BALLS

These quick bites are great when you're short on time—and you don't even have to turn on the oven. I like to make them a day or two ahead to allow the flavors to blend.
—**CARMELETTA DAILEY** WINFIELD, TX

START TO FINISH: 25 MIN.
MAKES: 5 DOZEN

- 1 cup (6 ounces) semisweet chocolate chips
- 3 cups confectioners' sugar
- 1¾ cups crushed vanilla wafers (about 55 wafers)
- 1 cup chopped walnuts, toasted
- ⅓ cup orange juice
- 3 tablespoons light corn syrup
  Additional confectioners' sugar

1. In a large microwave-safe bowl, melt the chocolate chips; stir until smooth. Stir in confectioners' sugar, vanilla wafers, walnuts, orange juice and corn syrup.
2. Shape into 1-in. balls; roll in additional confectioners' sugar. Store in an airtight container.

Cook to Cook

Finely chop the walnuts, and instead of orange juice, add ⅓ cup rum or bourbon! Yummy! —**SEEKER OF KNOWLEDGE**

NOTES

_____
_____
_____
_____
_____
_____

SHORTCUT STRAWBERRY-VANILLA DESSERT

My no-fuss treat is just scrumptious. It's loaded with fresh strawberries and a creamy pudding topping. Make sure you make plenty—it disappears quickly!

—CHRISTINE JOHNSON RICETOWN, KY

PREP: 15 MIN. + STANDING
MAKES: 7 SERVINGS

- 2 **cups fresh strawberries, sliced**
- 1 **teaspoon sugar**
- 1½ **cups cold 2% milk**
- 1 **package (3.4 ounces) instant vanilla pudding mix**
- 2 **cups whipped topping, divided**
- 1 **loaf (10-¾ ounces) frozen pound cake, thawed**

1. In a small bowl, mix strawberries and sugar; let stand 30 minutes.
2. Meanwhile, in a large bowl, whisk milk and pudding mix 2 minutes. Let stand 2 minutes or until soft-set. Fold in 1 cup whipped topping and set aside.
3. Cut cake into 14 slices. Layer seven cake slices with 2 tablespoons of the strawberries, ⅓ cup pudding mixture and another cake slice. Top with the remaining strawberries and the whipped topping.

NOTE *While the strawberries are standing, make the pudding mixture and slice the cake. Assemble the dessert right before serving.*

Cook to Cook

I had this at a friend's house and found it to be great. I got the recipe from her and have sent it on to others. I make it often. It's so easy! I think that I'll add chopped walnuts some of the time. It'll be especially nice in the summer, when temps get to be above 100 degrees and you can just pop it into the microwave!
—CALCITE

EASY APPLE CRISP

If you want a perfect ending to a hearty meal, turn to my apple crisp. It's ideal in fall, when it seems that everyone has a bag of fresh apples to give away!
—**TERRI WETZEL** ROSEBURG, OR

START TO FINISH: 20 MIN.
MAKES: 6 SERVINGS

- 4 **medium tart apples, peeled and thinly sliced**
- ⅓ **cup all-purpose flour, divided**
- ¼ **cup sugar**
- 2 **teaspoons lemon juice**
- ¾ **teaspoon ground cinnamon, divided**
- ⅔ **cup old-fashioned oats**
- ½ **cup packed brown sugar**
- 3 **tablespoons cold butter**
  Vanilla ice cream, optional

1. In a large bowl, combine the apples, 1 tablespoon flour, sugar, lemon juice and ¼ teaspoon cinnamon. Pour into a greased microwave-safe 9-in. deep-dish pie plate.
2. In a small bowl, combine the oats, brown sugar and remaining flour and cinnamon. Cut in butter until crumbly; sprinkle over apple mixture.
3. Cover with waxed paper. Microwave on high 5-7 minutes or until apples are tender. Serve with ice cream if desired.

NOTE *This recipe was tested in a 1,100-watt microwave.*

LEMON BURST TARTLETS

You'll love the taste of raspberry and lemon and in these bites. They're perfect for a party or as a simple dessert. The flavors complement each other so well that I'll bet you can't stop at just one!

—**PAM JAVOR** NORTH HUNTINGDON, PA

START TO FINISH: 20 MIN.
MAKES: 2½ DOZEN

- 1 **jar (10 ounces) lemon curd**
- 1 **carton (8 ounces) frozen whipped topping, thawed**
- 5 **to 6 drops yellow food coloring, optional**
- ⅔ **cup raspberry cake and pastry filling**
- 2 **packages (1.9 ounces each) frozen miniature phyllo tart shells**
- 30 **fresh raspberries**

1. In a large bowl, mix the lemon curd, whipped topping and food coloring, if desired, until smooth.

2. Spoon 1 teaspoon raspberry filling into each tart shell. Pipe or spoon the lemon mixture over filling. Garnish each with a raspberry. Store in the refrigerator.

NOTE *This recipe was tested with Solo brand cake and pastry filling. Look for it in the baking aisle.*

GRILLED PEACHES 'N' BERRIES

Highlight the natural sweetness of peak summertime fruit with brown sugar, butter and a squeeze of lemon juice. Foil packets make this a go-anywhere dessert.
—**SHARON BICKETT** CHESTER, SC

START TO FINISH: 30 MIN.
MAKES: 3 SERVINGS

- 3 **medium ripe peaches, halved and pitted**
- 1 **cup fresh blueberries**
- 2 **tablespoons brown sugar**
- 2 **tablespoons butter**
- 1 **tablespoon lemon juice**

1. Place two peach halves, cut side up, on each of three double thicknesses of heavy-duty foil (12 in. square). Top with blueberries, brown sugar, butter and lemon juice. Fold foil around mixture and seal tightly.
2. Grill, covered, over medium-low heat 18-20 minutes or until tender. Open the foil packet carefully to allow steam to escape.

NOTES
_____
_____
_____
_____
_____
_____
_____
_____
_____

BLACK & WHITE CEREAL TREATS

At 7 years old, my daughter asked to make a sweet treat for her school bake sale that everyone would rave about for years to come. While making Rice Krispies Treats, she had the brilliant idea of adding Oreo cookies to the mix. Now 24, she still asks for these on occasion; they're that good!

—TAMMY PHOENIX AVA, IL

PREP: 10 MIN. • **COOK:** 10 MIN. + COOLING
MAKES: 2 DOZEN

- ¼ cup butter, cubed
- 8 cups miniature marshmallows
- 6 cups Rice Krispies
- 2½ cups chopped double-stuffed Oreo cookies (about 16), divided
- 1⅓ cups white baking chips, melted

1. In a Dutch oven, melt butter over medium heat. Add marshmallows; cook and stir until melted. Remove from heat. Stir in cereal and 2 cups of Oreos. Press into a greased 13x9-in. baking pan.

2. Spread melted baking chips over the top; sprinkle with remaining Oreos, pressing gently to adhere. Cool to room temperature. Cut into bars.

Cook to Cook

I made these this morning to bring to a party this afternoon. I snuck a bite while slicing them up, so I can attest that they are delicious! I only used ⅔ cup of white chocolate chips—by far enough. I tinted the white chocolate with a drop or two of yellow food coloring, as I am trying for a Spring look. At first I wondered if the chocolate drizzle was really necessary. It is, because it makes the ½ cup of chopped Oreos that you sprinkle on top stay in place. I might try a milk or dark chocolate drizzle next time (which would certainly go with the black-and-white idea). I can see that these treats would be very popular at a bake sale. —MURPHYNJ

HAZELNUT CHOCOLATE MOUSSE

I love creamy chocolate, and this mousse takes just minutes to make. That means I can surprise my family with this dessert whenever I want. It is also good using chocolate fudge-flavored pudding mix. Feel free to add toppings of your choice.

—**KARLA KROHN** MADISON, WI

START TO FINISH: 10 MIN.
MAKES: 6 SERVINGS

- 1¾ **cups cold 2% milk**
- 1 **package (3.9 ounces) instant chocolate pudding mix**
- ½ **cup Nutella**
- 1¾ **cups whipped topping**
  Additional whipped topping

1. Whisk the milk and pudding mix in a large bowl 2 minutes. Let stand 2 minutes or until soft set. Whisk in the Nutella until smooth. Fold in the whipped topping.

2. Spoon into six dessert dishes. Chill until serving. Garnish servings with additional whipped topping.

Cook to Cook

My kids love chocolate just as much as I do, so when I saw this recipe I had to try it. Oh my goodness, it was good, easy to make and ready when dinner was over!
—**EFWYNNE**

9

JAZZ IT UP

Check out these easy ways to enhance salads, soups and side dishes.

4

14

When you're in a rush to put a meal on the table, the main dish gets most of your attention. Now you can add some pizzazz to basic side dishes with the suggestions that follow. Best of all, they take only a few minutes!

BREADS

1. Honey Butter
Beat ¼ cup softened butter and 1 to 2 tablespoons honey until blended. Serve with corn bread, biscuits or warm muffins.

2. Parmesan Refrigerated Biscuits
For 1 tube (10 oz.) refrigerated biscuits, mix ¼ cup melted butter with ¼ cup grated Parmesan cheese. Dip biscuits into butter mixture; bake as package directs.

3. Dill Biscuit Bites
For 1 tube (10 oz.) refrigerated biscuits, mix ¼ cup melted butter,

1 tablespoon minced onion and 1 teaspoon dill weed. Cut biscuits lengthwise in half; toss in butter mixture. Bake as package directs.

4. Poppy Seed Monkey Bread
Preheat oven to 400°. Mix ⅓ cup melted butter, 1 minced garlic clove, 1 teaspoon dried minced onion and 1 teaspoon poppy seeds. Separate biscuits from 2 tubes (12 oz. each) refrigerated biscuits. Dip biscuits in butter mixture; place in a greased 10-in. fluted tube pan. Bake 14-18 minutes until golden brown. Cool 5 minutes; invert from the pan and serve warm.

5. Herbed Monkey Bread
Preheat oven to 400°. Mix ⅓ cup melted butter, 1 minced garlic clove, 2 teaspoons dried parsley flakes, 1 teaspoon minced chives, ½ teaspoon dried basil and ½ teaspoon dried oregano. Separate biscuits from 2 tubes (12 oz. each) refrigerated biscuits. Dip biscuits in butter mixture; place in a greased 10-in. fluted tube pan. Bake 14-18 minutes until golden brown. Cool 5 minutes; invert from pan and serve warm.

6. Mini Focaccia
Preheat oven to 375°. Remove dough from 1 tube (11 oz.) refrigerated

breadsticks; cut into eight slices. Place on greased baking sheets; press each into a 4½-in. round. Brush with 2 teaspoons olive oil. Sprinkle with 1 teaspoon Italian seasoning and 2 tablespoons Parmesan cheese. Bake 10-15 minutes or until golden brown.

7. Buttery Parmesan Garlic Bread

Preheat oven to 400°. Mix ¼ cup softened butter, 2 tablespoons grated Parmesan cheese and 1 teaspoon garlic powder. Cut 1 loaf (8 oz.) French bread lengthwise in half. Spread butter mixture over cut sides of bread. Place on an ungreased baking sheet. Bake 10-12 minutes or until golden brown.

8. Oregano-Swiss Slices

Preheat oven to 400°. Mix 1 cup shredded Swiss cheese, 3 tablespoons mayonnaise, 1 tablespoon grated onion, 1½ teaspoons cider vinegar and ½ teaspoon dried oregano. Cut 1 loaf (8 oz.) French bread lengthwise in half. Spread cheese mixture over cut sides of bread. Place on an ungreased baking sheet. Bake 8-10 minutes or until cheese is melted and lightly browned.

NOODLES/PASTA

9. Buttered Italian Noodles

Mix 2 tablespoons melted butter, 2 tablespoons grated Parmesan cheese, 1 teaspoon dried parsley flakes, ¼ teaspoon salt, ¼ teaspoon garlic powder and ⅛ teaspoon pepper. Toss the seasoned butter with hot cooked noodles.

10. Poppy Seed Noodles

Add 1 tablespoon butter, 3 chopped green onions, 1½ teaspoons poppy seeds, ¼ teaspoon garlic salt and ¼ teaspoon pepper to 8 oz. of hot cooked noodles; stir until butter is melted. Stir in 1 cup sour cream.

11. Lemon Feta Pasta

In a large skillet, saute 2 minced garlic cloves in 2 tablespoons olive oil 1 minute. Stir in 8 oz. hot cooked pasta. Add 1 package (4 oz.) crumbled feta, 2 teaspoons grated lemon peel, ½ teaspoon dried oregano, ½ teaspoon salt and ½ teaspoon pepper; toss to coat.

12. Garlic Oil for Pasta

In a large skillet, saute 2 minced garlic cloves in ⅓ cup olive oil. Stir in 1 jar (4½ oz.) sliced mushrooms, ¼ cup sliced ripe olives, ¾ teaspoon dried basil, ¾ teaspoon dried parsley flakes, ¼ teaspoon pepper and ⅛ teaspoon garlic salt. Cook for 5 minutes. Pour over 8 oz. hot cooked pasta or noodles; toss to coat. Sprinkle with Parmesan cheese.

Last-Minute Pasta Touches

- Crumbled cooked bacon
- Fresh herbs
- Chopped fresh parsley and butter
- Pesto
- Jarred sliced roasted red peppers
- Oil-packed sun-dried tomatoes

POTATOES

13. Ranch Fries

Sprinkle 1 package (26 oz.) frozen French-fried potatoes with 2 tablespoons dried ranch dip mix. Bake as directed.

14. Cheese Fries

In a small saucepan, mix 1 can (10¾ oz.) undiluted condensed cheddar cheese soup, ¼ cup milk, ½ teaspoon garlic powder and ¼ teaspoon onion powder; heat through. Drizzle over cooked fries; sprinkle with paprika.

JAZZ IT UP

15. Herbed Steak Fries

Preheat oven to 450°. Toss 4 cups frozen steak fries with 1 tablespoon olive oil, 1½ teaspoons dried basil, 1½ teaspoons dried parsley flakes, ¼ teaspoon garlic salt and ¼ teaspoon seasoned salt. Arrange fries in a single layer in a greased 15x10x1-in. baking pan. Bake for 15-20 minutes or until lightly browned. Sprinkle with ¼ cup grated Romano cheese.

16. Lemon-Garlic Boiled Potatoes

In a small skillet, saute 2 minced garlic cloves in 2 tablespoons oil for 1 minute. Toss with 1 pound boiled potatoes. Add ¼ cup grated Parmesan cheese, 2 tablespoons lemon juice, ¼ teaspoon salt and ¼ teaspoon pepper. Toss to coat.

Last-Minute Potato Touches
- Crumbled cooked bacon
- Seasoned butters (see Vegetables for suggestions)
- Chopped fresh parsley, chives or dill
- Sour cream
- Steamed broccoli florets or cauliflowerets

RICE

17. Flavored Rice

Add 1 bouillon cube for every 1 cup of water before bringing water to a boil. Omit salt.

18. Sauteed Veggie Rice

In a skillet, saute one or a combo of the following vegetables in butter until tender: sliced or chopped fresh mushrooms, green and/or red sweet peppers, onions, celery and shallots. Stir into cooked rice.

19. Broccoli Rice

Five minutes before the rice is done, stir in chopped fresh broccoli.

20. Carrot Rice

Five minutes before the rice is done, stir in shredded carrots.

21. Spinach Rice

One or two minutes before the rice is done, stir in fresh baby spinach.

Last-Minute Rice Touches
- Crumbled cooked bacon
- Fresh herbs
- Thawed frozen peas
- Chopped nuts
- Dried cranberries
- Shredded cheese
- Chopped fresh parsley

SALADS

22. Jamming Salad Dressing

In a jar with a tight-fitting lid, combine ¼ cup raspberry jam, 2 tablespoons red wine vinegar and ¼ cup olive or canola oil. Shake until blended. Strawberry jam, peach jam and current jelly can be used in place of the raspberry jam. Use flavored vinegars in place of red wine vinegar.

23. Pantry Vinaigrette

In a small bowl, whisk ¼ cup cider vinegar, 3 tablespoons honey,

2 tablespoons olive or canola oil, ½ teaspoon honey mustard or Dijon mustard, ⅛ teaspoon salt and ⅛ teaspoon pepper. Substitute red or white wine vinegar for the cider vinegar. For herb vinaigrette, omit the honey and add 1 teaspoon each of dried basil, mint and parsley flakes and ½ teaspoon garlic powder.

24. Sugared Nuts
In a heavy skillet, melt 1 tablespoon butter. Add 1 cup pecans, walnuts or almonds; cook over medium heat until nuts are toasted, about 4 minutes. Sprinkle with 1-2 tablespoons sugar or brown sugar. If desired, sprinkle with pepper or cayenne. Cook and stir 2-4 minutes or until sugar is melted. Spread on foil to cool completely. Store in an airtight container up to 1 week.

25. Sauteed Apples or Pears
In a large skillet, heat 2 tablespoons butter and 2 teaspoons brown sugar until sugar is melted, stirring occasionally. Add 2 thinly sliced cored apples or pears; saute 2-3 minutes or until crisp-tender.

Last-Minute Salad Touches
- Cheese cubes
- Crumbled cooked bacon
- Dried cherries or cranberries
- Packaged croutons
- Sliced hard-cooked eggs
- Fresh berries
- Sliced fresh apples or pears
- Toasted nuts (see Vegetables for directions)

SOUPS

26. Parmesan Crisps
Preheat oven to 400°. For each crisp, drop a tablespoon of Parmesan cheese onto parchment paper-lined baking sheets about 1 in. apart. Spread each into a circle. Bake 5-6 minutes or until crispy and golden brown. Remove from pans. These are great on salads, too.

27. Tortilla Strips
Preheat oven to 400°. Cut two (8-in.) flour tortillas or two (6-in.) corn tortillas into ¼-in. strips. Place strips in a single layer on a baking sheet coated with cooking spray. Bake 6-10 minutes or until crisp.

Last-Minute Soup Touches
- Grated or shredded cheese
- Crumbled cooked bacon
- Popped popcorn
- Sliced green onions
- Broken tortilla chips or corn chips
- Sour cream
- Fresh herbs
- Croutons
- Chow mein noodles
- Lime or lemon wedges
- Chopped tomato

VEGETABLES

28. Herb Butter
Mix 2 tablespoons softened butter, 1/4 teaspoon chives, 1/8 teaspoon dried parsley, 1/8 teaspoon basil and a dash each paprika, salt and pepper. Toss with cooked vegetables.

29. Garlic Butter
Mix 2 tablespoons softened butter and 1/4 to 1/2 teaspoon garlic powder. Toss with cooked vegetables.

30. Maple Butter
Mix 2 tablespoons softened butter, 1 1/2 teaspoons maple syrup, 1/4 teaspoon dried parsley and a dash pepper. Toss with cooked vegetables.

31. Lemon-Tarragon Butter
Mix 2 tablespoons softened butter, 1/4 teaspoon grated lemon peel, 1/4 teaspoon dried tarragon, 1/8 teaspoon salt and 1/8 teaspoon dried thyme. Toss with cooked vegetables.

32. Balsamic Vinegar Glaze
In a saucepan, bring 1/2 cup balsamic vinegar and 2 tablespoons brown sugar to a boil; cook until liquid is reduced by half. Drizzle over cooked vegetables.

33. Toasted Bread Crumbs
In a small skillet, heat 1 tablespoon butter or olive oil. Stir in 1/4 cup bread crumbs or panko (Japanese) bread crumbs. Toast over medium heat 3-5 minutes or until golden brown, stirring occasionally. If desired, add 1 minced garlic clove during the last minute of toasting. Sprinkle over cooked vegetables.

34. Toasted Nuts or Seeds
In a dry nonstick skillet, spread nuts (whole, sliced or chopped), pine nuts, sesame seeds or sunflower kernels in a single layer; toast over low heat until lightly browned, stirring occasionally. Toss with cooked vegetables or with salads.

35. Sauteed Flavor
In a small skillet, saute one or a combination of the following vegetables in butter until tender: chopped onion, green or red sweet pepper, shallots, garlic and celery. Toss with cooked vegetables.

Last-Minute Vegetable Touches
- Grated or shredded cheese
- Splash of lemon or lime juice, wine vinegar, sesame oil or soy sauce
- Crumbled cooked bacon

GENERAL RECIPE INDEX

ALPHABETIC RECIPE INDEX